DE TO
LITIES

hool

rvices, Inc.

itted
ding
val
.

THE PARENT'S GUI
LEARNING DISABI

Helping the LD Child
Succeed at Home and Sc

Stephen B. McCarney, Ed.D.
Angela Marie Bauer, M.Ed.

Copyright © 1991 by Hawthorne Educational S

Printed in the
United States of America

Hawthorne
Educational Services, Inc.
800 Gray Oak Drive
Columbia, Missouri 65201
Telephone: (314) 874-1710

Table of Contents

I. Introduction

The **Parent's Guide to Learning Disabilities** was written to help the parents and learning disabled child experience more success at home and at school. The learning and behavior intervention strategies included have been tried and tested by parents of children with learning disabilities and are presented in the most convenient and practical manner possible.

The format chosen for the guide was designed for ease of use in identifying the learning or behavior problem the child encounters and providing a selection of strategies parents may implement to successfully deal with the problem. This format reduces the need for lengthy reading exercises, indecision over how or exactly what to do, and indecision over whether the intervention strategies are appropriate for the child. Because of differences in situations and the kinds of behaviors associated with learning disabilities, the interventions take several forms. Some interventions are appropriate for the prevention of problems, while others reduce problem behavior, increase the child's self-control of his/her behavior, or help the child learn more appropriate behavior. A variety of intervention strategies is presented for each problem associated with learning disabilities so that **parents** will be able to choose the interventions best suited to their child, in **their** home.

The majority of the intervention strategies in the guide are designed to help the learning disabled child be more successful in school.

By using the suggestions under Memory, Organization, Following Directions; General Academics; Reading; Written/Expressive Language and Speech; Math; Handwriting; and Self-Control; the parent will be able to help the student succeed in the regular or special education classroom. By conferring with the classroom teacher, specific areas such as math or reading can be pinpointed for the parent and student to work on at home. Teachers have been very enthusiastic about the use of the guide by parents to supplement the learning experiences in the classroom.

You will notice that, for some problems, there are as many as 50 possible solutions to the particular situation. The reason for this is that we believe there is no one best way to help children and youth be successful. We offer a variety of possible solutions in order that you will be able to find a solution that will work in your unique situation, based on all variables related to your family and considering the age, sex, maturity, abilities, etc., of your child. The variety is there in order for you to choose the interventions that are best for you and your child.

We believe it is extremely important that the intervention strategies employed to help a child succeed are those with which parents are most comfortable. Parents are likely to be more successful implementing those interventions they think are best for themselves and their child rather than attempting to implement interventions suggested by a third party who would not have the same insight the parents have relative to their child's behavior.

SBM

II. Behaviors & Solutions

1   Has to have several reminders

1. Establish rules for following directions (e.g., listen carefully to the directions, ask questions if you do not understand, follow the directions without having to be reminded, etc.). These rules should be consistent and followed by everyone in the home. Talk about the rules often.

2. Reward your child for not requiring reminders to do what he/she is told to do. Possible rewards include verbal praise (e.g., "Thank you for making your bed without having to be reminded."), a kiss on the cheek, a hug, having a friend over to play, staying up late, watching a favorite TV show, and playing a game with a parent. (See Appendix for Reward Menu.)

3. If there are other children or adolescents in the home, reward them for doing what they are told to do without requiring reminders.

4. Carefully consider your child's age and experience when giving your child a job to do or telling him/her to do something.

5. Demonstrate for your child what he/she should do when given a chore (e.g., show your child how to take out the trash when told to do so).

6. When your child requires a reminder(s) to do something, explain what he/she did wrong, what should have been done and why.

For example: You told your child to set the table before dinner. It is now five minutes until dinner time and the table is not set. Go to your child, tell him/her that this is a reminder to set the table and that it needs to be done immediately because dinner is ready.

7. Make sure your child is paying attention to you when you tell him/her to do something. Have your child look directly at you to know he/she is listening and have your child repeat the direction to check for understanding.

8. Do not give directions to your child from another room. Go to your child, get his/her undivided attention, and tell him/her what should be done.

9. Write a contract with your child.

For example: I, William, will make my bed without having to be reminded to do so for 5 days in a row. When I accomplish this, I can watch 30 extra minutes of TV.

The contract should be written within the ability level of your child and should focus on only one behavior at a time. (See Appendix for an example of a Behavior Contract.)

10. Allow natural consequences to occur as a result of your child's failure to do what he/she is told (e.g., forgetting to put a bike in the garage may result in it being stolen, leaving a toy in the street may result in it being run over by a car, etc.).

11. Make certain that your child sees the relationship between his/her behavior and the consequences which follow (e.g., failing to retrieve a toy from the street results in having a broken toy).

12. Along with a directive, provide an incentive statement (e.g., "You may have a bowl of ice cream after you get ready for bed.").

13. Do not give your child more than two or three steps to follow in one direction. Directions that involve several steps can be confusing and cause your child to have difficulty following them. An example of a two-step direction is: "Please brush your teeth and go to bed."

14. Deliver directions in a supportive, rather than threatening, manner (e.g., "Please take out the trash." rather than "You had better take out the trash or else!").

15. Provide your child with a list of daily chores, weekly chores, etc., and put it where it will be seen often (e.g., on the closet door, on his/her desk, on the refrigerator, etc.). (See Appendix for List of Chores.)

16. Let your child know that directions will only be given once and that you will not remind him/her to follow the directions.

17. When giving your child a chore to do, tell your child when it needs to be done, how long he/she has to do the chore, and how long you think it will take to do it.

For example: William, please set the table before dinner. You have thirty minutes until then and it will probably take you 10 minutes.

18. Help your child begin a chore, such as cleaning up his/her room, in order to get your child started.

19. Make certain to give directions in a very simple manner and be specific as to what you want your child to do.

20. Make certain that your child has all the materials needed in order to perform the chore.

21. Establish a regular routine for your child to follow in order to help your child learn to perform chores without requiring reminders.

22. Give your child special responsibilities (e.g., answering the door, serving food, cleaning, etc.) in order to teach your child to follow directions.

23. Do not criticize. When correcting your child, be honest yet supportive. Never cause your child to feel bad about himself/herself.

24. Be consistent when expecting your child to follow directions. Do not allow your child to fail to follow directions one time and then expect him/her to follow directions the next time.

25. Use a timer to help your child know how much time he/she has to follow through with directions.

26. Do not punish your child for forgetting, being interrupted, etc.

27. In order to help your child remember directions, reduce distractions (e.g., turn off the TV, give directions in a room away from friends, etc.).

28. Make a written list of directions you want your child to follow.

29. Have your child do those things that need to be done when they are discussed instead of later (e.g., put swimsuits in the car now so that when you go to the pool later this afternoon, they will not be forgotten; etc.).

30. Make certain that the responsibilities given to your child are appropriate for his/her level of development and ability.

31. Assist your child in performing responsibilities. Gradually require your child to independently assume responsibility as he/she demonstrates success.

A Reminder: We all have to be "reminded" sometimes to do things we do not particularly enjoy doing.

1. Make sure you have your child's undivided attention when you are talking to him/her. Stand close to your child, maintain eye contact, and have your child repeat what you say.

2. Be sure your child hears what you have said by having him/her acknowledge you (e.g., saying, "Okay!" "Will do!" etc.).

3. Make certain your child knows that you expect him/her to listen to you (e.g., by saying, "William, it is very important that you listen carefully to what I have to say. You need to feed the dog now!").

4. Establish rules for listening (e.g., look at the person who is talking; ask questions if necessary; acknowledge understanding by saying, "Okay!" etc.). These rules should be consistent and followed by everyone in the home. Talk about the rules often.

5. Reward your child for not ignoring you. Possible rewards include verbal praise (e.g., "I like it when you do what I ask." "Thank you for looking at me when I talk to you." etc.), a kiss on the cheek, a hug, having a friend over to play, staying up late, watching a favorite TV show, and playing a game with a parent. (See Appendix for Reward Menu.)

6. If there are other children or adolescents in the home, reward them for not ignoring you.

7. Do not ignore your child when he/she wants to tell you something. When you ignore your child, you teach your child that it is acceptable to ignore people.

8. Write a contract with your child.

For example: I, William, for 7 days in a row, will look at my parents when they talk to me. When I accomplish this, I can buy a Matchbox car at the store.

The contract should be written within the ability level of your child and should focus on only one behavior at a time. (See Appendix for an example of a Behavior Contract.)

9. Have your child's hearing checked if you have not done so in the past year.

10. Allow natural consequences to occur as a result of your child's ignoring you (e.g., the child misses a favorite TV show because he/she ignores you when you say it is time for the show to begin).

11. Do not give your child more than two or three steps to follow in one direction. Directions that involve several steps can be confusing and cause your child to ignore you. An example of a two-step direction is: "Please turn off the TV and go to bed."

12. When your child ignores you, let your child know that he/she is ignoring you and that he/she needs to listen to what you say.

13. Do not talk to your child across a room or from another room. Your child may not be able to hear you and/or may not know that you are talking directly to him/her.

14. Make certain that your child sees the relationship between his/her behavior and the consequences which follow (e.g., failing to acknowledge that he/she was told to let in the dog may mean that the dog will get lost or run away from home).

15. Along with a directive, provide an incentive statement (e.g., "When you do what I ask, you may have a cookie.").

16. In order to determine if your child has heard what you have said, have your child repeat it.

17. Talk to your child in a supportive, rather than a threatening, manner (e.g., "Please take out the trash." rather than "You had better take out the trash or else!").

18. Talk to your child before going into a public place and remind your child of the importance of listening to what is said.

19. Treat your child with respect. Talk in an objective manner at all times.

20. Provide your child with written directions, chores, rules, etc. (See Appendix for List of Chores.)

21. Evaluate your child's chores and responsibilities in order to determine if they are too complicated for him/her to complete successfully.

22. Make certain your child knows what the consequences will be in your home for ignoring to do what he/she is told (e.g., privileges taken away, loss of freedom, etc.).

23. Tell your child exactly what he/she is to do (e.g., "You need to put away your bike now." etc.).

24. When giving your child directions to follow, reduce distractions (e.g., turn off the TV or radio, send friends home, etc.) so that your child can understand what it is you want him/her to do.

25. Make certain grandparents, baby-sitters, visitors in your home, etc., are aware of consequences for inappropriate behavior and the importance of maintaining consistency.

26. Maintain a regular routine of chores, meals, bedtime, TV, sports, etc., so your child knows what is expected at all times.

27. After asking your child to do something, explain why it is necessary to do what you ask.

28. Before going into a store, the shopping mall, a friend's house, etc., remind your child of the importance of listening to what he/she is told.

29. After you tell your child "no," explain exactly why he/she cannot do what he/she wants to do.

30. Be careful to avoid embarrassing your child by giving him/her orders, demands, etc., in front of others.

31. Speak to your child quietly and privately to provide reminders about behavior, when to come home, etc.

32. Make certain your child is aware of the dangers involved in ignoring to do what he/she is told (e.g., getting lost, frightening others, etc.).

3 Puts off doing things

1. Carefully determine if your child is capable of performing the expected responsibilities on his/her own. Do not give your child too many chores to do at once, make sure he/she gets up early enough to get to school on time, provide more than enough time to perform a chore, and do not always expect perfection.

2. Establish rules for performing everyday expectations (e.g., get up on time for school, do your chores right after you get home from school, finish your homework before you watch TV, etc.). These rules should be consistent and followed by everyone in the home. Talk about the rules often and reward your child for following the rules.

3. Establish a routine for your child to follow for getting ready for school, doing chores, completing homework, etc. This will help your child remember what is expected.

4. Reward your child for getting things done on time. Possible rewards include verbal praise (e.g., "You're on time for school. Good for you!" "Thank you for remembering to finish your homework before you turned on the TV." etc.), a kiss on the cheek, a hug, having a friend over to play, staying up late, watching a favorite TV show, and playing a game with a parent. (See Appendix for Reward Menu.)

5. If there are other children or adolescents in the home, reward them for getting things done on time.

6. Model for your child the appropriate way to get things done on time. Show your child how to follow a routine by following one yourself and getting things done on time.

7. When your child does not get something done on time, explain exactly what he/she did wrong, what should have been done and why.

For example: Your child is supposed to catch the school bus at 7:45 a.m. and is still getting dressed when the bus arrives. Tell your child that he/she missed the bus because he/she was not ready on time. Explain that it is unacceptable to miss the bus because you don't have time to take him/her to school.

8. Write a contract with your child.

For example: I, William, will be ready and waiting for the school bus at 7:40 a.m. for 3 days in a row. When I accomplish this, I can watch 30 extra minutes of TV.

The contract should be written within the ability level of your child and should focus on only one behavior at a time. (See Appendix for an example of a Behavior Contract.)

9. Make certain that your child sees the relationship between his/her behavior and the consequences which follow (e.g., failing to feed the dog will cause the dog to go hungry).

10. Allow natural consequences to occur due to your child putting off doing things (e.g., the child's bike being stolen because it was not put in the garage overnight).

11. Along with a directive, provide an incentive statement (e.g., "After you get ready for bed, you may watch TV.").

12. Provide your child with written reminders (e.g., a list posted in the bathroom indicating what his/her chores are and when they need to be done). (See Appendix for Sample List.)

13. Tell your child when it is time to set the table, feed the dog, etc.

14. Allow your child to help decide what his/her routine chores will be.

15. Limit the number of chores for which your child is responsible and gradually increase the number of chores as your child demonstrates the ability to get them done on time.

16. Have your child perform the same chores each day, week, etc.

17. Reduce distracting activities which interfere with your child performing responsibilities (e.g., turning off the TV when it is time to set the table, not allowing friends to come over when it is time to do homework, etc.).

18. Show your child how to perform a new chore (e.g., setting the table) several times before expecting him/her to do it independently.

19. Make sure your child has all the necessary materials needed in order to get chores done on time.

20. Explain to your child that responsibilities not done on time will have to be done at other times (e.g., playtime, TV time, weekends, etc.).

21. Have everyone in the family work together at the same time in order to help your child get responsibilities done on time.

22. Make certain your child knows what the consequences will be in your home for putting off doing things (e.g., loss of privileges, responsibilities taken away, etc.).

23. Tell your child exactly what to do (e.g., "You need to pick up your clothes right now.").

24. Assist your child in performing responsibilities. Gradually require your child to independently assume responsibility as he/she demonstrates success.

25. Make certain that the responsibilities assigned are appropriate for your child's level of development and ability.

26. In order to help your child get things done on time, get chores done, etc., reduce distractions (e.g., turn off the TV, give directions in a room away from friends, etc.).

27. Have your child do those things that need to be done when they are discussed instead of at a later time (e.g., put swimsuits in the car now so that when you go to the pool later this afternoon, they will not be forgotten; etc.).

28. Make sure your child is paying attention to you when you tell him/her to do something. Have your child look directly at you to know he/she is listening and have your child repeat the direction to check for understanding.

29. Use a timer to help your child know how much time he/she has to follow through with directions.

30. Make certain grandparents, baby-sitters, visitors in your home, etc., understand the importance of maintaining consistency in the discipline of your child.

A Reminder: Your child needs to understand that things not done at the appropriate time will have to be made up during recreational time.

1. Make certain your child's hearing has been checked recently.

2. Reward your child for listening. Possible rewards include verbal praise, (e.g., "Thank you for listening to what I told you to do without requiring me to repeat it several times."), a kiss on the cheek, a hug, having a friend over to play, watching a favorite TV show, and playing a game with a parent. (See Appendix for Reward Menu.)

3. Speak to your child and explain (a) what your child is doing wrong (e.g., failing to listen to directions, explanations, and instructions), and (b) what your child should be doing (e.g., listening to directions, explanations, and instructions).

4. If there are other children or adolescents in the home, reward them for listening.

5. Reward your child for listening based on the length of time your child can be successful. Gradually increase the length of time required for listening as your child demonstrates success.

6. Write a contract with your child.

For example: I, William, will listen to directions the first time they are given, for two days in a row. When I accomplish this, I can watch 30 extra minutes of TV.

The contract should be written within the ability level of your child and should focus on only one behavior at a time. (See Appendix for an example of a Behavior Contract.)

7. Have your child question any directions or instructions which are not understood.

8. Determine what it is in the environment that interferes with your child's ability to listen (e.g., others talking, the TV, music playing, etc.) and remove what interferes when you are talking to your child.

9. Have your child close books, put away writing materials, put away toys, etc., when you are talking to your child, giving directions, etc.

10. Reduce those things in the environment that distract your child when you are talking (e.g., close the door, turn off the TV, ask friends to leave, etc.).

11. Talk to your child on a one-to-one basis. Gradually include more people in the conversation as your child demonstrates success in listening.

12. Maintain eye contact when delivering information to your child.

13. Reward your child for attending to the source of information. Continuous eye contact is not necessary for rewarding.

14. When speaking to your child, speak in a clear and concise manner.

15. Deliver information in both verbal and written form (e.g., write down your child's chores on a piece of paper to hang on the refrigerator and give your child the chore list verbally). (See Appendix for List of Chores.)

16. Determine if the level of information given to your child is presented at a level your child can understand.

17. Make certain information is given loudly enough to be heard by your child.

18. Stand so your child can see you when you are talking, giving directions, etc.

19. Make certain that your child is not engaged in activities that interfere with listening (e.g., looking at a book, playing with toys, talking to others, etc.).

20. Have your child repeat the information just given in order to check for understanding.

21. Teach your child listening skills (e.g., keep hands free of toys, paper, etc., and pay attention to the person who is talking).

22. Let your child know when directions are going to be given.

23. Allow natural consequences to occur as a result of your child's failure to listen (e.g., not putting a swimsuit in the pool bag will result in not swimming at the pool, not putting toys away will result in them being hard to find the next day, etc.)

24. Use multiple modalities (e.g., auditory, visual, tactile, etc.) when giving directions, explanations, and information. Determine which modality is stronger and utilize the results.

25. Make the subject manner meaningful to your child (e.g., explain the purpose of an assignment, relate the subject matter to the child's environment, etc.).

26. Stop at various points during the presentation of information to check your child's comprehension.

27. Tell your child what to listen for when being given directions, receiving information, etc.

5 Fails to demonstrate short-term memory skills

1. Make certain your child's hearing has been checked recently.

2. Reward your child for demonstrating short-term memory skills. Possible rewards include verbal praise (e.g., "Thank you for remembering to take out the trash without a reminder from me."), a kiss on the cheek, a hug, having a friend over to play, staying up late, watching a favorite TV show, playing a game with a parent. (See Appendix for Reward Menu.)

3. Write a contract with your child.

For example: I, William, will remember to take out the trash every morning without having to be reminded, for 5 days in a row. When I accomplish this, I can watch 30 extra minutes of TV.

The contact should be written within the ability level of your child and should focus on only one behavior at a time. (See Appendix for an example of a Behavior Contract.)

4. Determine if some memory tasks are too difficult for your child (e.g., two- or three-step directions, too much information presented at one time, etc.).

5. Have your child question any directions, explanations, and instructions which are not understood.

6. Have your child act as a messenger. Give your child a verbal message to deliver to a brother, sister, parent, etc. Increase the length of the message as your child demonstrates success.

7. Review the schedule of morning or afternoon activities for your child and have your child repeat the sequence. Increase the length of the sequence as your child demonstrates success.

8. Have your child play concentration games with a limited number of symbols. Gradually increase the number of symbols as your child demonstrates success.

9. Reward your child for remembering to have things ready (e.g., book bag by the door and ready for school, bringing both gloves home, returning library books, etc.).

10. At the end of the day have your child recall three things that he/she did during the day. As success is demonstrated, gradually increase the number of activities your child is required to recall.

11. After a trip to the store, a fun activity, a day at a friend's home, etc., have your child sequence the activities which occurred.

12. After reading a story, have your child identify the main characters, sequence the events, and give the outcome of the story.

13. Have your child deliver the sequence of the day's events (e.g., going to the store, a friend's house, the movies, etc.) to a brother, sister, or parent.

14. Teach your child to use memory clues.

15. Use multiple modalities (e.g., auditory, visual, tactile, etc.) when presenting directions, instructions, explanations to your child.

16. Record a message on a tape recorder. Have your child write the message after listening to it. Increase the length of the message as your child demonstrates success.

17. Have your child practice repetition of information in order to increase short-term memory skills (e.g., repeating names, telephone numbers, dates or events, etc.)

18. Teach your child how to organize information into smaller units (e.g., break number sequence 132563 into units of 13, 25, 63).

19. Show your child an object or a picture for a few seconds. Ask your child to recall what the object or picture looked like, what color it was, how big it was, etc.

20. Talk to your child in a clear manner and at an appropriate pace.

21. Have your child practice making notes for specific information which needs to be remembered.

22. Teach your child to recognize key words and phrases related to information in order to increase your child's short-term memory.

23. Make certain your child is attending to the source of information (e.g., eye contact is being made, hands are free of toys, others are not distracting your child, etc.).

24. Reduce distracting stimuli when talking to your child (e.g., turn off the, TV send friends home, close the door, etc.).

25. Stop at various points in a conversation with your child to check for understanding of what is being discussed.

26. Give your child only one task to perform at a time. Introduce the next task only when your child has successfully competed the first task.

27. Have your child memorize the first sentence or line of a poem, song, etc. Have your child memorize more as success is demonstrated.

28. Teach your child information-gathering skills (e.g., listen carefully, write down important points, ask for clarification, wait until all information is received before beginning, etc.).

29. Have your child repeat/paraphrase directions, explanations, and instructions.

30. Provide your child with written lists of things to do.

31. Establish a regular routine for your child to follow in performing chores, tasks, etc. (e.g., first brush your teeth and wash your face, next get out your pajamas, last climb in to bed).

1. Reward your child for demonstrating logical thinking. Possible rewards include verbal praise (e.g., "Thank you for thinking about what you were going to so rather than rushing into something."), a kiss on the cheek, a hug, having a friend over to play, staying up late, watching a favorite TV show, and playing a game with a parent. (See Appendix for Reward Menu.)

2. If there are other children or adolescents in the home, reward them for logical thinking.

3. Have your child question any directions, explanations, and instructions which are not understood.

4. Give your child responsibilities which require logical thinking (e.g., instruct your child to water the plants; and provide a watering can and a glass, telling your child to use the most appropriate container).

5. Each day provide your child with a problem solving situation which requires logical thinking (e.g., "A stranger takes you by the arm in a department store. What do you do?" "You see smoke coming out of the neighbor's house and no one is home. What do you do?" etc.).

6. Make certain your child experiences the consequences of not using logical thinking (e.g., appropriate behavior results in positive consequences while inappropriate behavior results in negative consequences).

7. Provide your child with a list of questions, involving logical thinking, which can be answered orally (e.g., "Why do we post wet paint signs?" "Why do we have stop sign at intersections?" "Why do we wear seatbelts?" etc.)

8. When something is broken, lost, etc., have your child identify what could have been done to prevent the situation. When possessions are properly organized, maintained, and serviced, have you child discuss the value of such practices.

9. Read stories to your child involving a moral (e.g., "The Tortoise and the Hare," "The Boy Who Cried Wolf," etc.) and explain the reason for the outcome of the story.

10. Have your child read short stories without endings. Require the student to develop logical endings for the stories.

11. Describe situations/pictures and have your child explain the effects of the variables (e.g., "Snow is falling; the wind is blowing. Is the temperature hot or cold? What should you wear outdoors?").

12. Have your child sequence cartoon strips, after they have been cut apart and rearranged, and explain the logic of the sequence created.

13. Give your child fill-in-the-blank statements requiring an appropriate response from multiple-choice possibilities (e.g., The boy's dog was dirty so the boy decided to give his dog a ___ (dog, biscuit, bath, toy).).

14. Show your child pictures of dangerous situations and have your child explain why they are dangerous (e.g., a child running into the street between parked cars, a child riding a bicycle without using hands, etc.).

15. Use cause-and-effect relationships as they apply to nature and people. Discuss what led up to a specific situation in a story or picture, what could happen next, etc.

16. Make certain that your child can verbalize the reasons for real-life outcomes of behavior (e.g., why the child had to go home early, why the bike was taken away, etc.).

17. Have your child make up rules and explain the need for the rules.

18. Have your child identify appropriate consequences for rules (e.g., consequences for following rules and consequences for not following rules). Have your child explain the choice of consequence he/she identifies.

19. Have your child explain the answers to questions such as, "Why do we have rules?" "Why do we need to be a certain age before we can drive a car?" etc.

20. Have your child answer analogy situations (e.g., a garage is to a car as a house is to a ___).

21. Set aside time each day for a problem-solving game, analogies, decision-making activities, assigned responsibilities, etc.

22. Make certain your child is attending to the source of information (e.g., eye contact is being made, hands are free of materials, your child is looking at his/her work, etc.).

1. Have your child write down important information that should be remembered.

2. Have your child tape record important information that may need to be repeated.

3. If your child has difficulty remembering information in written form, present the information auditorily.

4. Have your child repeat/paraphrase important information that needs to be remembered.

5. Have your child outline, highlight, underline, or summarize information that should be remembered.

6. Use concrete examples and experiences when sharing information with your child.

7. Teach your child to recognize main points, important facts, etc.

8. Make certain your child has adequate opportunities for repetition of information through different experiences in order to enhance your child's memory.

9. Make certain information is presented to your child in the most clear and concise manner possible.

10. Reduce distracting stimuli when your child is attempting to remember important information.

11. Teach your child to rely on resources in the environment to recall information (e.g., notes, pictures, books, etc.).

12. When your child is required to recall information, provide auditory cues to help your child remember the information (e.g., key words, a brief oral description to help cue the child, etc.).

13. When your child is required to recall information, remind your child of the situation in which the information was originally presented (e.g., "Remember yesterday when we talked about going to Grandma's house..." "Remember last week when we talked about the library books you checked out..." etc.).

14. Assess the meaningfulness of situations, information, etc., to your child. Remembering is more likely to occur when the information is meaningful and your child can relate to real experiences.

15. Relate the information being presented to your child's previous experiences.

16. Have your child make notes, lists, etc., of things that need to be remembered. Have your child carry the reminders in a pocket, purse, book bag, etc.

17. Have your child follow a regular routine of daily events to establish consistency in your child's routine.

18. Have your child repeat to himself/herself information just heard in order to help your child remember important facts.

19. Make certain your child is not required to learn more information than he/she is capable of at any one time.

20. Give your child a choice of answers (e.g., more than one possible answer, multiple-choice on a worksheet, etc.). This increases your child's opportunity for recognizing the correct answer.

21. Use daily drill activities to help your child memorize math facts, vocabulary words, etc.

22. Provide reminders throughout your child's home environment in order to help your child be more successful in remembering information (e.g., rules, lists, schedules, etc.).

23. Help your child employ memory aids in order to recall words (e.g., a name might be linked to another word; for example, "Mr. Green is a very colorful person.").

24. Make certain your child has adequate opportunities for repetition of information through different experiences in order to enhance his/her memory.

25. Review, on a daily basis, those skills, concepts, tasks, etc., which have been previously introduced to help your child remember information previously learned.

26. As soon as your child learns a new skill or information, make certain that he/she applies it to other situations (e.g., when your child learns to count by fives, have him/her practice adding nickels; vocabulary words learned should be pointed out in reading selections; etc.).

27. Identify your child's most efficient learning mode and use it consistently to increase the probability of understanding (e.g., If your child fails to understand directions or information given verbally, present them in written form. If your child has difficulty understanding written directions or information, present them verbally.).

8 Requires slow, sequential, broken-down directions or explanations

1. Make certain that your child's hearing has been checked recently.

2. Reward your child for listening to what is said. Possible rewards include verbal praise (e.g., "Thank you for listening to what I said!"), a kiss on the cheek, a hug, having a friend over to play, staying up late, watching a favorite TV show, and playing a game with a parent. (See Appendix for Reward Menu.)

3. Speak to your child to explain (a) what your child is doing wrong (e.g., failing to listen to word endings, key words, etc.), and (b) what your child should be doing (e.g., listening for word endings, key words, etc.).

4. Reward your child for listening carefully based on the length of time your child can be successful. Gradually increase the length of time required for listening as your child demonstrates success.

5. Evaluate the level of difficulty of the information to which your child is expected to listen (e.g., information communicated on the child's ability level).

6. Have your child question any directions, explanations, and instructions which are not understood.

7. Have your child repeat or paraphrase what is said to him/her in order to determine what was heard.

8. Give your child short directions, explanations, instructions to follow. Gradually increase the length of the directions, explanations, and instructions as your child demonstrates success.

9. Maintain consistency in the delivery of verbal directions.

10. Make certain your child is attending to the source of information (e.g., making eye contact, hands free of toys, away from other noises, etc.).

11. Provide your child with written directions and instructions to supplement verbal directions and instructions.

12. Emphasize or repeat word endings, key words, etc.

13. Speak clearly and concisely when delivering directions, explanations, and instructions.

14. Place your child near the source of information.

15. Reduce distracting stimuli (e.g., noise and motion in the room) in order to enhance your child's ability to listen successfully.

16. Use multiple modalities (e.g., auditory, visual, tactile, etc.) when presenting directions, explanations, and instructional content. Determine which modality is stronger and utilize the results.

17. Use concrete examples and experiences when teaching concepts and sharing information with your child.

18. Review, on a daily basis, those skills, concepts, tasks, etc., which have been previously introduced.

9 Does not hear all of what is said

1. Make certain your child's hearing has been checked recently.

2. Reward your child for hearing all of what is said. Possible rewards include verbal praise (e.g., "I like it when you listen and hear everything I say."), a kiss on the cheek, a hug, having a friend over to play, staying up late, watching a favorite TV show, and playing a game with a parent. (See Appendix for Reward Menu.)

3. Speak to your child to explain (a) what he/she is doing wrong (e.g., failing to listen to word endings, key words, etc.) and (b) what your child should be doing (e.g., listening for word endings, key words, etc.).

4. Reward your child for listening carefully based on the length of time your child can be successful. Gradually increase the length of time required for listening as your child demonstrates success.

5. Evaluate the difficulty of information to which your child is expected to listen (e.g., be sure information communicated is on your child's ability level).

6. Have your child question any directions, explanations, and instructions which are not understood.

7. Have your child repeat or paraphrase what is said to him/her in order to determine what was heard.

8. Give your child short directions, explanations, and instructions to follow. Gradually increase the length of directions, explanations, and instructions as the student demonstrates success.

9. Maintain consistency in the verbal delivery of information.

10. Make certain your child is attending to the source of information (e.g., making eye contact, hands free of toys, in a quiet area, etc.).

11. Provide your child with written directions and instructions along with verbal directions and instructions.

12. Emphasize or repeat word endings, key words, etc.

13. Speak clearly and concisely when delivering directions, explanations, and instructions.

14. Make certain your child is near the source of information when directions are being given.

15. Reduce distracting stimuli (e.g., noise and motion in the room) in order to increase your child's ability to listen successfully.

16. Stop at key points when delivering directions, explanations, and instructions in order to determine your child's comprehension.

17. Deliver directions, explanations, and instructions at an appropriate pace for your child.

18. Identify a list of word endings, key words, etc., that your child will practice listening for when someone is speaking.

19. Use multiple modalities (e.g., auditory, visual, tactile, etc.) when presenting directions, explanations, and instructional content. Determine which modality is stronger and utilize the results.

20. Stop at various points during the presentation of information to check your child's comprehension.

21. Teach your child listening skills (e.g., stop working, look at the person delivering questions and directions, have necessary note-taking materials, etc.).

22. Tell your child what to listen for when being given directions, receiving information, etc.

23. Make certain that all directions, questions, explanations, and instructions are delivered loud enough for your child to hear.

24. Play games to teach listening skills (e.g., "Mother May I?" "Red Light-Green Light," "Simon Says," etc.).

25. Have your child silently repeat information just heard to help him/her remember important facts.

10 Is unsuccessful in activities requiring listening

1. Make certain that your child's hearing has been checked recently.

2. Reward your child for listening. Possible rewards include verbal praise (e.g., "Thank you for listening to what I said."), a kiss on the cheek, a hug, having a friend over to play, staying up late, watching a favorite TV show, and playing a game with a parent. (See Appendix for Reward Menu.)

3. Speak to your child to explain (a) what your child is doing wrong (e.g., not listening to directions, explanations, and instructions) and (b) what your child should be doing (e.g., listening to directions, explanations, and instructions).

4. If there are other children or adolescents in the home, reward them for listening.

5. Write a contract with your child.

For example: I, William, for 7 days in a row, will listen to my parents when they talk to me. When I accomplish this, I can buy a Matchbox car at the store.

The contract should be written within the ability level of your child and should focus on only one behavior at a time. (See Appendix for an example of a Behavior Contract.)

6. Evaluate the difficulty of information to which your child is expected to listen (e.g., be sure information communicated is on your child's ability level).

7. Identify a sibling or friend to act as a model for your child to imitate appropriate listening skills.

8. Have your child question any directions, explanations, and instructions which are not understood.

9. Make certain your child is near the source of information when listening is necessary.

10. Make certain your child is attending when you are speaking to your child (e.g., making eye contact, hands free of toys or other materials, etc.).

11. Make certain that competing sounds (e.g., talking, movement, noises, etc.) are silenced when you are speaking to your child.

12. Deliver a predetermined signal (e.g., calling your child by name, a hand signal, etc.) before beginning to speak to your child.

13. Stand directly in front of your child when speaking to your child.

14. Call your child by name prior to giving directions or instructions.

15. Have another child or adolescent in the home provide your child with the information he/she has missed.

16. Along with verbal directions, instructions, and explanations, give your child written directions, instructions, and explanations.

17. Maintain visibility to and from your child when you are speaking in order to ensure that your child is listening.

18. Reduce distracting stimuli in the immediate environment (e.g., call your child into the room to speak to him/her, leave a room where there are distractions, etc.). This is used as a means of reducing distracting stimuli and not as a form of punishment.

19. Have your child verbally repeat or paraphrase information.

20. Teach your child listening skills (e.g., listen carefully, write down important points, ask for clarification, wait until all directions are given before beginning a job, etc.).

21. Have your child practice activities designed to develop listening skills (e.g., following one-, two-, three-step directions; etc.).

22. Give directions in a variety of ways in order to enhance your child's ability to attend (e.g., verbally, in written form, etc.).

23. Stop at various points when speaking to your child in order to ensure that your child is attending.

24. Speak to your child when speaking to your child in order to ensure that your child is attending.

25. Demonstrate directions, explanations and instructions as they are given to your child (e.g., help your child od the first few homework problems, help your child get started cleaning the bedroom, etc.).

26. Use pictures, diagrams, and gestures when delivering information to your child.

27. Deliver information slowly to your child.

28. Present one concept at a time. Make certain your child understands each concept before presenting the next.

29. Rephrase directions, explanations, and instructions in order to increase the likelihood of your child understanding what is being presented.

30. Present directions, explanations, and instructions as simply and clearly as possible (e.g., "Get your book bag and your lunch box and wait by the door for the bus.").

31. When speaking to your child, be certain to use vocabulary that is within your child's level of comprehension.

32. Have your child practice listening skills by taking notes when directions, explanations, and instructions are presented.

33. Play games designed to teach listening skills (e.g., "Simon Says," "Red Light-Green Light," "Mother May I," etc.).

34. Have your child practice listening skills (e.g., "Get your math homework and a pencil, open your book and get ready for us to review your math homework.").

35. Teach your child when to ask questions, how to ask questions, and what types of questions to ask.

36. Have your child repeat to himself/herself information just heard to help your child remember the important facts.

37. Request listening or study guides form your child's teacher to use at home.

38. Along with a directive, provide an incentive statement (e.g., "When you eat your peas, you may have dessert." "You may watch TV after you get ready for bed." etc.).

39. Allow natural consequences to occur due to your child's failure to listen to directions or instructions (e.g., schoolwork not being done on time, missing out on going to the store when not ready on time, leaving his/her book bag at home, etc.).

40. Do not talk to your child from another room. Before beginning to talk, go to the room where your child is.

41. Make certain that games, activities, etc., in which your child participates are appropriate to your child's level of development.

42. Play games with your child that require listening in order to increase your child's ability to listen.

43. Use multiple modalities (e.g., auditory, visual, tactile, etc.) when presenting directions, explanations, and instructional content. Determine which modality is stronger and utilize the results.

44. Teach your child direction-following skills (e.g., stoop doing other things, listen carefully, write down important points, wait until all directions are given, question any directions not understood, etc.).

45. Interact frequently with your child. Make certain that eye contact is being made in order to ensure that your child is attending.

46. Have your child tape record directions, explanations, and instructions in order that he/she may replay information as often as needed.

47. Identify your child's most efficient learning mode and use it consistently to increase the probability of understanding (e.g., if your child fails to understand directions or information given verbally, present it in written form).

11 Does not bring home notes about field trips, the book fair, etc.

1. Establish rules for taking care of responsibilities (e.g., bring notes home). These rules should be consistent and followed by everyone in the home, including the parents. Talk about the rules often.

2. Reward your child for "remembering" to bring notes home. Possible rewards include verbal praise (e.g., "You did a great job of remembering to bring your note home." etc.), a kiss on the cheek, a hug, having a friend over to play, staying up late, watching a favorite TV show, and playing a game with a parent. (See Appendix for Reward Menu.)

3. If there are other children or adolescents in the home, reward them for "remembering" to bring notes home.

4. Carefully consider your child's age and experience when expecting him/her to remember to bring notes home.

5. Make certain that your child sees the relationship between his/her behavior and the consequences which follow (e.g., forgetting to bring field trip notes home will result in not being able to go on the field trip).

6. When your child "forgets" to bring notes home, explain exactly what he/she did wrong, what should have been done, and why.

For example: "William, you need to put notes in your backpack and bring them home to me to sign and return."

7. Write a contract with your child indicating what behavior is expected (e.g., bringing notes home) and what reward he/she will earn when the terms of the contract have been met. The contract should be written within the ability level of your child and should focus on only one behavior at a time. (See Appendix for an example of a Behavior Contract.)

8. Allow natural consequences to occur due to your child's "forgetting" to take care of responsibilities (e.g., notes not being signed will result in your child not participating in activities, etc.).

9. Provide an incentive statement for your child to help him/her bring notes home (e.g., "When you bring notes home, you may stay up 10 minutes later in the evening." etc.).

10. Be consistent when expecting your child to bring notes home. Do not allow your child to fail to bring notes home one time and then expect him/her to bring them home the next time.

11. Do not punish your child for accidentally forgetting to bring notes home, for accidents that interfere with bringing notes home, etc.

12. Make certain to be specific when telling your child what you want him/her to do.

13. Make certain that the responsibilities given to your child are appropriate for your child's level of development and ability.

14. Provide your child with a book bag to carry notes to and from school.

15. Remind your child before leaving for school to bring home all notes that need to be signed.

16. Maintain open communications with school personnel in order to make certain that your child is putting notes in his/her book bag, to make certain that notes are getting back to school, etc.

17. Do not accept excuses. Your child must understand that, regardless of the reason, it is necessary that he/she takes responsibility for bringing notes home, getting notes back to school, etc.

12 Is disorganized with possessions

1. Establish a rule for putting things back where they belong so they can be easily found the next time they are needed. This rule should be consistent and followed by everyone in the home. Talk about the rule often.

2. Reward your child for putting things back where they belong. Possible rewards include verbal praise (e.g., "Thank you for putting your toys in the toy box!"), a kiss on the cheek, a hug, having a friend over to play, staying up late, watching a favorite TV show, and playing a game with a parent. (See Appendix for Reward Menu.)

3. If there are other children or adolescents in the home, reward them for being organized.

4. Carefully consider your child's age before expecting him/her to be organized. Help him/her put away toys, clothes, etc.

5. Teach your child to put things back where they belong by returning things to their places after you use them.

6. When your child forgets to put things back where they belong, explain exactly what he/she did wrong, what he/she was supposed to do and why.

For example: Your child forgets to put a toy back where it belongs. Go to your child and explain that he/she forgot to put away the toy and that it needs to be put back where it belongs so it can be found when he/she wants it in the future.

7. Write a contract with your child.

For example: I, William, for 5 days in a row, will put my toys back where they belong after I'm finished with them. When I accomplish this, I can watch a favorite TV show.

The contract should be written within the ability level of your child and should focus on only one behavior at a time. (See Appendix for an example of a Behavior Contract.)

8. Make certain that your child sees the relationship between his/her behavior and the consequences which follow (e.g., not putting away toys will result in not being able to find them and possibly losing them).

9. Allow natural consequences to occur as a result of your child's failure to put things back where they belong (e.g., not being able to find them, the items being damaged and possibly lost, etc.).

10. Along with a directive, provide an incentive statement (e.g., "You may watch TV after you put your clothes where they belong.").

11. Make certain there is a designated place for all items in and around the home.

12. Require your child to put his/her coat, gloves, hat, etc., in a designated place upon entering the home.

13. Set aside time each week for your child to straighten his/her room, clothes, toys, etc.

14. Make a list of your child's most frequently used items and/or materials and have your child make sure that each item and/or material is put in its designated place each day.

15. Identify a place for all members of the household to keep frequently used items (e.g., coats, boots, gloves, hats, keys, pens and pencils, purses, etc.).

16. Set aside time each evening when all family members put things in their proper places and organize their possessions for the next day (e.g., school clothes, books, lunches, etc.).

17. Have your child put away toys, clothes, etc., before getting out new things to play with or wear.

18. Require that your child's room be neat and organized so there will always be a place to put toys, games, clothes, etc.

19. When your child has a friend over, have them pick up toys and games 15 minutes before the friend leaves so he/she can help your child.

20. If your child fails to pick up his/her clothes, games, toys, etc., before going to bed, pick up the items and take them away from the child for a period of time.

21. Make certain to be consistent when expecting your child to pick up toys (e.g., do not leave the house with toys in the yard one time and expect the toys to be picked up the next time).

22. Do not expect your child to pick up toys and games that friends failed to put away. Encourage your child's friends to pick up toys and games when playing at your house.

23. Communicate with the parents of your child's friends to make certain that your child helps pick up toys when he/she is spending time at a friend's house.

24. Tell baby sitters or others who are involved with your child that he/she is responsible for picking up and putting away his/her own materials.

25. Show your child the proper way to take care of his/her things (e.g., shining shoes, hosing off his/her bike, taking care of dolls, etc.). This will teach your child a sense of responsibility with his/her own belongings.

26. Do not buy additional toys, games, etc., for your child if he/she is not able to take care of what he/she has.

27. Have your child pay for things he/she wants (e.g., a baseball mitt, a new doll, a new pair of jeans, etc.). If the child has spent some of his/her own money on an item, he/she may be more willing to take care of it.

28. Provide your child with shelving, containers, organizers, etc., for his/her possessions. Label the storage areas and require your child to keep his/her possessions organized.

29. Limit your child's use of those things he/she is not responsible for putting away, returning, etc.

30. Make certain your child understands that he/she must replace things which are lost, broken, or destroyed.

31. Make certain that the responsibilities given to your child are appropriate for your child's level of development and ability.

32. Assist your child in performing his/her responsibilities. Gradually require your child to independently assume more responsibility as he/she demonstrates success.

33. Discuss your child's responsibilities at the beginning of each day so he/she knows what is expected of him/her.

13 Does not prepare for school assignments

1. Establish rules for school assignments (e.g., start school assignments when you get home from school, finish school assignments before you watch TV or play with others, ask for help when necessary, etc.).

2. Reward your child for following the rules. Possible rewards include verbal praise (e.g., "Thank you for finishing your school assignments before playing outside."), a kiss on the cheek, a hug, having a friend over to play, staying up late, watching a favorite TV show, and playing a game with a parent. (See Appendix for a Reward Menu.)

3. If there are other children or adolescents in the home, reward them for following the rules for school assignments.

4. Make sure your child has a quiet and well lighted place in which to do his/her school assignments.

5. Reduce distractions (e.g., turn off the radio and/or TV, have people talk quietly, etc.) in order to help your child complete his/her school assignments.

6. Remind your child when it is time to do his/her school assignments.

7. Encourage your child to ask for help when necessary.

8. Ask your child's teacher to send home explanations of how to help your child with his/her school assignments if necessary.

9. Sit with your child when he/she is working on his/her school assignments. You could read, do needlework, etc., while your child works.

10. Write a contract with your child.

For example: I, William, will complete my school assignments for 4 days in a row. When I accomplish this, I can stay up an hour later on Friday night.

The contract should be written within the ability level of your child and should focus on only one behavior at a time. (See Appendix for an example of a Behavior Contract.)

11. Make certain that your child sees the relationship between his/her behavior and the consequences which follow (e.g., forgetting to complete his/her school assignments will result in a low grade).

12. Allow your child to do something enjoyable (e.g., playing a game, watching TV, talking with a friend on the phone, etc.) after completing his/her school assignments for the evening.

13. Allow natural consequences to occur due to your child's failure to complete his/her school assignments (e.g., receiving low grades, being excluded from extra-curricular activities, etc.).

14. If you feel that your child is being assigned too many school assignments, talk with his/her teacher about your concerns.

15. Allow your child to have a friend come over so they can do their school assignments together.

16. Have your child put a star or check mark beside each assignment he/she completes and allow him/her to turn in the stars or check marks for rewards.

17. Make positive comments about school and the importance of completing assignments.

18. Have your child begin his/her assignments as soon as he/she gets home from school in order to prevent your child from putting it off all evening.

19. Find a tutor (e.g., a volunteer in the community, one of your child's classmates, etc.) to help your child complete his/her school assignments.

20. Arrange to pick up a list of your child's school assignments each day if he/she has difficulty "remembering" to bring it home.

21. Help your child study for tests, quizzes, etc.

22. If your child appears to need a break, allow him/her some playtime between school assignments.

23. Set up an assignment system with your child's teacher (e.g., 2 days a week drill with flash cards, 3 days a week work on book work sent home, etc.). This will add some variety to your child's school assignments.

24. Let your child set up an "office" where he/she can finish school assignments.

25. Develop an assignment sheet with your child's teacher so you are aware of the work that should be completed each night. Sign and send back the assignment sheet the next day so your child's teacher is aware that you saw the sheet.

26. Play educational games with your child so it is more interesting for him/her to do school assignments (e.g., a spelling bee, math races, let your child teach the materials to you, etc.).

27. Check over your child's assignments when he/she is finished so you can be certain that everything is complete.

28. Assist your child in performing his/her school assignments. Gradually require him/her to independently assume more responsibility as he/she demonstrates success.

29. Make certain you are familiar with the school district's homework policy (e.g., 15 minutes a day for 1st-3rd grade, 30 minutes a day for 4th-6th grade, etc.). If your child is receiving more assignments than the district requires, talk with your child's teacher.

30. Along with a directive, provide an incentive statement (e.g., "When you finish your school assignments, you may watch TV." etc.)

31. Make certain your child understands that school assignments not completed and turned in on time must still be completed and turned in.

32. Review your child's assignment responsibilities with him/her after school so your child knows what he/she is expected to do that evening.

33. Have another child (e.g., brother, sister, friend) help your child with school assignments each evening.

34. Have your child and a classmate who has the same assignment do their homework together (e.g., right after school at one home or the other).

35. Set aside quiet time each night when the family turns off TV's and radios to read, do school assignments, write letters, etc.

36. Hire a tutor to help your child complete school assignments.

37. Make sure your child has all the necessary materials to perform school assignments (e.g., pencils, paper, erasers, etc.).

A Reminder: If your child cannot be successful completing assignments at home, speak to his/her teacher(s) about providing time at school for assignment completion.

14 Does not read or follow directions

1. Establish rules for following directions (e.g., read directions, ask questions about directions if you do not understand, follow the directions, etc.). These rules should be consistent and followed by everyone in the home. Talk about the rules often and reward your child for following the rules.

2. Reward your child for following directions. Possible rewards include verbal praise (e.g., "You did a great job picking up your clothes!" "I like the way you follow directions!" etc.), a kiss on the cheek, a hug, having a friend over to play, staying up late, watching a favorite TV show, and playing a game with a parent. (See Appendix for Reward Menu.)

3. If there are other children or adolescents in the home, reward them for following directions.

4. Carefully consider your child's age and experience when giving him/her directions to follow.

5. Demonstrate the appropriate way to follow directions (e.g., give your child directions to feed the dog and then you feed the dog with him/her).

6. When your child does not follow a direction, explain exactly what he/she did wrong, what was supposed be done and why.

For example: You tell your child to clean up his/her room before 5:00. At 5:00, you tell your child that the room has not been cleaned up and that he/she needs to follow the direction to clean the room now.

7. Write a contract with your child.

For example: I, William, for three days in a row, will follow directions without having to be told more than once. When I accomplish this, I can watch 30 extra minutes of TV.

The contract should be written within the ability level of your child and should focus on only one behavior at a time. (See Appendix for an example of a Behavior Contract.)

8. Allow natural consequences to occur due to your child's failure to follow directions (e.g., his/her bike being stolen, loss of school books, schoolwork not done on time, etc.).

9. Make certain that your child sees the relationship between his/her behavior and the consequences which follow (e.g., failing to follow the direction to bring in his/her bike at night may result in the bike being stolen).

10. Along with a directive, provide an incentive statement (e.g., "When you eat your peas, you may have dessert." "You may watch TV after you get ready for bed." etc.).

11. When your child has difficulty following directions in front of others (e.g., at the grocery store, in the mall, playing a game with family members, etc.) remove him/her from the situation until he/she can demonstrate self-control and follow directions.

12. In order to help your child be able to follow directions, reduce distractions (e.g., turn off the TV, give directions in a room away from his/her friends, etc.).

13. Do not give your child more than two- or three-step directions to follow. Directions that involve several steps can be confusing and cause your child to have difficulty following them. An example of a two-step directions is: "Please turn off your lights and go to bed."

14. In order to determine if your child heard a direction, have him/her repeat it.

15. Deliver directions in a supportive rather than a threatening manner (e.g., "Please take out the trash." rather than "You had better take out the trash or else!").

16. Give your child a special responsibility (e.g., answering the door, serving food, cleaning, etc.) in order to teach your child to follow directions.

17. Do not criticize your child. When correcting him/her, be honest yet supportive. Never cause your child to feel bad about himself/herself.

18. Be consistent when expecting your child to follow directions. Do not allow him/her to fail to follow directions one time and expect appropriate behavior the next time.

19. Use a timer to help your child know the amount of time he/she has to follow through with directions given to him/her.

20. Make a written list of directions you want your child to follow (e.g., feed the dog, take out the trash, etc.).

21. Talk to your child before going into a public place and remind him/her of the importance of following directions.

22. Establish a regular routine for your child to follow on a daily basis in order to help him/her "remember" to take care of his/her responsibilities. (See Appendix for Weekday or Saturday Schedule.)

23. Make sure your child is paying attention to you when you tell him/her to do something. Have your child look directly at you to know he/she is listening and have him/her repeat the directions to check for understanding.

24. Do not give directions to your child from another room. Go to your child, get his/her undivided attention, and tell him/her what to do.

25. Do not punish your child for forgetting, for accidents that interfere with following directions, etc.

26. Make certain to give directions in a very simple manner and be specific as to what you want your child to do.

27. Establish a certain time each day for your child to take care of his/her responsibilities (e.g., feeding the dog, completing homework, etc., right after school).

28. Sit down with your child and let him/her come up with a list of chores he/she would like to do.

29. Have your child do those things that need to be done when they are discussed instead of later (e.g., put swimsuits in the car now, so that when you go to the pool later this afternoon, they will not be forgotten; etc.).

30. Make certain that responsibilities given to your child are appropriate for your child's level of development and ability.

31. Assist your child in performing his/her responsibilities. Gradually require him/her to independently assume responsibility as he/she demonstrates success.

15 Is unable to follow a routine

1. Carefully determine if your child is capable of performing the responsibilities expected of him/her on his/her own. Do not give him/her too many chores to do at once, make sure he/she gets up early enough to get to school on time, provide him/her with more than enough time to perform a chore, and do not expect perfection.

2. Establish rules for performing everyday expectations (e.g., get up on time for school, do your chores right after you get home from school, finish your homework before you watch TV, etc.). These rules should be consistent and followed by everyone in the home. Talk about the rules often and reward your child for following the rules.

3. Establish a routine for your child to follow for getting ready for school, doing chores, completing homework, etc. This will help your child remember what is expected of him/her.

4. Reward your child for getting things done on time. Possible rewards include verbal praise (e.g., "You're on time for school. Good for you!" "Thank you for remembering to finish your homework before you turned on the TV" etc.), a kiss on the cheek, a hug, having a friend over to play, staying up late, watching a favorite TV show, and playing a game with a parent. (See Appendix for Reward Menu.)

5. If there are other children or adolescents in the home, reward them for getting things done on time and following a routine.

6. Model for your child the appropriate ways to get things done on time. Show him/her how to follow a routine by following one yourself and getting things done on time.

7. When your child does not get something done on time, explain exactly what he/she did wrong, what he/she was supposed to do and why.

For example: Your child is supposed to catch the school bus at 7:45 a.m. and he/she is still getting dressed when the bus arrives. Go to your child and tell him that he/she has missed the bus because he/she was not ready on time. Explain that it is unacceptable to miss the bus because you don't have time to take him/her to school.

8. Write a contract with your child.

For example: I, William, will be ready and waiting for the school bus at 7:40 a.m. for 3 days in a row. When I accomplish this, I can watch 30 extra minutes of TV.

The contract should be written within the ability level of your child and should focus on only one behavior at a time. (See Appendix for an example of a Behavior Contract.)

9. Make certain that your child sees the relationship between his/her behavior and the consequences which follow (e.g., failing to feed the dog will cause the dog to go hungry).

10. Allow natural consequences to occur due to your child putting off doing things (e.g., his/her bike being stolen because he/she did not put it in the garage overnight).

11. Along with a directive, provide an incentive statement (e.g., "After you get ready for bed, you may watch TV.").

12. Provide your child with written reminders (e.g., a list posted in the bathroom indicating what his/her chores are and when they need to be done). (See Appendix for Sample List.)

13. Tell your child when it is time to set the table, feed the dog, etc.

14. Allow your child to help decide what his/her chores will be.

15. Limit the number of chores for which your child is responsible and gradually increase the number of chores as your child demonstrates the ability to get them done on time.

16. Have your child perform the same chores each day, week, etc.

17. Show your child how to perform a new chore (e.g., setting the table) several times before expecting him/her to do it on his/her own.

18. Make sure your child has all the necessary materials in order to get his/her chores done on time.

19. Explain to your child that responsibilities not done on time will have to be done at other times (e.g., playtime, TV time, weekends, etc.).

20. Have everyone in the family work together at the same time in order to help your child get his/her responsibilities done on time.

21. Reduce distracting activities which interfere with your child performing his/her responsibilities (e.g., turning off the TV when it is time to set the table, not allowing friends to come over when it is time to do homework, etc.).

22. Have your child put a star or check mark beside each chore performed on time and allow your child to trade in the stars or check marks for rewards.

23. Set aside time each day for everyone in your home to do chores (e.g., after dinner, everyone does those chores assigned to him/her).

24. Do not accept your child's excuse of "forgetting" to do chores. Have your child make up the chores he/she forgot to do during free time, TV time, etc.

25. Provide an atmosphere where everyone works together to get things done around the house.

26. Set aside time each week for your child to straighten his/her room, clothes, toys, etc.

27. Have your child do those things that need to be done when they are discussed instead of at a later time (e.g., put swimsuits in the car now, so that when you go to the pool later this afternoon, they will not be forgotten; etc.).

28. Sit down and explain changes in routine to your child a few days before they happen, if possible.

29. Try to give your child as much structure and "sameness" in his/her life as possible.

30. Allow your child to participate in deciding when changes in his/her routine will occur.

31. Have a calendar of family activities and indicate on the calendar when guests will visit, doctor appointments will occur, baby sitters will come, etc.

32. Plan things for your child to do when changes in his/her routine will occur (e.g., caring for a younger brother or sister, going to see a movie, having a friend spend the night, etc.).

33. Be personally available when your child is dealing with changes in his/her routine (e.g., take your child to the first day of swim lessons, have the new baby-sitter come over to play a game with your child while you are at home, etc.).

34. Allow your child to take part in changing his/her routine (e.g., let your child decide which day he/she would like to visit Grandma, let him/her decide which baby-sitter he/she would like to have, etc.).

35. Carefully consider your child's age and maturity level before expecting him/her to accept changes in routine.

36. Have your child help plan special events (e.g., family gatherings, parties, etc.) in your home by choosing refreshments, planning a schedule of events, etc.

37. Provide your child with a revised schedule of daily events which identifies the activities for the day and the times when they will occur. (See Appendix for Weekday or Saturday Schedule.)

38. Provide your child with notes on the refrigerator, in his room, etc., to remind him/her of changes in routine.

39. Provide your child with a verbal reminder of changes in his/her routine.

40. Limit the number of changes in your child's established routine. Gradually increase the number of changes in routine as your child demonstrates success.

41. Make certain that anyone who assumes responsibility in your home (e.g., grandparents, baby-sitter, etc.) is provided with rules, schedules, mealtimes, bedtimes, appropriate activities, consequences, etc., in order that their supervision will be as consistent with yours as possible.

16 Begins things before receiving directions or instructions

1. Immediately remove your child from a situation when he/she begins doing things before receiving directions or instructions.

2. Do not allow your child to participate in a situation unless he/she can demonstrate self-control and listen to directions or instructions before beginning.

3. Closely supervise your child in order to monitor his/her behavior at all times.

4. Inform individuals who will be spending time with your child about his/her tendency to begin things before receiving directions or instructions.

5. Talk with your family doctor, a school official, a social worker, etc., about your child's behavior if it is causing him/her to have problems getting along with others, getting things done, etc.

6. Provide your child with a quiet place to go when he/she begins a task, chore, etc.

7. Teach your child to recognize when he/she is becoming overanxious and beginning things before receiving directions or instructions.

8. Reward your child for controlling his/her behavior. Possible rewards include verbal praise (e.g., "I'm so proud of you for waiting for directions before beginning the game."), a kiss on the cheek, a hug, having a friend over to play, staying up late, watching a favorite TV show, and playing a game with a parent. (See Appendix for Reward Menu.)

9. If there are other children or adolescents in the home, reward them for controlling their behavior and waiting for directions or instructions.

10. Treat your child with respect. Talk to him/her in a nonthreatening manner.

11. Discuss your child's behavior with him/her in private rather than in front of others.

12. When your child becomes overanxious, explain exactly what he/she is doing wrong, what should be done and why.

For example: You are playing a new game with your child and he/she starts to play before receiving directions. Stop the game, get your child's attention, and say, "William, you need to wait for directions. Others will not want to play with you if you cannot follow the rules."

13. Write a contract with your child.

For example: I, William, will not begin an activity until I know the directions. When I accomplish this, I can go to the movies on Saturday.

The contract should be written within the ability level of your child and should focus on only one behavior at a time. (See Appendix for an example of a Behavior Contract.)

14. Make certain that your child sees the relationship between his/her behavior and the consequences which follow (e.g., being avoided by others, not being able to participate in special activities, others making fun of him/her, chores and responsibilities not performed correctly, etc.).

15. Try to reduce or prevent your child from beginning something before receiving directions or instructions (e.g., sit next to him/her, do not give out materials until it is time to begin the task, etc.).

16. Teach your child how to handle feelings of frustration (e.g., ask for help, count to ten, etc.).

17. Before a competitive activity, remind your child of the importance of following directions and instructions, personal improvement, doing his/her best, contributing to team success, etc.

18. Encourage your child to play a game in such a manner that he/she can return and play it again tomorrow (e.g., do not behave foolishly or upset your opponent so that he/she will not want to compete against you again, begin the game after receiving directions or instructions).

19. Make certain that the activities, situations, etc., in which your child is involved are appropriate for your child's age, maturity, development level, etc. It may be that your child is not ready for such activities at this particular time.

20. Provide your child with a place to go when he/she gets overexcited (e.g., a quiet chair, his/her room, a corner, etc.).

21. Encourage your child to talk with you when he/she is overly anxious or excited.

22. Immediately remove your child from the attention of others when he/she becomes overly anxious or excited.

23. Do not place an emphasis on perfection. If your child feels he/she must meet up to your expectations and cannot, it may cause him/her to become frustrated.

24. Make certain you set an example by dealing in a socially acceptable way with situations which require you to sit through directions or instructions.

25. When your child becomes overly excited, tell him/her to calm down, count to ten, etc.

26. Reinforce your child for demonstrating self-control based on the length of time he/she can be successful. Gradually increase the length of time required for reinforcement as he/she demonstrates success.

27. Prevent frustrating or anxiety-producing situations from occurring (e.g., give your child chores, responsibilities, etc., on his/her ability level).

28. Make necessary adjustments in the environment to prevent your child from becoming overly excited or anxious (e.g., give out materials after giving directions or instructions).

29. Monitor the behavior of others (e.g., brothers, sisters, friends, etc.) to make certain they are not stimulating your child to become overly anxious or excited.

30. Look for the warning signs (e.g., getting up, walking around, etc.) that your child is overly anxious or excited.

31. Make certain that the activities in which your child engages are not too difficult for him/her.

32. Reduce the emphasis on competition. Highly competitive activities may cause your child to feel anxious or excited.

33. Encourage your child to avoid those activities which cause him/her to become overly excited. He/she can always participate in the activities at a later date.

34. Before competitive activities, discuss with your child the importance of waiting for directions or instructions.

35. If your child needs improvement in particular skill areas in order to be competitive, help him/her improve in those areas with more practice, additional coaching, etc.

A Reminder: Anyone would be frustrated by continued disappointment or failure. Make certain your child is not engaged in activities with which he/she cannot have some success.

17 Fails to follow necessary steps in doing things

1. Establish a rule (e.g., take your time and follow directions). This rule should be consistent and followed by everyone in the home. Talk about the rule often and reward your child for following the rule.

2. Attempt to be patient and follow necessary steps in doing things. If you are impatient, your child will learn to be impatient also.

3. Reward your child for being patient and following necessary steps. Possible rewards include verbal praise (e.g., "Thanks for using the lawn mower the right way."), a kiss on the cheek, a hug, having a friend over to play, staying up late, watching a favorite TV show, and playing a game with a parent. (See Appendix for Reward Menu.)

4. If there are other children or adolescents in the home, reward them for following necessary steps in doing things.

5. Give your child suggestions of things to do in order to learn to be more patient (e.g., counting to ten, saying the alphabet to himself/herself, walking away from the situation and then returning, etc.).

6. When your child is impatient, explain what he/she is doing wrong, what should be done and why.

For example: You see your child using an appliance inappropriately. Go to your child and say, "William, you are using the mixer the wrong way. You need to read the directions and start again."

7. Make certain that your child sees the relationship between his/her behavior and the consequences which follow (e.g., breaking things, chores not getting done, etc.).

8. Immediately remove your child from interacting with others when he/she begins to be impatient and doesn't follow directions.

9. Teach your child how to deal with his/her feelings of frustration in an appropriate manner.

10. Carefully consider your child's age and experience before expecting him/her to always be patient.

11. Encourage your child to ask for help when necessary.

12. Do not make your child wait for long periods of time to get your attention.

13. Remove your child from the presence of others when he/she begins to be impatient and is not following directions.

14. Identify the things with which your child is impatient (e.g., appliances, chores, homework, etc.). Remind your child to try to use patience before beginning to do things which cause him/her to be impatient.

15. Make certain that your child is able to get those things that he/she needs without having to ask others for help. Your child should be able to reach food, dishes, shampoo, clothes, etc., without needing someone's help.

16. Provide your child with a place to go when he/she becomes impatient (e.g., a quiet corner, his/her room, etc.).

17. Remind your child when he/she begins to get impatient (e.g., by saying, "You need to count to ten." "Calm down; you're becoming impatient." etc.).

18. Discourage your child from engaging in those activities which cause him/her to fail to follow directions.

19. Help your child to be able to identify when he/she is getting upset so he/she can do something to calm down (e.g., walk away, talk about his/her feelings in a socially acceptable way, seek help from an adult, etc.).

20. Involve your child in activities in which he/she can be successful and which will help him/her feel good about himself/herself. Repeated failures result in frustration and impatience.

21. Reinforce your child for demonstrating self-control based on the length of time he/she can be successful. Gradually increase the length of time required for reinforcement as your child demonstrates success.

22. Prevent frustrating or anxiety-producing situations from occurring (e.g., only give your child chores, responsibilities, etc., on his/her ability level).

23. Look for the warning signs (e.g., arguing, loud voices, etc.) that your child is getting upset or angry and intervene to change the activity.

24. Make certain the activities in which your child engages are not too difficult for him/her.

25. Do not allow your child to participate in a situation unless he/she can demonstrate self-control.

26. Make certain that the activities, situations, etc., in which your child is involved are appropriate for your child's age, maturity, developmental level, etc. It may be that your child is not ready for such activities at this particular time.

27. Help your child perform those activities which cause him/her to be impatient (e.g., putting a model together, making his/her bed, etc.). Provide less assistance as your child experiences success.

18 Fails to remember sequences

1. Reward your child for remembering sequences. Possible rewards include verbal praise (e.g., "Thank you for remembering to do all the things that I asked you to do.") a kiss on the cheek, a hug, having a friend over to play, staying up late, watching a favorite TV show, playing a game with a parent. (See Appendix for Reward Menu.)

2. If there are other children or adolescents in the home, reward them for remembering sequences.

3. Reward your child for remembering sequencings based on the number of times your child can be successful. Gradually increase the length of the sequences required for reinforcement as your child demonstrates success.

4. Evaluate the appropriateness of what is required of your child to determine: (a) if the requirements are too difficult and (b) if the length of time scheduled to complete the task is appropriate.

5. Have your child question any directions, explanations, instructions not understood.

6. Break the sequence into units and have your child learn one unit at a time.

7. Give your child short sequences (e.g., two components, three components, etc.) to remember. Gradually increase the length of the sequences as your child demonstrates success.

8. Provide your child with environmental cues and prompts (e.g., lists of jobs to perform, sequence of daily events, bell, timer, etc.).

9. Maintain consistency in sequential activities in order to increase the likelihood of your child's success (e.g., your child has lunch every day at noon, nap time at one o'clock, etc.).

10. Teach your child associative cues or mnemonic devices to remember sequences.

11. Have your child maintain notes, written reminders, etc., in order to remember sequences.

12. Actively involve your child in learning to remember sequences by having your child physically perform sequential activities (e.g., operating equipment, following recipes, solving homework problems, etc.).

13. Have your child be responsible for helping a peer or sibling remember sequences.

14. Have your child practice remembering sequences by engaging in sequential activities which are purposeful to your child (e.g., operating equipment, following recipes, opening a combination lock, etc.).

15. Teach your child to use environmental resources to remember sequences (e.g., calendar, dictionary, etc.).

16. Have your child maintain a notebook for keeping notes regarding necessary sequential information (e.g., lists of things to do, schedule of events, days of the week, months of the year, etc.).

17. Provide your child with frequent opportunities to recite sequences throughout the day in order to increase memory skills.

18. Give your child additional activities which require the use of sequences in order to enhance your child's ability to remember sequences.

19. Practice sequential memory activities each day for those sequences your child needs to memorize (e.g., important telephone numbers, addresses, etc.).

20. Provide your child with a schedule of daily events for each day's activities at school. (See Appendix for Schedule of Daily Events).

21. Teach your child to make reminders for himself/herself (e.g., a reminder that today is a P.E. day and he/she will need gym shoes, a reminder that there is a field trip at school and he/she will need a sack lunch, etc.).

19 Has difficulty retrieving, recalling, or naming objects, persons, places, etc.

1. Reward your child for remembering things. Possible rewards include verbal praise (e.g., "You did a wonderful job of remembering to do your chores today."), a kiss on the cheek, a hug, having a friend over to play, staying up late, watching a favorite TV show, and playing a game with a parent. (See Appendix for Reward Menu.)

2. Reward your child for demonstrating accurate memory skills based on the length of time your child can be successful. Gradually increase the length of time for reinforcement as your child demonstrates success.

3. Have your child act as a messenger. Give your child a verbal message to deliver to a brother/sister, a parent, a friend, etc. Increase the length of the message as your child demonstrates success.

4. Review the sequence of the morning or afternoon activities with your child and have your child repeat the sequence. Increase the length of the sequence as your child demonstrates success.

5. At the end of the day, have your child recall the activities of the day. Gradually increase the number of activities your child is asked to recall as your child demonstrates success.

6. After a special activity or event, have your child recall what occurred.

7. After reading a short story, have your child recall the main characters, sequence the events, and recall the outcome of the story.

8. Give your child specific categories and have your child name the category to which they belong (e.g., objects, persons, places, etc.).

9. Give your child a series of words or pictures and have your child name the category to which they belong (e.g., objects, persons, places, etc.).

10. Help your child employ memory aids in order to recall words (e.g., a name might be linked to another word, for example, "Mr. Green" is a very colorful person).

11. Describe objects, persons, places, etc., and have your child name the items described.

12. Give your child a series of words describing objects, persons, places, etc., and have your child identify the opposite of each word.

13. Encourage your child to play word games such as "Hangman," "Scrabble," "Password," etc.

14. Have your child complete "fill-in-the-blank" sentences with appropriate words (e.g., objects, persons, places, etc.).

15. Give your child a series of words (e.g., objects, persons, places, etc.) and have your child list all the words he/she can think of with similar meaning (synonyms).

16. Have your child compete against himself/herself by timing how fast he/she can name a series of pictured objects. Each time your child should try to increase his/her speed.

17. Have your child take notes in school in order to recall material needed to study at home.

18. Have your child make notes, lists, etc., of things he/she needs to be able to recall. Your child should carry these reminders in a purse, pocket, book bag, etc.

19. Have your child tape record important information that should be remembered.

20. Have your child outline, highlight, underline, or summarize information that needs to be remembered.

21. When your child is asked to recall information, help your child by giving clues about the information that should be recalled (e.g., "You remember when we were at Grandma's last week..." "Last week when we talked about going to Ann's house..." etc.).

22. Teach your child to recognize key words and phrases related to information in order to increase your child's memory skills.

23. Have your child practice repetition of information in order to increase accurate memory skills (e.g., repeating names, telephone numbers, dates of events, etc.).

24. Show your child an object or a picture of an object for a few seconds. Ask your child to recall specific attributes of the object (e.g., color, size, shape, etc.).

25. Label objects, persons, places, etc., in the environment in order to help your child be able to recall their names.

26. Make certain your child receives information from a variety of sources (e.g., in written form, verbally, through demonstrations, etc.) in order to enhance your child's memory/recall.

27. Make certain your child is attending to the source of information (e.g., eye contact is being made, hands are free of materials, your child is looking at his/her work, etc.).

28. Make certain your child has adequate opportunities for repetition of information through different experiences in order to enhance memory.

29. Review, on a daily basis, those skills, concepts, tasks, etc., which have been previously introduced.

30. Identify your child's most efficient learning mode and use it consistently to increase the probability of understanding (e.g., If your child fails to understand information presented verbally, present it in written form. If the child has difficulty understanding written information, present it verbally.).

1. Establish rules (e.g., put things away where they belong, return borrowed items in the same or better condition, etc.). These rules should be consistent and followed by everyone in the home. Talk about the rules often.

2. Reward your child for following the rules. Possible rewards include verbal praise (e.g., "Thank you for putting your dirty clothes in the hamper!" "I'm so proud of you for finishing your homework before watching TV" etc.), a kiss on the cheek, a hug, having a friend over to play, staying up late, watching a favorite TV show, and playing a game with a parent. (See Appendix for Reward Menu.)

3. If there are other children or adolescents in the home, reward them for organizing responsibilities.

4. Carefully consider your child's age and experience before assigning responsibilities to him/her.

5. Show your child how to return things to their proper places, return borrowed items in the same or better condition, complete chores, etc., before expecting him/her to perform the responsibilities on his/her own.

6. When your child is not responsible, explain exactly what was done wrong, what should be done and why.

For example: It is 9:00 p.m. and your child has not started his/her homework. Go to your child and explain that his/her homework has not been done and that he/she needs to be doing the homework because bedtime is at 9:30 p.m.

7. Write a contract with your child.

For example: I, William, will finish my homework by 8:00 p.m. every weeknight for 5 nights in a row. When I accomplish this, I can stay up until 11:00 p.m. on Friday night.

The contract should be written within the ability level of your child and should focus on only one behavior at a time. (See Appendix for an example of a Behavior Contract.)

8. Allow natural consequences to occur due to your child's failure to be responsible (e.g., forgetting to do homework will result in low grades).

9. Establish a certain time each day for your child to take care of responsibilities (e.g., feeding the dog, completing homework, etc., right after school).

10. Act as a model for your child by being responsible at all times.

11. Tell your child when it is time to complete homework, chores, etc.

12. Post a list of your child's responsibilities (e.g., 1. Take out the trash, 2. Feed the dog, 3. Set the table, etc.). Have your child put a check mark next to each chore he/she completes. Reward your child for completing his/her chores. (See Appendix for List of Chores.)

13. Discuss your child's responsibilities at the beginning of each day so he/she knows what is expected of him/her.

14. Help your child get out the materials necessary to complete his/her responsibilities (e.g., paper for homework, cleaning supplies for cleaning his/her room, etc.).

15. Help your child get started with his/her chores and explain to your child where things belong when he/she is finished using them.

16. Set aside a time each day for the family to put away all materials that have been used throughout the day (e.g., bikes, toys, lawn equipment, dishes, etc.).

17. Let your child know that materials not put away at the end of the day may be taken away for a period of time due to lack of responsibility.

18. Make a list of your child's frequently used items and/or materials and have your child make sure that each item is put in its designated place each day.

19. Make certain there is a designated place for all items in and around the home.

20. Require your child to put his/her coat, gloves, hat, etc., in a designated place upon entering the home.

21. Teach your child to return things to their places by putting things back where they belong after using them.

22. Make certain that responsibilities given to your child are appropriate for your child's level of development and ability.

23. Provide your child with shelving, containers, organizers, etc., for his/her possessions. Label the storage areas and require your child to keep his/her possessions together.

24. Assist your child in performing his/her responsibilities. Gradually require your child to independently assume more responsibilities as he/she demonstrates success.

25. Make certain your child understands that things which are lost, broken, destroyed, etc., must be replaced by him/her.

26. Do not buy additional toys, games, etc., for your child if he/she is not able to take care of the things he/she already has.

27. Limit your child's use of those things he/she is not responsible for putting away, returning, etc.

28. Help your child to get ready for things on time.

29. Make sure you are ready for things on time. Organize your time and show your child how to follow a routine in order to get ready for things on time.

30. Make certain that your child sees the relationship between his/her behavior and the consequences which follow (e.g., failing to be ready for school when the bus arrives will result in missing the bus).

31. Have your child keep a checklist of things that should be done in order to be ready for school on time (e.g., eat, brush teeth, dress, etc.) and put a star or check mark by each behavior after your child completes it. Allow your child to trade in the stars or check marks for rewards.

32. Make sure your child gets up in plenty of time to be ready when the bus arrives, knows what time you are leaving to go shopping, etc.

33. Establish a routine for getting ready for school (e.g., get up, make bed, eat breakfast, brush teeth, wash face, get dressed).

34. Have breakfast, lunch, and dinner at the same time each day in order to help your child organize his/her day.

35. Frequently remind your child of the time when he/she needs to be home, ready to go shopping, etc.

36. Use a timer to help your child know the amount of time he/she has to get ready for an activity (e.g., going shopping, meeting the school bus, eating meals, etc.).

37. In order to help your child get ready for things on time, reduce distractions (e.g., turn off the radio or TV, do not allow friends to visit, etc.).

38. Help your child prepare for the next day by selecting and laying out clothes, gathering school materials in one place, and reviewing any special activities or events which will occur the next day.

39. Do not allow your child to become involved in high interest activities just before it is time to get ready for another activity (e.g., going shopping, eating dinner, meeting the school bus, etc.).

40. Have your child begin getting ready 10 minutes before everyone else so he/she will be ready on time.

41. Use motivators for your child (e.g., "If you get ready for school on time, you can help decide what to have for breakfast." "If you pick up your toys before dinner, you can choose your seat at the table." "If you are ready to go shopping on time, you may buy something special." "If you are ready for dinner on time, you may have ice cream for dessert."etc.).

21 Is unable to perform homework independently

1. Reward your child for performing homework assignments independently. Possible rewards include verbal praise (e.g., "You are doing a great job of working on your homework."), a kiss on the cheek, having a friend over to play, staying up late, watching a favorite TV show, and playing a game with a parent. (See Appendix for Reward Menu.)

2. Speak to your child to explain: (a) what your child is doing wrong (e.g., asking for help when it is not necessary) and (b) what your child should be doing (e.g., asking for help when it is necessary).

3. Establish homework rules (e.g., turn off the TV, work quietly, ask for help only when it is needed, etc.). Talk about the rules before sitting down to do homework each evening.

4. If there are other children or adolescents in the home, reward them for doing their homework independently.

5. Reward your child for communicating needs to others based on the number of times your child can be successful. Gradually increase the number of times required for reinforcement as your child demonstrates success.

6. Write a contract with your child.

For example: I, William, will do my homework on my own for five nights in a row. When I accomplish this, I can watch 30 extra minutes of TV.

The contract should be written within the ability level of your child and should focus on only one behavior at a time. (See Appendix for an example of a Behavior Contract.)

7. Identify a sibling or a friend to act as a model for your child to imitate the performing of homework assignments independently.

8. Encourage your child to question any directions, explanations, and instructions not understood.

9. Evaluate the appropriateness of expecting your child to communicate needs to others.

10. Make yourself available during homework time in order that your child can ask questions if he/she needs to.

11. Offer your child assistance frequently throughout homework time.

12. Make certain that directions, explanations, and instructions are delivered at your child's ability level.

13. Structure the environment in order that your child is not required to communicate all needs to others (e.g., make certain your child's tasks are on his/her ability level, instructions are clear, and that you maintain frequent interactions with your child to ensure success).

14. In order to detect your child's needs, communicate with your child often.

15. Demonstrate behavior that is accepting of others (e.g., willingness to help others, making criticisms constructive and positive, demonstrating confidentiality in personal matters, etc.).

16. Communicate to your child an interest in his/her needs.

17. Teach your child communication skills (e.g., expressing needs in written and/or verbal form, etc.).

18. Encourage your child to communicate needs to others (e.g., friends' parents, grandparents, friends, etc.).

19. Communicate with grandparents, friends' parents, baby-sitters, etc., in order to inform them of your child's difficulty in communicating needs.

20. Teach your child to communicate needs in an appropriate manner (e.g., use a normal tone of voice when speaking, verbally express problems, etc.).

21. Recognize your child's attempts to communicate needs (e.g., facial expressions, gestures, inactivity, self-depreciating comments, etc.).

22. Have a friend do homework with your child in order that he/she will have a nonthreatening individual to answer questions.

23. Have your child keep a chart or graph representing the number of homework assignments completed independently.

24. Assess the degree of task difficulty in comparison with your child's ability level.

25. Break your child's homework assignments into shorter tasks to be done throughout the evening. Gradually increase the number of minutes your child works as success in demonstrated.

26. Present homework in the most interesting manner possible.

27. Reduce distracting stimuli in the immediate environment (e.g., turn off the TV, send friends home, put away all toys, etc.) when your child sits down to do homework.

28. Provide your child with step-by-step written directions for performing assignments.

29. Allow natural consequences to occur when your child will not perform homework assignments independently (e.g., homework incomplete, loss of free time, etc.).

30. Explain to your child that work not done during homework time will have to be finished during outside playtime, TV time, etc.

31. Maintain consistency in the daily routine.

32. Work the first few homework problems with your child in order to help your child get started.

33. Sit close to your child when he/she does homework.

34. Have homework time each evening when there are no other activities going on in the home.

35. Make certain your child has all necessary resources available for doing homework independently (e.g., textbooks, calculator, dictionary, paper, ruler, etc.).

36. Work on a project of your own as your child does homework each evening.

37. Make certain your child knows what is expected each evening in order to perform homework assignments (e.g., have directions for homework sent home to you, have the teacher send homework instructions home with your child, etc.).

38. Provide your child with a selection of homework assignments and require him/her to choose a minimum number of assignments to perform independently (e.g., present your child with two homework assignments from which one must be selected).

39. Communicate clearly with your child the length of time he/she has to complete homework. Your child may want to use a timer in order to complete homework within the given period of time.

40. Specify exactly what is to be done for the completion of the homework (e.g., indicate definite starting and stopping points, indicate the minimum requirements, etc.).

22 Does not complete homework

1. Establish homework rules (e.g., start homework when you get home from school, finish homework before you watch TV or play with others, ask for help when necessary, etc.).

2. Reward your child for following the rules. Possible rewards include verbal praise (e.g., "Thank you for finishing your homework before playing outside."), a kiss on the cheek, a hug, having a friend over to play, staying up late, watching a favorite TV show, and playing a game with a parent. (See Appendix for Reward Menu.)

3. If there are other children or adolescents in the home, reward them for following homework rules.

4. Make sure your child has a quiet and well lighted place in which to do homework.

5. Reduce distractions (e.g., turn off the radio and/or TV, have people talk quietly, etc.) in order to help your child complete his/her homework.

6. Remind your child when it is time to do homework.

7. Encourage your child to ask for help when necessary.

8. Ask your child's teacher to send home notes explaining how to help your child with homework if necessary.

9. Sit with your child when he/she is working on homework. You could read, do needlework, etc., while your child works.

10. Write a contract with your child.

For example: I, William, will complete my homework for 4 days in a row. When I accomplish this, I can stay up an hour later on Friday night.

The contract should be written within the ability level of your child and should focus on only one behavior at a time. (See Appendix for an example of a Behavior Contract.)

11. Make certain that your child sees the relationship between his/her behavior and the consequences which follow (e.g., forgetting to complete homework will result in a low grade).

12. Allow your child to do something enjoyable (e.g., playing a game, watching TV, talking with a friend on the phone, etc.) after completing homework for the evening.

13. Allow natural consequences to occur due to your child's failure to complete homework (e.g., low grades, being excluded from extracurricular activities, etc.).

14. If you feel that your child is being assigned too much homework, talk with the teacher about your concerns.

15. Allow your child to have a friend come over so they can do their homework together.

16. Have your child put a star or check mark beside each completed assignment and allow your child to turn in the stars or check marks for rewards.

17. Make positive comments about school and the importance of completing homework.

18. Have your child begin homework as soon as he/she gets home from school in order to prevent your child from putting if off all evening.

19. Find a tutor (e.g., a volunteer in the community, a classmate of your child, etc.) in order to help your child complete homework.

20. Arrange to pick up your child's homework each day if your child has difficulty "remembering" to bring it home.

21. Help your child study for tests, quizzes, etc.

22. If your child appears to need a break, allow some playtime between homework assignments.

23. Let your child set up an "office" where homework can be completed.

24. Set up a homework system with your child's teacher (e.g., 2 days a week work with drill flash cards, 3 days a week work on book work sent home, etc.). This will add some variety to your child's homework.

25. Develop an assignment sheet with your child's teacher so you are aware of the work that should be completed each night. Send back the assignment sheet the next day so your child's teacher is aware you saw the sheet.

26. Play educational games with your child so it is more interesting to do homework (e.g., a spelling bee, math races, let your child teach the material to you, etc.).

27. Check over your child's homework when he/she is finished so you can be certain that everything is complete.

28. Assist your child in performing homework responsibilities. Gradually require your child to independently assume more responsibility as he/she demonstrates success.

29. Make sure your child has all the necessary materials to perform homework (e.g., pencils, paper, erasers, etc.).

30. Along with a directive, provide an incentive statement (e.g., ''When you finish your homework, you can watch TV'', etc.).

31. Make certain your child understands that homework not completed and turned in on time must, nevertheless, still be completed and turned in.

32. Review your child's homework responsibilities after school so your child knows what he/she is expected to do that evening.

33. Have another child (e.g., brother, sister, friend) help your child with homework each evening.

34. Have your child and a classmate who has the same assignment do their homework together each day (e.g., right after school at one home or the another).

35. Set aside quiet time each night when the family turns off TV's and radios to read, do homework, write letters, etc.

36. Hire a tutor to work with your child to help him/her complete homework.

37. Make certain you are familiar with the school district's homework policy (e.g., 15 minutes a day for 1st-3rd grades, 30 minutes a day for 4th-6th grades, etc.). If your child is receiving more homework than the district requires, talk with your child's teacher.

A Reminder: Homework should be a form of ''practice'' for what your child has already been taught in school. You should not have to teach your child how to work each problem or activity. Talk with your child's teacher if this is a problem.

Note: If your child cannot be successful in completing homework at home, speak to the teacher(s) about providing time at school for homework completion.

23 Requires repeated drill and practice to learn schoolwork

1. Reduce the emphasis on competition. Competitive activities may cause your child to hurry and make mistakes.

2. Give your child fewer concepts to learn at any one time, spending more time on each concept until your child can learn it.

3. Have a sibling or friend spend time each day engaged in drill activities with your child.

4. Have your child use the new concepts frequently throughout the day.

5. Have your child highlight or underline key words, phrases, and sentences from reading assignments, newspapers, magazines, etc.

6. Develop crossword puzzles which contain only your child's spelling words and have your child complete them.

7. Write sentences, passages, paragraphs, etc., for your child to read which reinforce new concepts.

8. Have your child act as a tutor to a younger brother/sister to teach concepts just learned.

9. Have your child review new concepts each day for a short period of time rather than two or three times per week for longer periods of time.

10. Use pictures to introduce new concepts with visual images for your child to associate with previously learned concepts.

11. Initiate a "learn a concept a day" program with your child and incorporate the concept into the assigned school activities for the day.

12. Communicate with your child's teacher to get information on concepts that are going to be taught over the next week or two in order to review the concepts at home with your child.

13. Allow your child to use devices to help him/her successfully perform tasks (e.g., calculator, multiplication tables, abacus, dictionary, etc.).

14. Provide your child with various times throughout the day when he/she can engage in drill activities with a parent, peer, brother/sister, etc.

15. Provide your child with opportunities for drill activities in the most interesting manner possible (e.g., computer programs, using a calculator, playing educational games, watching a video, listening to a tape, etc.).

16. Provide your child with a list of key words, phrases, or main points to learn for each new concept introduced in school.

17. Underline, circle, or highlight important information from any material your child is to learn (e.g., science, math, geography, etc.).

18. Provide your child with information he/she needs to learn in the most direct manner possible (e.g., a list of facts, a summary of important points, an outline of important events, etc.).

19. Tape record important information your child can listen to as often as necessary.

20. Provide your child with a pleasant, functional "office" space of his/her own in which to study, drill, do homework, etc.

21. Make fun activities contingent upon completion of a short drill or study activity (e.g., first we go over spelling words and then you may watch TV, work ten math problems before going out to play, etc.).

22. Make certain your child is only drilling over material that still needs to be learned (i.e., if 20 spelling words are assigned and your child knows 12 of them, only the remaining eight need to be written again and again).

23. Provide practice in new concepts using a computer software program that gives your child immediate feedback.

24. Make certain that your child has mastery of concepts at each level before expecting him/her to understand a new skill level.

25. Have your child practice a new skill or assignment alone or with a brother/sister, friend, parent, etc., before trying it in front of peers at school or before performing it for a grade.

24 Does not have necessary study skills

1. Identify a particular place to study which is free of clutter (e.g., desk, table, etc.).

2. Identify and use a place to study which is quiet and free from movement or other distractions (e.g., no radio or TV, away from siblings, isolated from discussions or telephone calls, etc.).

3. Choose a time for studying which allows for maximum concentration (e.g., after school, after one hour of play and relaxation, after dinner, etc.). This will be an individual preference.

4. Have your child study at the same identified time each day. In the event he/she does not have an assignment, the time should be used for reading or reviewing.

5. Provide your child with materials needed in order to be organized at his/her work area (e.g., paper, pencils, pen, ruler, eraser, pencil sharpener, tape, crayons, colored pencils, scissors, stapler, dictionary, thesaurus). This will reduce the need for your child to interrupt his/her work to look for materials.

6. Keep the identified work area at a comfortable room temperature. A room kept too warm will make your child drowsy.

7. Have your child prioritize his/her assignments on the basis of due dates and then divide study time according to the assignments. (See Appendix for Assignment Sheet and Schedule of Daily Events.)

8. As a parent, be available to help or check for completion and/or accuracy. Being available does not mean sitting with your child. It is best to be in another room while available.

9. It is vital that your child is required to follow a routine of studying and preparing for school each day.

10. Have your child plan for short study breaks (e.g., drink of water, stretching break, restroom break, etc.).

11. Require your child to review nightly for two to three nights before a test.

12. Require your child to study graphics, pictures and captions within chapters.

13. After reading a chapter, require your child to summarize the chapter with a parent by using the Outline Form. (See Appendix.)

14. When reading for content, require your child to answer "Who, What, Where, When, How, and Why" using the Outline Form. (See Appendix.)

15. Require your child to use flash cards when preparing for tests. (See Appendix for Flash Card Study Aid.)

16. If your child regularly has difficulty remembering to bring necessary materials home, a set of school texts can be kept at home for his/her use (e.g., spelling book, reading book, science book, etc.).

17. Make sure your child is aware of those specified times when he/she can watch TV, visit with a friend, etc.

18. Provide an organizer for materials in your child's room.

19. At the end of each study period, require the child to show the progress made on assignments.

20. Evaluate the appropriateness of the task to determine: (a) if the task is too difficult, and (b) if the length of time scheduled to complete the task is appropriate.

21. Have your child question any written directions, explanations, instructions he/she does not understand.

22. Assign a peer to work with your child to help him/her follow written directions.

23. Teach your child written direction-following skills (e.g., read carefully, write down important points, ask for clarification, wait until all directions are received before beginning, etc.).

24. Give directions in a variety of ways to increase the probability of understanding (e.g., if your child fails to understand written directions, present them in verbal form).

25. Provide clearly stated written directions (e.g., make the directions as simple and concrete as possible).

26. Interact frequently with your child in order to help him/her follow written directions.

27. Require that assignments done incorrectly, for any reason, be redone.

28. Follow a less desirable task with a highly desirable task, making the completion of the first necessary to perform the second.

29. Prevent your child from becoming over-stimulated by an activity (e.g., frustrated, angry, etc.).

30. Present directions in both written and verbal form.

31. Tape record directions for your child to listen to individually and repeat as necessary.

32. Work the first problem or problems with your child to make certain that he/she follows the written directions accurately.

33. Teach your child note-taking skills (e.g., copy main ideas from the board, identify main ideas from lectures, condense statements into a few key words, etc.).

34. Provide a standard format for taking notes of directions and explanations (e.g., have paper and pencil or pen ready, listen for the steps in directions or explanations, write a shortened form of directions or explanations, ask to have any steps repeated when necessary).

35. Provide a standard format for taking notes during lectures (e.g., have paper and pencil or pen ready, listen for main ideas or important information, write a shortened form of main ideas or important information, ask to have any main ideas or important information repeated when necessary, etc.).

36. Have your child practice legible manuscript or cursive handwriting during simulated and actual note-taking activities.

37. Have your child keep his/her notes organized in a folder for each subject or activity.

38. Check your child's notes before he/she begins an assignment in order to determine if they are correct and adequate for the assignment.

39. Provide your child with samples of notes taken from actual instructions, directions, lectures, etc., given in the classroom in order that he/she may learn which information is necessary for note taking.

40. Provide delivery of information in short segments for your child to take notes. Gradually increase the length of delivery as the student experiences success in note taking.

41. Make certain that the vocabulary used in delivering instructions, directions, lectures, etc., is appropriate for your child's ability level.

42. Make certain your child has all necessary materials for note taking (e.g., paper, pencil, pen, etc.).

43. Make certain your child uses any necessary aids in order to facilitate note taking (e.g., eye-glasses, hearing aid, etc.).

44. Make certain your child has adequate surface space on which to write when taking notes (e.g., uncluttered desk top).

45. As an alternative to note taking, have your child tape record instructions, directions, lectures, etc.

46. Have your child listen and take notes for the "Who, What, Where, When, How, and Why" when concepts are presented. (See Appendix for Outline Form.)

47. Have your child prepare for tests using the "Who, What, Where, When, How, and Why" method. (See Appendix for Outline Form.)

48. Have your child takes notes when directions are being given following the "What, How, Materials, and When" format. (See Appendix for Assignment Form.)

49. Provide your child with earphones to wear if auditory stimuli interferes with his/her ability to function. Gradually remove the earphones as your child functions more successfully in the presence of auditory stimuli.

50. Require your child to be productive in the presence of auditory and visual stimuli for short periods of time. Gradually increase the length of time your child is required to be productive as he/she becomes successful.

51. Provide your child with shorter tasks which do not require extended attention in order to be successful. Gradually increase the length of the tasks as your child demonstrates success.

52. Model for your child appropriate behavior in the presence of auditory and visual stimuli in the home (e.g., continuing to work, asking for quiet, moving to a quieter part of the home, etc.).

53. Provide time at the beginning of each day/activity for your child to organize his/her materials (e.g., before school, after school, end of the day, etc.).

54. Act as a model for being prepared for activities.

55. Reduce the emphasis on competition. Competitive activities may cause your child to hurry and make mistakes.

56. Give your child fewer concepts to learn at any one time, spending more time on each concept until your child can learn it correctly.

57. Have your child use new concepts frequently throughout the day.

58. Have your child highlight or underline key words, phrases, and sentences from reading assignments, newspapers, magazines, etc.

59. Write sentences, passages, paragraphs, etc. for your child to read which reinforce new concepts.

60. Have your child review new concepts each day for a short period of time rather than two or three times per week for longer periods of time.

61. Require your child to use resources (e.g., encyclopedia, dictionary, etc.) to provide information to help him/her be successful when performing tasks.

62. Encourage your child to review new concepts each evening for a short period of time.

63. Provide your child with opportunities for drill activities in the most interesting manner possible (e.g., working with a computer, using a calculator, playing educational games, watching a film, listening to a tape, etc.).

64. Allow your child to use devices to help him/her successfully perform tasks (e.g., calculator, multiplication tables, abacus, dictionary, etc.).

65. Use concrete examples in teaching your child new information and concepts.

66. Teach your child to takes notes when he/she is in an early grade (i.e., third grade).

67. Teach your child to listen and look for key words (e.g., Christopher Columbus, Spain, New World, etc.).

68. Teach your child to listen and look for action words (e.g., sailed, discovered, founded, etc.).

69. Teach your child to listen and look for direction words (e.g., circle, underline, choose, list, etc.).

70. Teach your child, when taking notes, to write the key words and main ideas that answer "Who, What, Where, When, How, and Why." Your child should then be given time periodically to go back to fill in connecting details (e.g., your child writes, "Christopher Columbus - Spain - New World - 1492," and is given time to go back to fill in "sailed from - to discover - during the year," resulting in a complete statement: "Christopher Columbus sailed from Spain to discover the New World during the year of 1492.").

71. Teach your child to divide note-taking paper in the middle, writing main ideas and key words on the left side of the paper, filling in details and connecting points on the right side of the paper. These details and connecting points may be filled in after the lecture or during a pause.

72. Teach your child to learn and use abbreviations for words frequently used, in order to take notes more effectively. (See Appendix for Selected Abbreviations and Symbols.)

73. Teach your child that it is acceptable to write notes in incomplete sentences.

74. Teach your child how to organize information into smaller units (e.g., break the number sequence 132563 into units of 13, 25, 63).

75. Use sentence dictation to develop your child's short-term memory skills. Begin with sentences of three words and increase the length of the sentences as the student demonstrates success.

76. Have your child practice making notes for specific information he/she wants and/or needs to remember.

77. Provide your child with written lists of things to do, materials he/she will need, etc.

78. Teach your child to use associative cues or mnemonic devices to remember sequences.

79. Teach your child to recognize main points, important facts, etc. (See Appendix for Outline Form.)

80. Help your child employ memory aids in order to recall words (e.g., a name might be linked to another word, for example, "Mr. Green is a very colorful person.").

81. Make certain your child receives information from a variety of sources (e.g., texts, discussions, films, slide presentations, etc.) in order to enhance your child's memory/recall.

82. Have your child memorize the first sentence or line of poems, songs, etc. Require more to be memorized as your child experiences success.

83. Have your child be responsible for helping a peer remember sequences.

84. When your child is required to recall information, provide him/her with auditory cues to help him/her remember the information (e.g., key words, a brief oral description to clue your child, etc.).

85. Teach your child not to spend too much time on any one item on timed tests.

86. Teach your child to proofread all items on a test.

87. Give your child a practice test at home.

88. Provide your child with sample questions from a test.

89. Make certain your child knows what topic/areas will be covered by a test.

25 Does not demonstrate an understanding of left-right, forward-backward, east-west, etc.

1. Make certain to use the terms right and left as a part of directions you give to your child (e.g., refer to the windows on the left side of the room, the table on the right side of the room, etc.).

2. Identify directions in your home with signs (e.g., on the ceiling of your child's bedroom put up, on the floor put down, etc.).

3. Have your child practice following directions on paper. Instruct your child to make marks on the right, left, middle, top, and bottom parts of the paper according to the directions given.

4. Avoid the problem of mirror images by standing next to your child when giving right and left directions.

5. Design an obstacle course using materials in your home. Your child can step into the box, crawl over the coffee table, walk under the light, etc., when trying to convey an understanding of concepts.

6. Use concrete examples when teaching concepts of up/down, high/low, above/below, etc. Use books, balls, your child's toys, etc., when trying to convey these concepts.

7. Hang directional signs in your child's room (e.g., turn left, games under cabinet, etc.).

8. Play "Simon Says" for directions (e.g., "Raise your left hand." "Walk behind the chair." etc.).

9. Conduct scavenger hunts. Have your child look for a pencil in the desk, a bowl under the table, a glass on the chair, etc.

10. Teach north, south, east, and west using the neighbor's home, the neighborhood playground, etc.

11. Have your child sort left and right gloves, shoes, paper hand and foot cut-outs, etc.

12. Label strips of paper left and right and attach them to your child's wrists.

13. Have your child practice walking forward and backward, moving toy cars and trucks forward and backward, etc.

14. Have your child identify objects which move up and down (e.g., airplanes, teeter-totter, etc.).

15. Point out doors which are labeled push and pull and activities which require pushing and pulling (e.g., opening drawers, opening doors, etc.).

16. Have your child find things that represent the concept of in and out (e.g., we pour milk in a glass and pour it out, we walk in a room and walk out etc.).

17. Identify objects which represent over and under (e.g., a bridge is over water; people sleep under blankets; birds fly over our heads; rugs are under our feet, etc.).

18. Teach the concept of before and after with examples from your child's daily routine (e.g., we wake up before we eat breakfast; we go to school after we eat breakfast; we eat dinner after we do our homework, etc.).

19. Teach the concept of above and below with examples in your home (e.g., the ceiling is above our heads and the floor is below our feet, etc.).

20. Emphasize activities which require the action of off and on (e.g., we turn lights on for light and off when we do not need them; we turn the stove on to heat things and off when things are hot; we put clothes on to go to school; leaves fall off a tree in the fall; etc.).

26 Performs homework so carelessly as to be illegible

1. Reward your child for performing homework assignments neatly. Possible rewards include verbal praise (e.g., "Your handwriting looks wonderful on your math assignment."), a kiss on the cheek, a hug, having a friend over to play, staying up late, watching a favorite TV show, playing a game with a parent. (See Appendix for Reward Menu.)

2. Speak to your child to explain: (a) what your child is doing wrong (e.g., turning in work which has spelling errors or spacing errors, work that is illegible, etc.) and (b) what your child should be doing (e.g., taking time to check for spelling, spacing errors, etc.).

3. Establish homework rules (e.g., work on assignment, work quietly, remain in your room, etc.). Reiterate rules often and reinforce your child for following the rules.

4. If there are other children or adolescents in the home, reward them for doing their homework neatly and taking their time.

5. Reward your child for improving the quality of handwriting based on ability. Gradually increase the amount of improvement expected for reinforcement as your child is successful.

6. Write a contract with your child.

For example: I, William, for 5 days in a row, will do my homework in the best handwriting I can. When I accomplish this, I can buy Matchbox car at the store.

The contract should be written within the ability level of your child and should focus on only one behavior at a time. (See Appendix for an example of a Behavior Contract.)

7. Evaluate the appropriateness of the homework to determine: (a) if the task is too difficult and (b) if the length of time scheduled to complete the task is appropriate.

8. Have a sibling or a friend work with your child in order to provide an acceptable model for your child to imitate.

9. Allow your child to perform homework in a quiet place (e.g., in a bedroom, at the library, in the dining room, etc.).

10. Have your child do smaller amounts of homework several times throughout the evening.

11. Supervise your child during homework time in order to monitor handwriting quality.

12. Provide your child with clearly stated criteria for acceptable work.

13. Have your child read/go over schoolwork with the teacher in order that your child can become more aware of the quality of work.

14. Provide your child with samples of work which may serve as models for acceptable quality (e.g., your child is to match the quality of the sample before turning in the assignment).

15. Provide your child with additional time to perform homework in order to achieve quality.

16. Teach your child procedures for doing quality work (e.g., listen to homework directions, make certain directions are understood, make certain you bring all necessary materials home, make certain that you allow yourself enough time to do your work, etc.).

17. Make certain to go over your child's homework when it is completed.

18. Allow natural consequences to occur when your child does homework assignments carelessly (e.g., require that the homework be done over until it is done neatly).

19. Provide your child with quality materials to perform homework assignments (e.g., pencil with eraser, paper, handwriting sample, etc.).

20. Provide your child with an appropriate model of handwriting to use while doing homework (e.g., sample work, teacher samples, commercial samples, etc.).

21. Provide your child with ample opportunity to master handwriting skills (e.g., instruction in letter positioning, directions, spacing, etc.).

22. Act as a model for appropriate handwriting at all times for your child.

23. Provide a multitude of opportunities for your child to practice handwriting skills (e.g., writing letters to sports and entertainment figures, relatives, and friends; writing for free information on a topic of interest; etc.).

24. Have your child trace handwriting models and fade the model as your child develops the skill.

25. Gradually reduce the space between lines as your child's handwriting improves.

26. Use primary paper to assist your child in sizing upper-case and lower-case letters. Use standard lined paper when your child's skills improve.

27. Use paper that is also vertically lined (e.g., | | | | |) to teach your child appropriate spacing skills (e.g., | K | a | t | h | y |).

28. Use adhesive material (e.g., tape, Dycem material, etc.) to keep paper positioned appropriately for handwriting.

29. Use a pencil grip (e.g., three-side, foam rubber, etc.) in order to provide your child assistance in appropriate positioning of the pencil or pen.

30. Use handwriting models with arrows that indicate the direction in which your child should correctly form the letters.

31. Make certain that everyone who works with your child maintains consistent expectations of handwriting quality.

32. Speak to your child's teacher to see if assignments could be shortened for your child. Longer assignments may cause your child to fail to perform assignments neatly. The length of the assignments may be increased as your child demonstrates success.

33. Make certain your child has a number line and alphabet strip to use as a reference for correct form of letters and numbers in order to reduce errors.

34. Recognize your child's quality work (e.g., hang assignments on the refrigerator, show papers to brothers/sisters, etc.).

35. Check your child's pencil grip to make certain that he/she is holding the pencil correctly.

36. Have your child use a different size pencil or pencil grip.

27 Demonstrates visual perception problems

1. Make certain your child's vision has been checked recently.

2. Give your child the opportunity to find objects which are the same or different in size, shape, color, etc.

3. Have your child sort objects according to size, shape, color, etc.

4. Have your child use play equipment such as a ladder, jungle gym, blocks, teeter-totter, balance beam, etc., to become more aware of body positions in space.

5. Have your child complete partially drawn figures, words, numbers, etc.

6. Have your child use paper pictures from magazines, catalogs, etc., to assemble features and body parts.

7. Have your child build an object according to a pattern (e.g., Tinker Toys, blocks, etc.).

8. Have your child engage in sequencing activities (e.g., put numbers in order, place pictures in correct order, etc.).

9. Have your child pick out specific objects from pictures around the house or in the environment while outside playing.

10. Have your child perform a variety of activities such as tracing, cutting, coloring, pasting, etc.

11. Have your child complete jigsaw puzzles (e.g., beginning with simple self-made puzzles and progressing to more complex puzzles).

12. Develop a variety of activities for your child using a pegboard.

13. Provide your child with a variety of classifying activities (e.g., from simple classifying of types of clothes, cars, etc., to more complex classifying of items that would be located at certain stores; etc.).

14. Have your child find specific shapes in the home (e.g., the door is a rectangle, the clock is a circle, etc.).

15. Provide your child with simple designs to be reproduced with blocks, sticks, paper, etc.

16. Provide your child with dot-to-dot worksheets following specific patterns, etc.

17. Have your child identify objects by looking at the outlines of objects on a cardboard silhouette, etc.

18. Reduce visual stimuli on a worksheet or in a book by covering all of the page except the activity on which your child is working.

19. Have your child repeat the names of objects, shapes, numbers, or words that are presented to him/her for a limited period.

20. Provide your child with a variety of exercises in which he/she must identify the missing body parts, common objects, etc.

21. Provide your child with a variety of visual recall tasks (e.g., your child writes numbers, shapes, and words that were shown for a specific time, etc.).

22. Use a variety of colored tiles to make a pattern. Have your child duplicate the pattern while looking at the model and then complete the design from memory without using the model.

23. Place several items on a tray (e.g., a pencil, flower, penny, and piece of gum). Allow your child to look at the items, then take the items away and have your child identify the items that were on the tray.

24. Have your child practice tracing outlines of pictures. Work pages with dotted lines of pictures, letters, numbers, etc., can be used to develop eye-hand coordination.

25. Play a matching game like "Concentration" in which hidden pictures, numbers, or shapes are turned over one at a time and your child must remember where the matching picture is located.

26. Using pictures from magazines, remove any important part of the picture and ask your child to identify the missing part.

27. Speak to your child's teacher about reducing the amount of information on a page for your child.

28 Has difficulty classifying

1. Make certain your child understands that all objects, people, ideas, actions, etc., can be grouped based on how they are alike. Provide your child with concrete examples.

2. Give your child pairs of objects and ask your child to name all the ways in which they are alike and then ways in which they are different. Proceed from simple things which can be seen and touched to more abstract ideas which cannot be seen or touched.

3. Name a category or group and ask your child to identify as many things as possible which belong in the group. Begin with large categories (e.g., living things) and move to more specific categories (e.g., things which are green).

4. Explain that each new word which is learned is an example of some category. When defining a word, it should first be put into a category (e.g., a hammer is a kind of tool, anger is a kind of emotion, etc.).

5. Present a series of objects or words and have your child tell which one does not belong in the same category as the others.

6. Present a series of objects and have your child create a category into which they fit.

7. Give your child a list of words and have your child identify the categories into which the words belong (e.g., Love and hate are both emotions. Love fits into the specific category of good feelings and hate fits into the specific category of bad or unhappy feelings.).

8. Explain that words can be categorized according to many different attributes, such as size, function, texture, etc.

9. Ask your child to help make lists of some categories which fit inside larger categories (e.g., flowers, trees, and bushes are all categories which can be included in the plant category).

10. Play a game such as "I'm thinking of an object" in which an object is described and your child must guess the item based on the answers that are given to the questions that are asked.

11. Have your child help when grocery shopping by having your child make a list of items needed in a particular food group (e.g., dairy products, meats, etc.).

12. Have your child cut out pictures for a notebook of favorite foods, television shows, or other categories, and group them in appropriate arrangements.

13. Give your child specific categories and have your child name as many items as possible within the category (e.g., objects, persons, places, etc.).

14. Give your child a series of words or pictures and have your child name the category to which they belong (e.g., objects, persons, places, etc.).

15. Give your child a series of words (e.g., objects, persons, places, etc.) your child can think of which have similar meanings. (synonyms)

16. Stop at various points during the presentation of information to check your child's comprehension.

17. Use pictures, diagrams, a chalkboard, and gestures when delivering information.

29   Does not comprehend what he/she reads

1. Make certain that the reading material your child is reading is on your child's reading level.

2. Talk to your child's teacher in order to have reading material modified or adjusted to your child's reading level.

3. Outline reading material for your child using words and phrases on your child's reading level.

4. Tape record difficult reading material for your child to listen to while reading along.

5. Talk to your child's teacher to get upcoming readings in science, social studies, basal readers, etc., to preview with your child before they are read in class.

6. Arrange for a brother/sister or a friend to study with your child for quizzes, tests, etc.

7. Use a sight word vocabulary approach in order to teach your child key words and phrases when reading directions and instructions (e.g., key words such as circle, underline, match, etc.).

8. Use lower grade-level reading books from the library for outside reading material for your child.

9. Have your child tape record lectures at school to use as an additional source of information when studying.

10. Make a list of main points from your child's reading material, written on your child's reading level.

11. Reduce distracting stimuli in order to increase your child's ability to concentrate on what he/she is reading (e.g., turn the TV off, work in the dining room or bedroom, send friends home, etc.). This is used as a means of distracting stimuli and not as a form of punishment.

12. Provide your child with a quiet place to work while doing homework (e.g., an office, a bedroom, a dining room, etc.).

13. Teach your child to identify the main points in reading material in order to assess comprehension.

14. Have your child outline, underline, or highlight important points in reading material.

15. Provide your child with written direction-following activities in order to enhance comprehension (e.g., following a recipe, following directions to put together a model, etc.).

16. Provide your child with written one-, two- and three-step direction-following activities (e.g., make your bed, pick up your clothes, take out the trash, etc.).

17. Have your child take notes while reading in order to increase comprehension.

18. Have your child read progressively longer segments of reading material in order to build comprehension skills (e.g., begin with a single paragraph and progress to several paragraphs, a chapter, a short story, a novel, etc.).

19. Have your child tape record what he/she reads in order to enhance comprehension by listening to the material.

20. Teach your child to use context clues to identify words and phrases that he/she does not know.

21. Write paragraphs and short stories requiring skills that your child is currently developing in school. These passages should be of high interest to your child by using names of family members, friends, pets, interesting experiences, etc.

22. Have your child dictate stories which are then written for him/her to read, placing an emphasis on comprehension skills.

23. Have your child read high-interest signs, advertisements, notices, etc., from newspapers, magazines, movie promotions, etc.

24. Make certain that your child is practicing comprehension skills which are directly related to high interest reading activities (e.g., adventures, romance, mystery, sports, etc.).

25. Reduce the emphasis on competition among brothers/sisters or friends. Competitive activities may make it difficult for your child to comprehend what is read.

26. Underline or highlight important points before your child reads material silently.

27. Write notes and letters to your child to provide reading material which your child will want to read for comprehension. Your child may be encouraged to write notes and letters at a time set aside each day, once a week, etc.

28. Give your child time to read a selection more than once, emphasizing comprehension, rather than speed.

29. After your child reads a passage, discuss what was read.

30. Make it a habit every evening to turn off the TV and set aside silent reading time for the family.

31. Be a model for reading for enjoyment.

32. Reduce the amount of material your child reads at one time (e.g., reduce reading material to single sentences on a page, a single paragraph, etc.). Gradually increase the amount of material as your child experiences success.

33. Avoid subjecting your child to uncomfortable reading situations (e.g., reading aloud in front of others, reading with time limits, etc.).

34. Stop your child at various points throughout the reading selection to check for comprehension.

35. Reduce the amount of information on a page if it is causing visual distractions for your child (e.g., less print to read, fewer pictures, etc.).

36. Highlight or underline important information your child should pay close attention to when reading.

1. With the help of your child's teacher, create a list of words and phrases from your child's reading material which your child will not recognize (e.g., have the science teacher identify words your child will not recognize in the following week's assignment). These words and phrases will become the student's reading word list for the following week.

2. Have your child identify words and phrases which he/she does not recognize. Make these words a list to learn.

3. Make certain that your child's teacher has reading materials modified or adjusted to his/her reading level.

4. Outline reading material for your child using words and phrases on your child's reading level.

5. Teach your child to use context clues to identify words and phrases he/she does not know.

6. Emphasize that your child learn a root word sight vocabulary in order to be able to add various prefixes and suffixes to develop work attack skills.

7. Tape record difficult reading material for your child to listen to while reading along.

8. Use a highlight marker to identify key words and phrases for your child. These words and phrases become your child's sight word vocabulary.

9. Teach your child to use related learning experiences (e.g., videotapes, the museum, tape recordings, etc.).

10. Use the sight word vocabulary approach in order to teach your child key words and phrases when reading directions and instructions (e.g., key words such as circle, underline, match, etc.).

11. Arrange for a brother/sister or a friend to study with your child for quizzes, tests, etc.

12. Use library books on a lower grade level for extra reading material for your child.

13. Talk to your child's teachers in order to have lectures and test reviews tape recorded for your child.

14. Make a list of main points from your child's reading material, written on your child's reading level.

15. Write paragraphs and short stories requiring skill your child is currently developing at school. These passages should be of high interest to your child using family members, friends, pets, and interesting experiences.

16. Have your child dictate stories which are then written for your child; the emphasis should be placed on reading skills.

17. Have your child read high-interest signs, advertisements, notices, etc., from newspapers, movie promotions, magazines, etc., placing an emphasis on reading skills.

18. Make certain your child is practicing reading skills which are directly related to high-interest reading activities (e.g., adventures, romance, mystery, athletics, etc.).

19. Make certain that the reading demands of all subjects and assignments are within the ability level of your child. If they are not, modify or adjust the reading material to your child's ability level. A lower grade level text may be an alternative.

20. Make certain that your child's knowledge of a particular skill is being assessed rather than your child's ability to read directions, instructions, etc.

21. Have your child read aloud each day in order to provide evaluative feedback.

22. Reduce the amount of material your child reads at one time (e.g., reduce reading material to single sentences on a page, a single paragraph, etc.). Gradually increase the amount of material as your child demonstrates success.

23. Have your child practice vocabulary words from required reading material by writing them while saying the sounds.

31 Loses place when reading

1. Make certain that your child's reading material is adjusted to your child's ability level.

2. Use a highlight marker to identify key syllables, words, etc., for your child. These words and phrases become your child's sight word vocabulary.

3. Have your child point to syllables, words, etc., as he/she reads them in order to help your child recognize omissions.

4. Tape record your child's reading in order that he/she can hear omissions made.

5. Reduce the emphasis on competition among brothers/sisters or friends. Competitive activities may cause your child to hurry and omit words.

6. Have your child read aloud to you each day in order to provide evaluative feedback relative to omissions made.

7. Verbally correct your child's omissions as often as possible in order that your child hears the correct version of the reading material.

8. Make a list of those words for which your child makes omissions. Have your child practice reading these words.

9. Have your child use a paper strip to move down the page while reading each line.

10. Make a reading "window" for each textbook your child uses. Your child moves the reading "window" down and across the page while reading.

11. Enlarge the print your child is reading.

12. Reduce the amount of material your child reads at one time (e.g., reduce reading material to single sentences on a page, a single paragraph, etc.).

13. Provide a quiet place for your child to work (e.g., "office" space, the dining room, a bedroom, etc.).

14. Have your child highlight or underline the material he/she reads.

15. Have your child read aloud in order to help maintain his/her place while reading.

16. Have your child place a ruler under each line that is being read at the time. Your child then moves the ruler to the next line and so on.

17. Give your child time to read a selection more than once, emphasizing comprehension rather than speed.

18. Make certain that the reading demands of all subjects and assignments are within the ability level of your child. If they are not, modify or adjust the reading material to your child's ability level.

19. Make certain that your child's knowledge of a particular skill is being assessed rather than your child's ability to read directions, etc.

20. Reduce the amount of information on a page if it is causing visual distractions for your child (e.g., less print to read, fewer pictures, etc.).

21. Have your child point to every word read in order to hold his/her place.

1. Talk to your child's teacher and make a list of words and phrases from your child's reading material which he/she will not recognize (e.g., have the science teacher identify the words and phrases your child will not recognize in the following week's assignment). These words and phrases will become a part of your child's reading activities for the following week.

2. Make certain that your child's reading material has been adjusted or modified to his/her reading level.

3. Have your child identify words and phrases that are not recognized. Make these words your child's list to be learned.

4. Emphasize that your child learn a root word sight vocabulary in order to be able to add various prefixes and suffixes to develop word attack skills.

5. Use a highlight marker to identify key syllables, words, etc., for your child. These words and phrases become your child's sight word vocabulary.

6. Use a sight word vocabulary approach in order to teach your child key words and phrases when reading directions and instructions (e.g., key words such as circle, underline, match, etc.).

7. Tape record pronunciations of words on which your child commonly makes errors in order that your child can hear all the sounds.

8. Have your child point to syllables while reading in order to help recognize omissions, additions, substitutions, or reversals.

9. Tape record your child's reading in order for him/her to hear omissions, additions, substitutions, or reversals.

10. Make certain your child is learning basic word lists to assist in reading.

11. Reduce the emphasis on competition among brothers/sisters, friends, etc. Competitive activities may cause your child to omit, add, substitute, or reverse letters, words, or sounds when reading.

12. Have your child read aloud to you each day in order to provide evaluative feedback relative to omissions, additions, substitutions, and reversals.

13. Verbally correct your child's omissions, additions, substitutions, and reversals as often as possible in order that your child hears the correct version of the reading material.

14. Make a list of those words for which your child makes omissions, additions, substitutions, or reversal errors. Have your child practice reading these words.

15. Have your child write those letters, words, or sounds that are often omitted, added, substituted, or reversed in order for him/her to have a greater opportunity to see the correct version.

16. Make certain your child has an alphabet strip to have a reference for the correct form of letters in order to reduce reversal-related errors when reading.

17. Teach your child to use context clues in reading (i.e., have your child use the words which are around the unknown word to help him/her figure out the word, such as "Bob ran very _____ because he was afraid.").

18. Tape record difficult reading material for your child to listen to while he/she reads along.

19. Make certain that the reading demands of all subjects and assignments are within your child's ability level.

20. Make certain that your child's knowledge of a particular skill is being assessed rather than your child's ability to read directions, instructions, etc. Reading directions, instructions, etc., to your child can increase success.

21. Reduce the amount of material your child reads at one time (e.g., reduce reading material to single sentences on a page, a single paragraph, etc.). Gradually increase the amount of material as your child experiences success.

22. Reduce the amount of information on a page if it is causing visual distractions for your child (e.g., less print to read, fewer pictures on a page, etc.).

33 Reads words correctly in one context but not in another

1. Speak to your child's teacher to make certain that your child is reading material on the appropriate reading level.

2. Highlight or underline those words your child most frequently fails to recognize in different contexts.

3. Use library books on a lower grade level as outside reading material for your child.

4. Write paragraphs and short stories using those words your child most frequently fails to recognize in different contexts. These paragraphs should be of high interest to your child using family members, friends, pets, and interesting experiences.

5. Make a reading "window" for your child. Your child moves the reading "window" down and across the page while reading.

6. Have your child list those words he/she most frequently fails to recognize into categories such as people, food, animals., etc., in order to help your child recognize those words in different contexts.

7. Teach your child to use context clues to identify words that are not understood.

8. Identify words your child does not recognize in different contexts and put these words on flash cards. Have your child match these words to the same words in sentences, paragraphs, short stories, etc.

9. Have your child maintain a list with definitions of those words he/she frequently fails to recognize in different contexts.

10. Have your child print/write words which he/she frequently fails to recognize in different contexts.

11. Highlight or underline those words in reading material which your child is unable to recognize. Have your child identify those words while reading them.

12. Reduce distracting stimuli where your child is reading in order to increase your child's ability level to concentrate (e.g., turn the TV off, send friends home, go to a quiet place to read, etc.).

13. Provide your child with a quiet place (e.g., an "office," the dining room, a bedroom, etc.) for reading.

14. Reduce the emphasis on competition among brothers/sisters, friends, etc. Competitive activities may cause your child to hurry and fail to recognize words in a particular context.

15. Provide your child with a dictionary and require him/her to find the definitions of those words that are not recognized.

16. Have your child read short sentences in order to make it easier to recognize words in different contexts. Longer sentences are presented as your child demonstrates success.

17. Provide your child with large-print reading materials in order to increase the likelihood of your child recognizing words in different contexts.

18. Use daily drill activities to help your child memorize vocabulary words.

19. Tape record difficult reading material for your child to listen to as he/she reads along.

20. Write notes and letters to your child to provide reading material which includes words your child frequently has difficulty with.

21. Have your child read aloud to you each day in order to provide evaluative feedback.

22. Reduce the amount of information on a page if it is causing visual distractions for your child (e.g., less print to read, fewer pictures to look at, etc.).

23. Require your child to read a selection each day which includes the vocabulary currently being studied.

34 Does not read independently

1. Speak to your child's teacher to make certain that your child is reading material on the appropriate reading level.

2. With the assistance of your child's teacher, modify or adjust reading material to the ability level of your child.

3. Tape record reading material for your child to listen to while reading.

4. Provide your child with a quiet place (e.g., an "office," the dining room, a bedroom, etc.) for reading.

5. Write paragraphs and short stories for your child. These passages should be of high-interest to your child using family members, friends, pets, and interesting experiences.

6. Have your child dictate stories which are then written for your child to read.

7. Have your child read high-interest signs, advertisements, notices, etc., from newspapers, magazines, movie promotions, etc.

8. Provide your child with many high-interest materials (e.g., comic books, magazines relating to sports, fashion magazines, etc.).

9. Talk to your child and discuss the types of reading material that would be interesting for him/her to read.

10. Read, or have someone read, high-interest material to your child to promote your child's interest in reading.

11. Develop a library in your home that is appealing to your child (e.g., in a tent, a bean-bag chair, etc.).

12. Provide your child with high-interest reading material that is also short in length in order that your child can finish reading the material without difficulty.

13. Encourage interest in reading by having brothers/sisters, friends, etc., share interesting things they have read.

14. Have your child write to the author of material he/she reads in order to encourage an interest in reading more material by the same author.

15. Encourage your child to read material with many illustrations and a limited amount of print. Gradually encourage your child to read material with fewer illustrations and more print.

16. Read to your child and have your child read to you.

17. Be a model for your child by reading for enjoyment.

18. Have your child read lower grade level stories to younger brothers/sisters, friends, etc., in order to enhance your child's feelings of confidence relative to reading.

19. Include predictable reading books in your child's library. Predictability can make books more appealing to beginning readers and build confidence as well.

20. Avoid subjecting your child to uncomfortable reading situations (e.g., reading in front of brothers/sisters, friends, other adults, etc.).

21. Write periodic notes to your child and encourage your child to write back.

22. Expose your child to large print materials. Large print can appear less intimidating to the child who does not choose to read.

23. Provide assistance in helping your child find reading material according to his/her interests and reading level.

24. Set aside a fixed or random time (e.g., a half-hour daily, an hour a week, etc.) for silent reading in your home. Everyone, parents included, chooses a book to read for pleasure.

25. Offer your child memberships in paperback book clubs.

26. Have your child act as a peer tutor to read to a younger brother/sister, friend, etc.

27. Make certain your child has mastery of reading skills before expecting him/her to read independently.

28. Encourage your child to find books about different subjects being taught or discussed in school (e.g., when studying electricity, encourage your child to read a book about Thomas Edison, etc.).

35 Does not discriminate between similar letters and words

1. Make certain that your child's hearing has been checked recently.

2. Each day have your child practice those letters and words that he/she can not discriminate.

3. Take every opportunity throughout the day to emphasize a designated letter or word your child cannot discriminate (e.g., identify the sound when speaking, writing, reading, etc.).

4. Use highlight markers (e.g., pink and yellow) to have your child mark the letters and words in a passage that he/she does not discriminate (e.g., all m's marked with the pink marker and all n's marked in yellow marker).

5. Make a list of words your child cannot discriminate. Have your child and a brother/sister, friend, etc., work together with flash cards to develop your child's ability to recognize the differences in the letters and words.

6. Tape record stories and paragraphs your child can listen to while reading along.

7. Have your child read aloud to you each day in order to provide evaluative feedback relative to your child's ability to discriminate letters and words.

8. Verbally correct your child as often as possible when he/she does not discriminate between letters and words in order that your child hears the correct version of the reading material.

9. Have your child use context clues in reading. These skills will be particularly helpful when your child is unable to discriminate letters and words.

10. Have your child write those letters and words that he/she has difficulty discriminating in order to have greater opportunity to conceptualize the correct version.

11. Make certain your child looks closely at word endings as well as beginnings in order to discriminate similar words (e.g., cap and cat).

12. Identify a letter or word each day which your child has difficulty discriminating. Have your child underline or highlight that letter or word each time it is read that day.

13. Make certain your child has an alphabet strip as a reference when reading or performing assignments.

14. Make certain that the reading demands of all subjects and assignments are within the ability level of your child. If they are not, modify or adjust the reading material to your child's ability level.

15. Make certain that your child's knowledge of a particular skill is being assessed rather than your child's ability to read directions, instructions, etc.

16. Have your child cut letters out of magazines or newspapers and glue the letters to make words, sentences, etc.

36 Does not know all the letters of the alphabet

1. Reward your child for knowing letters of the alphabet. Possible rewards include verbal praise (e.g., "I'm so proud of you for knowing the first three letters of the alphabet."), a kiss on the cheek, a hug, a special outing with a parent, etc.

2. Make certain that your child has an alphabet strip to use as a reference for the alphabet.

3. Hang the letters of the alphabet on the wall in your child's bedroom (e.g., an alphabet chart, a letter chain, etc.)

4. Each day have your child print those letters of the alphabet that he/she does not know.

5. Have your child work with a brother/sister, friend, etc., on one letter of the alphabet each day (e.g., tracing the letter, printing the letter, recognizing the letter in words in a paragraph, etc.).

6. Have your child read and write friends' first names which include letters your child does not recognize.

7. Introduce letters to the student as partners (e.g., Aa, Bb, Cc, Dd, etc.). This may make it easier for your child to remember the names of the letters.

8. Have your child say the letters of the alphabet in sequence. Repeat by rote several times a day.

9. Identify a letter your child does not know. Have your child find that letter in all the words in a paragraph or a page of a book.

10. Present the alphabet to your child on flash cards. This is an appropriate activity for a brother/sister to conduct with your child each day.

11. Start by teaching the names of the letters in your child's name only. When your child has mastered the letters in his/her first name, go on to the last name, parents' name, etc.

12. Give your child a word which begins with each letter of the alphabet (e.g., a-apple, b-bad, c-cat, etc.). Go over several of the words each day, stressing the alphabet letters being learned.

13. Take every opportunity throughout the day to emphasize a designated letter for that day (e.g., identify the letter when speaking, writing, reading, etc.).

14. Teach your child the alphabet song and sing it several times a day with your child.

15. Read alphabet books, listen to alphabet tapes, and watch alphabet videotapes with your child in order to add variety to the ways your child sees and hears the alphabet.

16. Use daily drill activities to help your child memorize the alphabet.

37 Understands what is read to him/her but not what he/she reads silently

1. Talk to your child's teacher to make certain that your child is reading material on the appropriate reading level.

2. With help from your child's teacher, modify or adjust reading material to your child's ability level.

3. Outline reading material which your child reads silently by using words and phrases on the ability level of your child.

4. Tape record difficult reading material for your child to listen to while reading along.

5. Use lower grade-level library books for your child to read as enjoyable outside reading.

6. Make a list of main points from your child's reading material, written on your child's reading level.

7. Reduce distracting stimuli in order to increase your child's ability to concentrate on reading (e.g., turn off the TV, send friends home, have your child go to a quiet place to read, etc.). This is used as a means of reducing distracting stimuli and not as a form of punishment.

8. Provide your child with a quiet place (e.g., an "office," the dining room, the bedroom, etc.) for reading activities.

9. Have your child verbally paraphrase material that has just been read in order to assess comprehension.

10. Teach your child to identify the main points in material read in order to assess comprehension.

11. Have your child outline, underline, or highlight important points in reading material.

12. Have your child take notes while reading in order to increase comprehension.

13. Have your child read progressively longer segments of reading material in order to build comprehension skills (e.g., begin with a single paragraph and progress to several paragraphs, chapters, short stories, etc.).

14. Have your child tape record what he/she reads in order to enhance comprehension by listening.

15. Teach your child to use context clues (e.g., the general idea of what is being read) to identify words and phrases which are not known.

16. Have your child read high-interest signs, advertisements, notices, etc., from newspapers, magazines, movie promotions, etc., placing an emphasis on comprehension skills.

17. Write paragraphs and short stories requiring reading skills your child is currently developing. These passages should be of high interest to your child using family members, friends, pets, and interesting experiences.

18. Have your child dictate stories which are then written for your child to read, placing an emphasis on comprehension skills.

19. Make certain your child is practicing comprehension skills which are directly related to high-interest reading activities (e.g., adventures, romances, mysteries, athletics, etc.).

20. Have your child underline or highlight important points in reading materials.

21. Underline or highlight important points before your child reads assigned material.

22. Write notes to your child to provide reading material which your child will want to read for comprehension. Your child may be encouraged to write notes to friends or relatives at a time set aside each day, once a week, etc.

23. Give your child time to read a selection more than once, emphasizing accuracy in understanding, not speed.

24. Use a sight word vocabulary approach in order to teach your child key words and phrases when reading directions and instructions (e.g., key words such as circle, underline, match, etc.).

25. Make certain your child is not required to learn more information than he/she is capable of at any one time.

26. Tape record difficult reading material for your child to listen to as he/she reads along.

27. Make certain that the reading demands of all subjects and assignments are within the ability level of your child. If they are not, modify or adjust the reading material to your child's ability level.

28. Have your child read aloud when reading to himself/herself.

29. Make certain that your child's knowledge of a particular skill is being assessed rather than your child's ability to read directions, instruc-- tions, etc. Reading directions, instructions, etc., to your child can increase his/her success.

30. Reduce the amount of material your child reads at one time (e.g., reduce reading material to single sentences on a page, a single paragraph, etc.). Gradually increase the amount of material as your child demonstrates success.

31. Stop at various points while your child is reading silently in order to check comprehension.

32. Reduce the amount of information on a page if it is causing visual distractions for your child (e.g., less print to read, fewer pictures to look at, etc.).

38 Does not compose complete sentences or express complete thoughts when writing

1. Reward your child for composing complete sentences and expressing complete thoughts when writing. Possible rewards include verbal praise (e.g., "I love your writing. That is one of the best stories you have ever written."), a kiss on the cheek, a hug, etc. (See Appendix for Reward Menu.)

2. Reduce the emphasis on competition among brothers/sisters, friends, etc. Competition may cause your child to hurry and fail to complete sentences or express complete thoughts when writing.

3. Identify the qualities a good writer possesses (e.g., writing in complete sentences or thoughts, using correct vocabulary, etc.) and help your child to achieve those characteristics.

4. Have your child identify someone who he/she thinks is a good writer and tell why.

5. Have a brother/sister, friend, etc., act as a model for writing in complete sentences or thoughts. Have that child work with your child to help improve writing skills.

6. Be certain to act as a model for your child to imitate writing in complete sentences or thoughts.

7. Require your child to proofread all written work before turning it in as homework.

8. Give your child a series of written phrases and have your child tell you which phrases express a complete thought.

9. Have your child correct a series of written phrases, making each a complete sentence.

10. After reading a piece of written work, have your child explain why specific sentences do not express complete thoughts.

11. Give your child a subject and have him/her write as many complete sentences about it as possible.

12. Recognize quality work (e.g., display your child's work, congratulate your child, etc.).

13. Make groups of cards containing subjects, verbs, adjectives, etc. Have your child combine the cards in various ways to construct complete sentences.

14. Give your child several short sentences and have your child combine them in order to make one long, complete sentence (e.g., The dog is big. The dog is brown. The dog is mine. becomes The big, brown dog is mine.).

15. Give your child a list of transition words (e.g., therefore, although, because, etc.) and have your child make sentences using each word.

16. Make certain your child understands that a complete sentence has to express a complete though about a subject and what that subject is or does.

17. Have your child write a daily log, expressing thoughts in complete sentences.

18. Have your child write letters to friends, relatives, etc., in order to practice writing complete sentences or thoughts.

19. Encourage your child to read his/her written work aloud, in order to help identify incomplete sentences and thoughts.

20. Give your child a group of related words (e.g., author, love, bestseller, etc.) and have your child make up a paragraph including all the words.

21. Provide your child with clearly stated criteria for acceptable work (e.g., neatness, complete sentences, etc.).

22. Check your child's written work at various points throughout the assignment to make certain your child is using complete sentences in written work.

23. Provide your child with appropriate time limits for the completion of written homework assignments.

24. Read orally to your child to stimulate his/her thought and writing process.

1. Reward your child for correctly organizing writing activities. Possible rewards include verbal praise (e.g., "I love the story you wrote. You did a nice job of telling the readers exactly how things happened."), a kiss on the cheek, a hug, etc. (See Appendix for Reward Menu.)

2. Have your child practice organizational skills in writing activities by engaging in writing activities designed to cause him/her to want to be successful (e.g., writing a letter to a friend, rock star, famous athlete, etc.).

3. Have your child regularly write an account of the previous week, past weekend, etc., with primary attention given to organization (e.g., sequencing events, developing a paragraph, using correct word order, etc.).

4. Require your child to proofread all written work before turning it in as homework.

5. Have your child write a daily log, expressing thoughts in complete sentences.

6. Have your child create personal stories about topics which are of interest. Your child is more likely to try to be successfully when writing about something of interest.

7. Have your child read his/her own written work aloud to help identify errors in organization.

8. Make certain your child knows that paragraphs, essays, etc., need an introduction, a middle where information is contained, and a conclusion or ending.

9. Have your child arrange a series of statements on a topic in an appropriate order so that they make sense in a paragraph.

10. Help your child "brainstorm" ideas about a topic and then show your child how to put those ideas into outline form, combining some ideas and discarding others.

11. Provide your child with a paragraph in which a statement does not belong. Have your child find the inappropriate statement.

12. Have your child write step-by-step directions (e.g., steps in making a cake) so your child can practice sequencing events.

13. Give your child a group of related words (e.g., author, read, love, bestseller, etc.) and have your child make up an appropriately organized paragraph including each word.

14. Using a written essay that your child has not seen, cut the paragraphs apart and have your child reconstruct the essay by putting the paragraphs in an appropriate order.

15. Reduce the emphasis on competition. Competitive activities may cause your child to hurry and fail to correctly organize writing activities.

16. Reduce distracting stimuli when your child is involved in a writing activity (e.g., turn off the TV, send friends home, have your child work in a quiet place, etc.). This is meant as a means of reducing distracting stimuli and not as a form of punishment.

17. Make certain your child is not interrupted or hurried when engaging in writing activities.

18. Have your child read sentences, paragraphs, stories, etc., written by peers who demonstrate good organizational skills in writing.

19. When correcting your child's organizational skills in writing, be certain to provide evaluative feedback which is designed to be instructional (e.g., help your child rewrite for better organization, rewrite passages for your child, etc.).

20. Have your child develop an outline or "skeleton" of what he/she is going to write. From the outline your child can then practice organizational skills in writing.

21. Have your child practice writing letters, words, and sentences by tracing over a series of dots.

22. Make certain your child has a number line and alphabet strip to use as a reference for correct form of letters and numbers in order to reduce errors.

23. Require your child to proofread all written work. Reinforce your child for each correction made.

24. Recognize quality work (e.g., display your child's work, congratulate your child, etc.).

25. Use a computer or typewriter as an alternative writing tool.

26. Be certain that your child has only the necessary materials when working on homework assignments.

27. Provide your child with quality materials to perform homework assignments (e.g., pencil with eraser, paper, dictionary, handwriting sample, etc.).

40 Omits, adds, or substitutes words when writing

1. Speak to your child to explain what he/she is doing wrong (e.g., not writing in clear and complete sentences, leaving words out, etc.) and what should be done (e.g., writing in clear and complete sentences, rereading what was written, etc.).

2. Reduce the emphasis on competition. Competitive activities may cause your child to hurry and omit words when writing.

3. Have your child proofread all written work for omissions, additions, or substitutions.

4. Encourage your child to read all written work aloud in order to detect omissions, additions, or substitutions.

5. Give your child several sentences and have your child combine them to practice making complete sentences (e.g., The car is new. The car is red. The car is mine. becomes The new, red car is mine.).

6. Give your child a list of transition words (e.g., therefore, although, because, etc.) and have your child make sentences using each word.

7. Have your child write a daily log or diary expressing thoughts in complete sentences.

8. Encourage your child to create stories about topics which are of interest in order to provide more experiences in writing.

9. Have your child complete "fill-in-the-blank" stories and sentences and then read them aloud.

10. Make certain your child is aware of the types of errors that are being made (e.g., omits is, omits final s, etc.) in order to be more conscious of them when writing.

11. Make certain your child is not interrupted or hurried when engaged in writing activities.

12. Have your child engage in writing activities designed to cause a desire to be successful in writing (e.g., writing a letter to a friend, rock star, famous athlete, etc.).

13. When reviewing your child's work, be certain to provide evaluative feedback which is designed to be instructional (e.g., point out all omissions, additions, and substitutions; suggest more appropriate words, phrases, etc.; help your child rewrite work to make corrections in the omissions, additions, substitutions, etc.).

14. Give your child the scrambled words of a sentence and have your child put them in the correct order to form the sentence.

15. Give your child a group of related words (e.g., baseball, fans, glove, strikeout, etc.) and have your child make up a paragraph including each word.

16. Reduce distracting stimuli when your child is engaged in writing activities (e.g., turn off the TV, send friends home, have your child work in a quiet place, etc.). This is used as a means of reducing distracting stimuli and not as a form of punishment.

17. Make a list of your child's most common omissions, additions, and substitutions and have your child refer to the list when engaged in writing activities in order to check for errors.

18. Have your child practice writing simple sentences successfully without omissions, additions, or substitutions. Have your child write more complex sentences, paragraphs, short stories, etc., as success is demonstrated.

19. Make certain your child has written work proofread by someone (e.g., older brother/sister, parent, teacher, etc.) for omissions, additions, substitutions before turning in written work.

20. Recognize quality work (e.g., display your child's work, congratulate your child, etc.).

21. Check your child's work at various points throughout a writing homework assignment in order to detect any omissions, additions, or substitutions.

22. Require your child to proofread all written work. Reinforce your child for each correction made.

41 Spells words correctly in one context but not in another

1. Reward your child for spelling words correctly in all contexts. Possible rewards include verbal praise (e.g., "The story you wrote is great. You did a wonderful job of spelling in the story."), a kiss on the cheek, a hug, etc. (See Appendix for Reward Menu.)

2. Reduce the emphasis on competition. Competitive activities may cause your child to hurry and make mistakes in spelling.

3. Give your child fewer words to learn to spell at any one time (e.g., learn three words a night rather than spending every night of the week on every spelling word), spending more time on each word until your child can spell the word correctly.

4. Have an older brother/sister, friend, etc., spend time each day engaged in drill activities with your child on spelling words.

5. Have your child use spelling words in sentences as a practice activity.

6. Write sentences, paragraphs, etc., for your child to read which repeat his/her spelling words throughout the material.

7. Have your child write spelling words in different locations throughout your home as your child is learning the words (e.g., notes on the refrigerator, notes on your child's bedroom door, etc.).

8. Have your child use the dictionary to find the correct spelling of any word he/she cannot spell correctly. The emphasis on this situation becomes spelling accurately rather than memorizing spelling words.

9. Have your child use correct spelling in a meaningful manner which would cause your child to want to be successful (e.g., writing a letter to a friend, rock star, famous athlete, etc.).

10. Make certain your child knows why he/she is learning each spelling word (e.g., provide your child with a concrete example of how each word can be used in daily experiences).

11. Have your child identify a list of spelling words (e.g., 5, 10, 15) each week which your child wants to learn to spell. If your child is interested in cars, words from automotive magazines, advertisements, etc., can be identified.

12. Try various activities to help strengthen and reinforce the visual memory of spelling words (e.g., flash cards, lists on the refrigerator, a list in your child's room, etc.).

13. Make certain your child has had adequate practice in writing the spelling words (e.g., drill activities, sentence activities, etc.).

14. Make certain your child has adequate time to perform homework assignments.

15. Reduce distracting stimuli when your child is working on spelling activities (e.g., turn off the TV, send friends home, have your child work in a quiet room, etc.). This is used as a means of reducing distracting stimuli and not as a form of punishment.

16. Have your child maintain a folder of all spelling words. Have your child refer to the list when engaged in writing activities in order to check spelling.

17. Make certain your child learns to "use" spelling words rather than simply memorizing the spelling of words for testing purposes (e.g., have your child use the words in writing notes, sentences, letters to relatives, etc.).

18. Require your child to proofread all written work for spelling errors before turning in homework.

19. Have your child keep a dictionary of "most misspelled words" to have as a reference when uncertain of the spelling of a word.

20. Have your child write spelling words frequently over a period of time in order to increase your child's visual memory of the spelling words.

21. Make certain your child is not being required to learn too many spelling words at one time.

22. Speak to your child's teacher to make certain that your child's spelling words are seen on a routine basis, rather than infrequently, in order to assure correct spelling and use of the words.

23. Arrange with your child's teacher to use weekly vocabulary words as weekly spelling words.

24. Speak to your child's teacher to make certain that your child is able to read the words that are given as spelling words. If your child is unable to read the spelling words, it is unlikely that your child will be able to spell the words.

25. Recognize quality work (e.g., display your child's work, congratulate your child, etc.).

26. Make certain your child is not required to learn more information than your child is capable of at any one time.

42 Requires continued drill and practice in order to learn spelling words

1. Reward your child for learning spelling words. Possible rewards include verbal praise (e.g., "You have done a great job of learning your spelling words this week."), a kiss on the cheek, a hug, etc.

2. Reduce the emphasis on competition. Competitive activities may cause your child to hurry and make mistakes in spelling.

3. Give your child fewer words to learn to spell at any one time (e.g., work on three words a night rather than all spelling words each night), spending more time on each word until your child can spell it correctly.

4. Have an older brother/sister, a peer, etc., spend time each day engaged in drill activities with your child on weekly spelling words.

5. Have your child use spelling words in sentences each day.

6. Have your child highlight or underline spelling words in passages from reading assignments, newspapers, magazines, etc.

7. Develop crossword puzzles which contain only your child's spelling words and have your child complete them.

8. Have your child act as a tutor to teach spelling words to a younger brother/sister, a younger friend, etc.

9. Write sentences, passages, paragraphs, etc., for your child to read which repeat your child's spelling words throughout the material.

10. Have your child post spelling words in different locations throughout your home as your child is learning them (e.g., a list on the refrigerator, a list on a desk, in your child's room, etc.).

11. Have your child indicate when a spelling word has been mastered. As your child demonstrates that the word is mastered, remove the spelling word from the study list.

12. Use visual images such as pictires for the student to associate with the letter sound.

13. Have your child's current spelling list in his/her bedroom with the requirement that the words practiced whenever your child has a few extra minutes. Reward your child for practicing spelling words.

14. Have your child review spelling words each day for a short period of time rather than two or three times per week for longer periods of time.

15. Have your child use a dictionary to find the correct spelling of any word that is difficult to spell. The emphasis in this situation becomes spelling accurately rather than memorizing spelling words.

16. Have your child quiz brothers/sisters, friends, etc., over his/her spelling words.

17. Speak with your child's teacher to make certain that your child's spelling instruction is on a level where success can be met.

18. Initiate a "learn to spell a word a day" program with your child.

19. Use words for your child's spelling list which are commonly found in daily surroundings (e.g., commercials, hazard signs, directions, lunch menu, etc.).

20. Have your child's current list of spelling words on the refrigerator at all times.

21. Have your child use current spelling words in a meaningful manner which would cause your child to want to be successful (e.g., writing a letter to a friend, rock star, famous athlete, etc.).

22. Require your child to proofread all written work for spelling errors.

23. Have your child identify a list of words (e.g., 5, 10, 15) each week which he/she wants to learn to spell. If your child is interested in cars, identify words from automotive magazines, advertisements, etc.

24. Speak to your child's teacher to make certain that your child is able to read the words that are given as spelling words. If your child is unable to read the spelling words, it is unlikely that he/she will be able to spell the words.

25. Recognize quality work (e.g., display your child's work, congratulate your child, etc.).

26. Make certain your child is not required to learn more information than he/she is capable of at any one time.

27. Provide practice on spelling words by using a computer software program that gives your child immediate feedback.

43 Has a limited speaking vocabulary

1. If there are other children or adolescents in the home, reward them for using an extended vocabulary.

2. Tape record your child's spontaneous speech, noting specific words that are used; and then have your child make a list of other words (synonyms) which could be substituted for these words.

3. Select relevant and appropriate reading material and have your child underline each unfamiliar word. Make a list of these words and review their meanings with your child until your child can use them when speaking.

4. Reward your child for using new or more difficult words when speaking.

5. Have your child keep a diary or log of all unfamiliar words which your child encounters each day. Include their meanings.

6. Give your child a list of words and ask your child to tell the opposite of each word.

7. Have your child make up sentences or stories using new words recently learned.

8. Name a category and have your child identify things within the category. Introduce new words which belong in the same group.

9. Explain to your child where he/she can go to find word meanings (e.g., dictionary, thesaurus, encyclopedia, etc.).

10. Encourage your child to read newspapers, novels, magazines, or other materials for enjoyment.

11. Be a model for your child by reading newspapers, novels, magazines, etc.

12. Give your child a "word of the day" which is to be incorporated into conversations. Reinforce your child with praise or "points" each time the word is used.

13. During conversation, repeat phrases used by your child, revising the vocabulary to include a larger speaking vocabulary (e.g., Your child says, "The TV show was good." Repeat by saying, "I'm glad the TV show was so entertaining.").

14. Use a new word to complete a sentence. Have your child explain how the word changes the sentence meaning (e.g., I like Jerry because he is ____ (sincere, humorous, competitive).).

15. Before your child reads, prepare a list of new words which will be encountered. Help your child look up the words and practice saying them and using them in sentences.

16. Explain to your child how to use context clues to determine the meaning of words heard or seen (e.g., looking at the surrounding words and determining what type of word would be appropriate).

17. Explain to your child how to classify new words as to category, function, antonym and synonym, etc., so your child will have a way of "filing" the word to remember it.

18. Have an older brother/sister, an older friend, etc., act as a model to expand your child's speaking vocabulary.

19. Review on a daily basis new vocabulary words and their meanings. Have your child use the words daily.

20. Review on a daily basis previously learned vocabulary words and meanings. Have your child incorporate previously learned vocabulary words into daily conversation and activities.

21. Have your child maintain a notebook of all new vocabulary words to call upon for daily conversation and activities.

22. Use pictures to help your child understand the meanings of new vocabulary words.

23. Make certain your child is not expected to learn more vocabulary words and meanings than he/she is capable of comprehending.

24. Make certain your child has mastery of vocabulary words at each level before introducing new words.

25. Be certain to take time each day (e.g., after school, at the dinner table, etc.) to have each member of the family tell about their day. When your child describes his/her day, ask questions to encourage the extended use of vocabulary.

44 Does not complete statements or thoughts when speaking

1. Reward your child for using complete statements or thoughts when speaking. Possible rewards include verbal praise (e.g., "You did a nice job of telling me what you wanted for lunch.").

2. If there are other children or adolescents in the home, reward them for speaking in complete statements or thoughts.

3. Allow your child to speak without being interrupted or hurried.

4. Tape record a spontaneous monologue given by your child. Transcribe your child's speech from the tape and have your child listen to the tape. Have your child correct errors and practice speaking in more complete statements or thoughts.

5. Have your child keep a list of times and/or situations in which he/she is nervous, anxious, etc., and has more trouble with speech than usual. Help your child identify ways to feel more successful with those situations.

6. Demonstrate acceptable and unacceptable speech, using complete/incomplete statements and thoughts, and have your child critique each example.

7. When your child has difficulty during a conversation, remind your child that this occasionally happens to everyone and not to become upset.

8. When your child fails to use complete thoughts (e.g., says, "Ball," and points) elaborate on what was said (e.g., "So you want to play ball?"). This provides a model for more complete statements and thoughts.

9. Have your child role-play various situations in which good speech is important (e.g., during a job interview, etc.).

10. Make a list of the attributes that are likely to help a person become a good speaker (e.g., takes time, thinks of what to say before starting, etc.).

11. Reduce the emphasis on competition. Competitive activities may cause your child to hurry and fail to speak in complete statements or thoughts.

12. Break down the qualities a good speaker possesses (e.g., rate, diction, volume, vocabulary, etc.) and have your child evaluate the characteristics in his/her own speaking. Set a goal for improvement in only one or two areas at a time.

13. Have an older brother/sister, an older friend, etc., act as a model for speaking in complete statements or thoughts.

14. Make a list of the most common incomplete statements or thoughts your child says. Spend time with your child practicing how to make these statements or thoughts complete.

15. Verbally correct your child when complete sentences are not used so your child can hear the correct version.

16. Have your child practice saying descriptive statements or thoughts which can be used when speaking.

17. Be certain to act as a model for your child to imitate speaking in complete statements or thoughts (e.g., speak clearly, slowly, concisely, and in complete sentences, statements, and thoughts).

18. When your child is required to recall information, provide visual and/or auditory cues to help him/her remember the information (e.g., key words, expose part of a picture, etc.).

19. Be certain to take time each day (e.g., after school, at the dinner table, etc.) to have each member of the family tell about their day. When your child describes his/her day, ask questions to encourage your child to complete statements or thoughts when speaking.

45 Dysfluent speech interferes with daily communication

1. Make certain your child's hearing has been recently checked.

2. Reward your child for speaking fluently. Possible rewards include verbal praise (e.g., "Thank you for speaking clearly; it is much easier to understand what you are trying to say."), a kiss on the cheek, a hug, etc. (See Appendix for Reward Menu.)

3. Familiarize yourself and your child with the terms of fluency, dysfluency, stuttering, easy speech, etc. Keep these words as neutral as possible, without negative connotations.

4. Evaluate the appropriateness of requiring your child to speak without dysfluency (e.g., developmentally, young children experience normal dysfluency in their speech and all persons are occasionally dysfluent).

5. Provide your child with an appropriate model of slow, easy speech. Lengthen the pauses between words, phrases, and sentences.

6. Identify an older brother/sister, an older friend, etc., to act as a model for appropriate speech.

7. During conversation, calmly delay your verbal responses by one or two seconds.

8. Use a tape recorder so your child may listen to and evaluate his/her own speech.

9. Develop a list of the attributes which are likely to help a person become a good speaker and have your child practice each attribute.

10. During oral reading, underline or highlight words which are difficult for your child to say, and provide reinforcement when your child says them fluently.

11. Have your child identify the times and/or situations that are likely to make him/her nervous or uncomfortable. Discuss the reasons for this and seek solutions to the difficulty experienced.

12. Have your child speak in unison with you while you are modeling slow, easy, speech.

13. Have your child practice techniques for relaxing (e.g., deep breathing, tensing and relaxing muscles, etc.) which he/she can be employed when he/she starts to become dysfluent.

14. Have your child identify the specific words on which he/she becomes dysfluent, and practice these words or phrases.

15. Encourage your child to maintain eye contact during all speaking situations. If the child is noticeably more fluent when eye contact is averted, attempt to increase eye contact on a gradual basis.

16. Reward your child's moments of relative fluency and emphasize that these occurred when your child was speaking slowly and easily.

17. Empathize with your child and explain that he/she is not more or less valuable as a person because of stuttering. Emphasize your child's positive attributes.

18. Empathize with feelings of anger which your child may be experiencing.

19. When your child is speaking fluently, try to extend the positive experience by allowing your child ample opportunity to continue speaking.

20. Reward your child each time a question is answered or your child makes a spontaneous comment.

21. If your child is speaking too rapidly, remind your child to slow down and take more time. Develop a private signal (e.g., raising a finger, touching earlobe, etc.) to avoid calling too much attention to your child's speech in front of others.

22. Try to give your child your undivided attention so your child will not feel a need to hurry or to compete with others for attention.

23. If your child is more dysfluent when involved in another activity at the same time he/she is talking, encourage your child to stop the other activity.

24. If your child is highly excited, wait until your child is calm before requiring any verbal interactions. A high level of excitement often precipitates an anxiety level that interferes with fluency.

25. During moments of dysfluency, use nonverbal activities to relax your child (e.g., deep breathing, eyes closed, etc.).

26. Do not interrupt or finish your child's sentences even if you can anticipate what your child is going to say. This can be extremely frustrating and may decrease your child's willingness to engage in future communicative interactions.

27. Help your child learn to identify periods of dysfluency and periods of slow, easy speech.

28. Help your child learn to identify situations in which he/she is more fluent and less fluent. Determine the aspects of the fluent situations that seem to enhance fluency and try to transfer those features to the less fluent situations.

29. When your child is dysfluent during conversations, explain that this happens to everyone at times.

30. Have your child make a list of his/her strong points or the things he/she does well in order to improve his/her overall level of confidence.

31. Point out to your child that he/she is capable of fluent speech and is in control in many situations.

32. Model slow, easy speech for your child and encourage your child to speak at a similar rate. Practice with your child for a short time each day until he/she is able to match the rate.

33. Provide your child with a list of sentences and encourage your child to read at a slow rate.

34. Prepare simple oral reading passages in written form in which phrases are separated by large spaces (indicating "pauses"). Have your child practice reading the passages aloud.

35. Teach your child ways to restate or rephrase a misunderstood message rather than continuing to repeat the original message with the same error patterns.

36. When your child experiences a severe episode of dysfluency, respond by reiterating the content of your child's message to communicate that the message has been understood.

37. Meet with your child's teacher to determine the level of dysfluency at school, teachers' reactions to the dysfluency, and successful strategies the teachers might employ when dealing with dysfluent speech.

46 Does not understand the concept of skip counting

1. Have your child count nickels, dimes, quarters, etc. (e.g., five cents, ten cents, fifteen cents, etc.).

2. Have an older brother/sister, an older friend, etc., work with your child to help your child understand the concept of skip counting (e.g., counting Oreo cookies by 2's, counting eggs by 3's, etc.).

3. Have your child use a number line (e.g., a line of numbers, 1, 2, 3, 4, 5, 6, 7, 8, 9, 10, 11, 12, 13, 14, 15, 16, 17, 18, 19, 20, etc.) as he/she counts by 2's, 5's, 10's, etc., in order that your child can see the increments that are being added.

4. Have your child count by 2's, 5's, 10's, etc., and write the numbers as your child counts. Your child can then go back to the numbers that were written and see that the increment of 2, 5, 10, etc., is added to each number.

5. Have your child use tangible objects (e.g., pennies, paper clips, etc.) when counting by 2's, 5's, 10's, etc., in order to see that the total number is increasing in successive increments.

6. Have your child use a calculator when skip counting, adding 2, 5, 10, etc., to each successive number in order to see that skip counting increases by the increment used in counting (e.g., 2 + 2 = 4, + 2 = 6, + 2 = 8, + 2 = 10, etc.).

7. Make certain your child knows why he/she is learning a math concept. Provide your child with concrete examples and opportunities to apply these concepts in real-life situations.

8. Have your child use a clock in the home to count by 5's, 10's, 15's, etc.

9. Make certain your child understands number concepts (e.g., "What does 3 mean?" "What does 5 mean?" etc.) and the relationships of symbols to the numbers of objects (e.g., the number 3 means three things, the number 5 means five things, etc.), before requiring your child to solve math problems.

10. Make certain your child has a number line (e.g., a line of numbers, 1, 2, 3, 4, 5, 6, 7, 8, 9, 10, 11, 12, 13, 14, 15, 16, 17, 18, 19, 20, etc.) to use as a reference.

11. Use manipulative objects (e.g., abacus, base ten blocks, etc.) to teach your child the concept of skip counting.

12. Make certain your child is not required to learn more information than he/she is capable of at any one time.

13. Have your child act as a tutor to teach a younger brother/sister, friend, etc., a concept he/she has mastered. This can serve as reinforcement for your child.

14. Provide practice in skip counting using a computer software program that gives your child immediate feedback.

15. Make certain your child has mastery of math concepts at each level before introducing a new skill level.

47 Does not remember math facts

1. Reward your child for improving retention of math facts. Possible rewards include verbal praise (e.g., "I am so proud of you for knowing 5 new math facts."), a kiss on the cheek, a hug, etc. (See Appendix for Reward Menu.)

2. Reduce the emphasis on competition. Competitive activities may cause your child to hurry and make mistakes in math problems.

3. Beginning with the addition and subtraction facts, separate the basic facts into "sets," each to be memorized successively by the student.

4. Using the tracking technique to help your child learn math facts, present a few facts at a time. Gradually increase the number of facts your child must remember as your child demonstrates success.

5. Provide your child with many concrete experiences to help your child learn and remember math facts. Use popsicle sticks, tongue depressors, paper clips, buttons, etc., to form groupings to teach math facts.

6. Use fingers to teach your child to form addition and subtraction combinations. Have your child hold up fingers and add or subtract other fingers to find the correct answer.

7. Have your child use a calculator to reinforce learning of the math facts. Have your child solve several problems each day using the calculator.

8. If there is a computer available, provide practice of math facts using a computer with software programs that provide immediate feedback for your child.

9. Use daily drill activities to help your child memorize math facts (e.g., written problems, flash cards, etc.).

10. Allow your child to keep basic addition, subtraction, multiplication, and division charts to use in solving math problems.

11. Build upon math facts your child already knows, reinforcing facts your child has mastered. Add one fact at a time as your child demonstrates success.

12. Have your child perform timed drills to reinforce basic math facts. Your child "competes" against his/her best work.

13. Have your child use a number line when working addition and subtraction problems.

14. Choose one fact your child is unsuccessful with and review it several times a day. Make that fact your child's "fact of the day."

15. Have your child complete math facts and then have your child use a calculator to check and correct the problem.

16. Have an older brother/sister, an older friend, etc., work with your child each day on drill activities (e.g., flash cards).

17. Avoid going on to multiplication and division facts until addition and subtraction facts have been mastered.

18. Have your child use math fact records and tapes for math fact drill activities.

19. Use manipulative objects (e.g., peg board, abacus, base ten blocks, etc.) to teach your child basic math facts while providing a visual image.

20. Have your child use a calculator for drill activities of basic math facts.

21. Find opportunities for your child to apply math facts in real-life situations (e.g., getting change at a restaurant, measuring the length of objects, etc.).

22. Have your child solve half of the math homework problems with a calculator and half of the problems without a calculator.

23. Make certain your child is not required to learn more information than he/she is capable of at any one time.

24. Review, on a daily basis, those skills, concepts, tasks, etc., which have been previously introduced.

48 Does not understand the concept of time

1. Reward your child for telling time correctly. Possible rewards include verbal praise (e.g., "Thank you for telling me that is was time to take you to school."), a kiss on the cheek, a hug, etc. (See Appendix for Reward Menu.)

2. If there is a computer available, provide practice in telling time using computer software programs that give immediate feedback to your child.

3. Have your child work with an older brother/sister, friend, etc., each day practicing skills required for telling time (e.g., telling time to the hour, half hour, quarter hour, etc.).

4. Make certain your child understands all the concepts involved in telling time (e.g., there are five minutes between each number on the clock; counting by 5's, 10's, 15's; the big hand and the little hand, etc.).

5. Make certain your child understands which seasons come before and after other seasons.

6. Make certain your child understands the concepts of morning, afternoon, evening, and night.

7. Make certain your child understands the concept of the length of a minute, five minutes, ten minutes, fifteen minutes, one hour, ninety minutes, twenty-four hours, etc.

8. Make certain your child has a standard clock in his/her room to use as a visual reference.

9. Make certain your child knows the number of hours in a day, days in a week, weeks in a year, etc.

10. Make certain your child understands the terms used in telling time (e.g., a quarter 'til, half past, a quarter after, etc.).

11. Make certain your child can count by common divisors of time (e.g., one minute, two minutes, three minutes, five minutes, 10 minutes, 15 minutes, 60 minutes, 90 minutes, one hour, two hours, three hours, etc.).

12. Have your child recognize when events occur in the environment (e.g., lunch, naptime, bedtime, etc.).

13. Have your child indicate when the clock is on the hour.

14. Have your child indicate when the clock is on the half hour.

15. Have your child indicate when the clock is on the quarter hour.

16. Give your child word problems involving math concepts on your child's ability level (e.g., "At 10 minutes after 9 o'clock, you will begin walking to school. It takes 10 minutes to walk to school. What time will it be when you arrive?").

17. Make certain your child has a clock with a face and hands to manipulate when learning to tell time.

18. Have your child set the hands on a clock as you indicate the time of the day.

19. Use a large face clock to set the hands and have your child indicate the time. Begin with the hours, the half hours, the quarter hours, etc.

20. Make certain your child can read a digital clock or watch.

21. If possible, provide your child with a wrist-watch to wear while learning to tell time.

22. Make certain your child has a number line (e.g., a line of numbers, 1, 2, 3, 4, 5, 6, 7, 8, 9, 10, 11, 12, 13, 14, 15, 16, 17, 18, 19, 20, etc.) to use as a reference.

23. Make certain your child knows why he/she is learning a math concept. Provide your child with concrete examples and opportunities to apply these concepts in real-life situations.

24. Have your child talk through math problems as he/she is solving them in order to identify errors your child is making.

25. Recognize quality work (e.g., display your child's work, congratulate your child, etc.).

26. Make certain your child has mastery of math concepts at each level before introducing a new skill level.

27. Reduce the amount of information on a page if it is causing visual distractions for your child (e.g., fewer math problems, less print, etc.).

1. Make certain to use terms when speaking to your child which convey concepts to describe tangible objects in the environment (e.g., larger, smaller, square, triangle, etc.).

2. Identify tangible objects in the home with signs that convey abstract concepts (e.g., larger, smaller, square, triangle, etc.).

3. Use concrete examples when teaching abstract concepts (e.g., number of objects to convey more than and less than, rulers and yardsticks to convey concepts of height and width, etc.).

4. Play "Simon Says" to enhance understanding of abstract concepts (e.g., "Find the largest desk." "Touch something that is a rectangle." etc.).

5. Conduct a scavenger hunt. Have your child look for the smallest pencil, tallest chair, etc., in your home.

6. Teach shapes using common objects in the environment (e.g., round clocks, rectangle tables, square tiles on the floor, etc.).

7. Evaluate the appropriateness of expecting your child to understand abstract concepts (e.g., is it too difficult for your child).

8. Teach abstract concepts one at a time before pairing the concepts (e.g., dimensionality, size, space, shape, etc.).

9. Provide repeated physical demonstrations of abstract concepts (e.g., identify things far away and close to your child, point out a small box in a large room, etc.).

10. Review, on a daily basis, those abstract concepts which have been previously talked about. Talk about new abstract concepts only after your child has mastery of those previously talked about.

11. When introducing abstract concepts, rely on tangible objects (e.g., boxes for dimensionality, family members for size, cookie cutters for shape, etc.). Do not introduce abstract concepts by using their descriptive titles such as square, rectangle, triangle, etc.

12. Have your child match the names of abstract concepts with objects (e.g., triangle, square, circle, etc.).

13. Give your child direction-following chores (e.g., "Go to the swing which is farthest away." "Go to the nearest sandbox.", etc.).

14. Have a peer spend time each day with your child pointing out abstract concepts in the classroom (e.g., the rectangle-shaped light switch plate, the round light fixture, the tallest girl, etc.).

15. Make certain your child is attending to the source of information (e.g., eye contact is being made, hands are free of materials, etc.) when directions are delivered that involve abstract concepts.

16. Label abstract concepts throughout the home (e.g., triangle shapes on the walls, left and right sides of a desk, etc.) to help your child understand the concepts.

17. Make certain your child is not required to learn more abstract concepts than your child is capable of learning at any one time.

50 Has trouble using money to make purchases, make change, etc.

1. Reward your child for correctly solving problems involving money. Possible rewards include verbal praise (e.g., "You did a great job of figuring out the money word problems."), a kiss on the cheek, a hug, having a friend over to play, staying up late, watching a favorite TV show, and playing a game with a parent. (See Appendix for Reward Menu.)

2. Have your child use a calculator to reinforce learning to solve problems involving money. Have your child solve several problems each day using the calculator.

3. Use real-life situations for your child to practice money problems (e.g., paying for lunch in the cafeteria line, making purchases from the store, purchasing a soft drink, etc.).

4. Use actual coins in teaching your child coin values; counting by fives, tens, etc.; matching combinations of coins; etc.

5. Make certain your child recognizes all coins (e.g., penny, nickel, dime, quarter, half-dollar).

6. Make certain your child recognizes common denominations of paper money (e.g., one-dollar bill, five-dollar bill, etc.).

7. Have a peer or a sibling work with your child every day practicing coin values, paper money values, money combinations, etc.

8. Have your child match equal values of coins (e.g., two nickels to a dime, two dimes and a nickel to a quarter, five nickels to a quarter, etc.).

9. Make certain your child understands all math operation concepts involved in using money (e.g., addition, subtraction, multiplication, division, decimals, etc.).

10. Make certain your child can solve the necessary math problems involved in the use of money (i.e., your child can solve math problems of the same difficulty as those involving money).

11. Make certain your child can count by pennies, nickels, dimes, quarters, half-dollars.

12. Have your child use actual money to simulate transactions (e.g., purchasing lunch, groceries, snacks, clothing, etc.). Have your child practice acting as both a customer and a clerk.

13. Provide your child with math word problems involving the use of money, making certain the appropriate operation is clearly stated.

14. Provide your child with a daily shopping list of items and include the cost of each item. Have your child determine the cost of his/her purchase.

15. Collect a selection of menus and have your child select items for a meal and compute the cost of the items.

16. Have your child use a newspaper or catalog and make a list of things advertised which he/she would like to purchase. Have your child determine the total cost of the items selected.

17. Have your child earn a hypothetical income and engage in money-related math problems (e.g., taxes, social security, savings, rent, food, clothing, auto payments, recreation, etc.). The degree of difficulty of the problems should be matched to your child's ability level.

18. Have your child talk through money math problems while solving them in order to identify errors.

19. Make certain your child knows why he/she is learning the concept of money. Provide your child with concrete examples and opportunities to apply these concepts in real-life situations.

20. Make certain your child is not required to learn more information than your child is capable of at any one time.

21. Provide practice in solving money problems using a computer software program that gives your child immediate feedback.

22. Review, on a daily basis, those skills, concepts, tasks, etc., which have been previously introduced.

51 Has trouble with measurement in day-to-day activities

1. Reward your child for using measurement in day-to-day activities. Possible rewards include verbal praise (e.g., "You did a nice job of using the ruler to measure the space you needed for your project." etc.), a kiss on the cheek, a hug, having a friend over to play, staying up late, watching a TV show, and playing a game with a parent. (See Appendix for Reward Menu.)

2. Reduce the emphasis on competition. Competitive activities may cause your child to hurry and solve measurement problems incorrectly.

3. Discuss and provide your child with a list of words/phrases which usually indicate measurement problems (e.g., pounds, inches, millimeter, kilogram, etc.).

4. Have a peer or sibling act as a model for your child to demonstrate how to solve measurement problems.

5. Evaluate the appropriateness of your child learning measurement skills to determine: (a) if the task is too difficult and (b) if the length of time scheduled for the task is appropriate.

6. Find opportunities for your child to apply measurement facts to real-life situations (e.g., cooking, measuring lengths of objects, etc.).

7. Develop a measurement reference sheet (e.g., 12 inches = 1 foot, 8 ounces = 1 cup, etc.) for your child to keep with him/her.

8. Provide your child with enjoyable activities in measurement (e.g., computer games, math games, etc.).

9. Make certain that the language used to communicate with your child about measurement is consistent (e.g., meters, grams, etc.).

10. Make certain that your child has mastery of measurement concepts at any level before introducing a more difficult level.

11. Have your child practice measuring items in the environment to find their length, weight, etc.

12. Work the first problem or two of a measurement assignment with your child in order to make certain that your child understands directions and the operations necessary to solve the problems.

13. Have your child practice basic measurement concepts (e.g., pound, ounce, inch, foot, etc.) using everyday measurement devices found in the environment (e.g., rulers, measuring cup, etc.).

14. Make certain your child knows the basic concepts of fractions before requiring him/her to solve problems involving measurement (e.g., 1/4 inch, 1 1/2 inch, etc.).

15. Have your child complete measurement problems that he/she will want to be able to successfully perform (e.g., following a recipe to cook, building a model, etc.).

16. Have your child practice using smaller units of measurement to create larger units of measurement (e.g., twelve inches to make one foot, three feet to make one yard, eight ounces to make one cup, four cups to make one quart, etc.).

17. Have your child begin solving problems using measurement which require same and whole units (e.g., 10 pounds minus 8 pounds, 24 inches plus 12 inches, etc.). Introduce fractions and mixed units (e.g., pounds and ounces, etc.) only after your child has demonstrated success with same and whole units.

18. Have your child use a calculator to solve measurement problems, check the accuracy of the problems that have been worked, etc.

19. Have your child use computer software programs to practice measurement skills.

20. Have your child solve beginning measurement problems by using measurement devices before solving the problems on paper (e.g., 5 inches plus 4 inches using a ruler, 3 liquid ounces plus 5 liquid ounces using a measuring cup, etc.).

21. Make certain your child knows why he/she is learning measurement concepts. Provide your child with concrete examples and opportunities to apply these concepts in real-life situations.

22. Make certain your child is not required to learn more information than he/she is capable of at any one time.

23. Review, on a daily basis, those skills, concepts, tasks, etc., which have been previously introduced.

24. Have your child participate in an actual "hands on" experience by following simple recipes (e.g., making Jell-O, peanut butter cookies, etc.).

52 Confuses operational signs when working math problems (e.g., +, -, ×, ÷)

1. Speak to your child to explain: (a) what your child is doing wrong (e.g., not recognizing operational symbols) and (b) what your child should be doing (e.g., following operational symbols).

2. Evaluate the appropriateness of tasks to determine: (a) if the task is too difficult, and (b) if the length of time scheduled for the task is appropriate.

3. Have your child practice recognizing operational symbols (e.g., flash cards of ÷, +, -, ×).

4. Use a written reminder beside math problems to indicate which math operation is to be used (e.g., addition, subtraction, multiplication, division). Gradually reduce the use of reminders as your child demonstrates success.

5. Make the math operation symbols next to the problems extra large in order that your child will be more likely to observe the symbol.

6. Color code math operation symbols next to the problems in order that your child will be more likely to observe the symbols.

7. Require your child to go through math problems on each homework assignment, highlighting or otherwise marking the operation of each problem before beginning to solve the problems.

8. Work the first problem or two of the math assignment for your child in order that he/she knows what math operations to use.

9. Use a separate piece of paper for each type of math problem. Gradually introduce different types of math problems on the same page.

10. Place the math operation symbols randomly around your child's room and have your child practice identifying the operation involved as he/she points to each symbol.

11. Have your child solve his/her math problems using a calculator.

12. Provide your child with a math operation symbol reference sheet to keep and use while working on homework (e.g., + means to add, - means to subtract, × means to multiply, and ÷ means to divide).

13. Talk to your child's teacher and ask that a math operation symbol reminder be provided for your child at the top of each sheet of math problems (e.g., + means to add, - means to subtract, × means to multiply, and ÷ means to divide).

14. Have your child practice matching math operation symbols to the words identifying the operations by using flash cards (e.g., +, -, ×, ÷; add, subtract, multiply, divide).

15. Have a sibling or a friend work with your child to act as a model and provide reminders as your child solves his/her math problems.

16. Make certain your child knows why he/she is learning a math concept. Provide your child with concrete examples and opportunities to apply these concepts in real-life situations.

17. Have your child check his/her math assignments using a calculator. The calculator can also be used to reinforce the learning of math facts.

18. Make certain your child is not required to learn more information than he/she is capable of at any one time.

19. Provide practice in operational signs using a computer software program that gives your child immediate feedback.

20. Make certain your child has mastery of math concepts at each level before introducing a new skill level.

21. Highlight operational signs so that your child is sure to notice the signs before beginning the operation.

53 Does not make use of columns when working math problems

1. Reward your child for making use of columns when working math problems. Possible rewards include verbal praise (e.g., "I like the way you worked your math problems by using the columns."), having a friend over to play, staying up late, watching a favorite TV show, and play a game with a parent. (See Appendix for Reward Menu.)

2. Identify a sibling or a friend to act as a model for your child to demonstrate the use of columns when working math problems.

3. Use manipulative objects (e.g., base ten blocks, connecting links, etc.) to teach your child the use of columns when working math problems.

4. Make certain your child has the prerequisite skills to learn place value (e.g., able to count orally, write numbers to 100, etc.).

5. Make certain your child knows the concepts and terminology necessary to learn place value (e.g., set, column, middle, left, digit, etc.).

6. Make certain your child understands that the collective value of ten "ones" is equal to one ten and that ten "tens" is equal to one hundred.

7. Provide your child with learning experiences in grouping tangible objects into groups of tens, hundreds, etc.

8. Have your child practice labeling columns to represent ones, tens, hundreds, etc.

9. Have your child practice regrouping a number in different positions and determining its value (e.g., 372, 627, 721).

10. Make certain your child understands the zero concept in place value (e.g., there are no tens in the number "207," so a zero is put in the tens column).

11. Have your child use a calculator to solve math problems involving the use of columns.

12. Money concepts will help your child learn place value by association (e.g., $1.26 is the same as six pennies or six ones; two dimes or two tens; one dollar or one hundred).

13. Use vertical lines on graph paper to help your child visualize columns and put a single digit in a column.

14. Make certain your child understands that math problems of addition, subtraction, and multiplication move from right to left beginning with the ones column.

15. Provide your child with many opportunities to indicate the value of columns in multiple-digit numbers (e.g., 56 = __ tens and __ ones; 329 = __ hundreds, __ tens, and __ ones; etc.).

16. Teach your child the concept of filling each column and moving on to the next column from ones to tens, hundreds, thousands, etc.

17. Talk to your child's teacher about developing a marked column format on a master which can be copied for your child to use in solving all math problems (e.g., | thousands | hundreds | tens | ones |).

18. Require your child to check all of his/her math assignments for accuracy. Reinforce your child for each correction made in the use of columns.

19. Make certain your child knows why he/she is learning a math concept. Provide your child with concrete examples and opportunities to apply these concepts in real-life situations.

20. Have your child talk through math problems as he/she is solving them in order to identify errors that are being made.

21. Provide practice of using columns in math by using a computer software program that gives your child immediate feedback.

54 Fails to correctly solve math problems requiring addition

1. Reward your child for correctly solving addition problems. Possible rewards include verbal praise (e.g., "You did a great job of solving your addition problems."), having a friend over to play, staying up late, watching a favorite TV show, and playing a game with a parent. (See Appendix for Reward Menu.)

2. Provide your child with a quiet place to work (e.g., "office," desk, etc.). This is used as a means of reducing distracting stimuli and not as a form of punishment.

3. Reduce the emphasis on competition. Competitive activities may cause your child to hurry and solve addition problems incorrectly.

4. Have your child solve addition problems by manipulating objects and stating the process(es) used.

5. Discuss and provide your child with a list of words/phrases which indicate an addition operation in word problems (e.g., together, altogether, sum, in all, both, gained, received, total, saved, etc.).

6. Have a sibling or a friend act as a model for your child to demonstrate how to solve addition problems.

7. Evaluate the appropriateness of the task to determine: (a) if the task is too difficult, and (b) if the length of time scheduled to complete the task is appropriate.

8. Provide your child with many concrete experiences to help him/her learn and remember math facts. Use popsicle sticks, tongue depressors, paper clips, buttons, fingers, etc., to form groupings to teach addition facts.

9. Have your child use a calculator to reinforce learning addition. Have your child solve several problems each day using a calculator.

10. Provide practice of addition facts using a computer with software programs that give immediate feedback to your child.

11. Use daily drill activities to help your child memorize addition facts (e.g., written problems, flash cards, etc.).

12. Have your child use a calculator for drill activities of basic addition facts.

13. Have your child use a number line (e.g., a line of numbers, 1, 2, 3, 4, 5, 6, 7, 8, 9, 10, 11, 12, 13, 14, 15, 16, 17, 18, 19, 20) to solve addition problems.

14. Find opportunities for your child to apply addition facts to real-life situations (e.g., getting change in a restaurant, measuring the length of objects, etc.).

15. Have your child perform timed drills in addition in order to reinforce basic math facts. Your child "competes" against his/her own best time.

16. Develop math facts reference sheets for addition for your child to use when solving math problems.

17. Have your child solve half of his/her problems each day and use the calculator as reinforcement to complete the other half of the assignment.

18. Make certain your child understands number concepts and the relationships of numbers of objects before requiring him/her to solve math problems requiring addition.

19. Make certain your child knows the concepts of more than, less than, equal, and zero. The use of tangible objects will facilitate the learning process.

20. Have your child make sets of objects and add the sets together to obtain a sum total.

21. Provide your child with opportunities for tutoring from siblings or friends. Allow your child to tutor others when he/she has mastered a concept.

22. Reinforce your child for attempting math assignments. Emphasize the number correct, then encourage him/her to see how many more he/she can correct without help. Have your child maintain a personal chart of math performance.

23. Provide your child with enjoyable math activities (e.g., computer games, math games, manipulatives, etc.).

24. Make certain that the language used to communicate with your child about addition is consistent (e.g., "Add the numbers." "What is the total?" or "Find the sum.").

25. Have your child recheck all math work. Reinforce your child for each error he/she corrects.

26. Provide your child with shorter math homework tasks, but give more of them throughout the evening (e.g., four problems given three times a night, etc.).

27. Work the first problem or two of the math homework assignment with your child in order to make certain that your child understands directions and the operation necessary to solve the problems.

28. Teach your child to use resources in the environment to help him/her solve problems (e.g., counting numbers of objects, using a calculator, etc.).

29. Have your child talk through the math problems as he/she solves them in order to identify errors your child is making.

30. Have your child add numbers of objects. Have your child then pair number symbols with the numbers of objects while he/she performs simple addition problems. Gradually remove the objects as your child demonstrates success in solving simple addition problems.

31. Make certain your child knows why he/she is learning a math concept. Provide your child with concrete examples and opportunities to apply the concept in real-life situations.

32. Make certain your child is not required to learn more information than he/she is capable of at any one time.

33. Have your child act as a tutor to teach a younger brother/sister, friend, etc., a concept he/she has mastered. This can serve as reinforcement for your child.

34. Make certain your child has mastery of math concepts at each level before introducing a new skill level.

35. Make certain that all directions, questions, explanations, and instructions are delivered in a clear and concise manner and at an appropriate pace for your child.

55 Fails to correctly solve math problems requiring subtraction

1. Reward your child for correctly solving math problems involving subtraction. Possible rewards include verbal praise (e.g., "You did a great job of solving your subtraction problems."), having a friend over to play, staying up late, watching a favorite TV show, and playing a game with a parent. (See Appendix for Reward Menu.)

2. Provide your child with a quiet place to work (e.g., "office," desk, etc.). This is used as a means of reducing distracting stimuli and not as a form of punishment.

3. Reduce the emphasis on competition. Competitive activities may cause your child to hurry and do subtraction problems incorrectly.

4. Have your child solve math problems by manipulating objects and stating the process(es) used.

5. Discuss words and phrases which usually indicate subtraction operations (e.g., difference, between, from, left, how many more or less, how much taller, how much farther, etc.).

6. Have a sibling or a friend act as a model for your child to demonstrate how to solve subtraction problems.

7. Evaluate the appropriateness of the task to determine: (a) if the task is too difficult, and (b) if the length of time scheduled to complete the task is appropriate.

8. Provide your child with many concrete experiences to help him/her learn and remember math facts. Use popsicle sticks, paper clips, fingers, etc., to form groupings to teach subtraction facts.

9. Have your child use a calculator to reinforce learning subtraction. Have your child solve several problems each day using a calculator.

10. Provide practice of subtraction facts using a computer with software programs that give immediate feedback for your child.

11. Use daily drill activities to help your child memorize subtraction facts (e.g., written problems, flash cards, etc.).

12. Have your child perform timed drills in subtraction to reinforce basic math facts. The student "competes" against his/her own best time.

13. Have your child use a number line (e.g., a line of numbers, 1, 2, 3, 4, 5, 6, 7, 8, 9, 10, 11, 12, 13, 14, 15, 16, 17, 18, 19, 20) to solve subtraction problems.

14. Have your child use a calculator for drill activities of basic subtraction facts.

15. Find opportunities for your child to apply subtraction facts to real-life situations (e.g., getting change in a restaurant, measuring the length of objects, etc.).

16. Have your child solve half his/her subtraction problems each day and use a calculator as reinforcement to solve the rest of the problems.

17. Make certain your child understands number concepts and the relationships of number symbols to numbers of objects before requiring your child to solve math problems requiring subtraction.

18. Make certain your child knows the concepts of more than, less than, equal, zero, etc. The use of tangible objects will facilitate the learning process.

19. Provide your child with opportunities for tutoring from siblings and friends. Allow your child to tutor others when he/she has mastered a concept.

20. Reinforce your child for attempting and completing work. Emphasize the number correct, then encourage your child to see how many more he/she can correct without help. Have your child maintain a personal "chart" of math performance.

21. Provide your child with enjoyable math activities (e.g., computer games, math games, manipulatives, etc.).

22. Make certain that the language used to communicate with your child about subtraction is consistent (e.g., "Subtract the numbers." "What is the difference?" etc.).

23. Have your child check all math work. Reinforce your child for each error corrected.

24. Make certain your child has mastery of math concepts at each level before introducing a new skill level.

25. Provide your child with shorter math assignments, but give more of them throughout the evening (e.g., four problems given three times throughout the evening, etc.).

26. Work the first problem or two of the math homework assignment with your child in order to make certain that he/she understands the directions and the math operation necessary to do the problems.

27. Teach your child to use resources in the environment to help him/her solve math problems (e.g., counting numbers of objects, using a calculator, etc.).

28. Have your child talk through math problems as he/she solves them in order to identify errors that are made.

29. Have your child subtract numbers of objects. Have your child then pair number symbols with the number of objects while he/she performs simple subtraction problems. Gradually remove the objects as your child demonstrates success in solving simple subtraction problems.

30. Require that your child check subtraction problems by adding (i.e., the difference plus the subtrahend equals the minuend). Reinforce your child for each error he/she corrects.

31. Make certain your child learns the concept of take away (e.g., "You have 3 toys and I take away 2 of them. How many do you have left?").

32. Make certain your child knows why he/she is learning a math concept. Provide your child with concrete examples and opportunities to apply these concepts in real-life situations.

33. Make certain your child is not required to learn more information than he/she is capable of at any one time.

34. Make certain that all directions, questions, explanations, and instructions are delivered in the most clear and concise manner and at an appropriate pace for your child.

1. Reward your child for correctly solving math problems requiring multiplication. Possible rewards include verbal praise (e.g., "I like the way you solved your multiplication problems."), a kiss on the cheek, a hug, having a friend over to play, staying up late, watching a favorite TV show, and playing a game with a parent. (See Appendix for Reward Menu.)

2. Provide your child with a quiet place to work (e.g., "office," desk, etc.). This is used as a means of reducing distracting stimuli and not as a form of punishment.

3. Reduce the emphasis on competition. Competitive activities may cause your child to hurry and do multiplication problems incorrectly.

4. Have your child solve math word problems by manipulating objects and stating the process(es) involved.

5. Discuss words/phrases which usually indicate a multiplication operation (e.g., area, each, times, product, double, triple, twice, etc.).

6. Have a sibling or a friend act as a model for your child to demonstrate how to solve multiplication problems.

7. Evaluate the appropriateness of the task to determine: (a) if the task is too difficult, and (b) if the length of time scheduled for the task is appropriate.

8. Provide your child with many concrete experiences to help in learning and remembering math facts. Use popsicle sticks, tongue depressors, paper clips, buttons, fingers, etc., to form groupings to teach multiplication facts.

9. Have your child use a calculator to reinforce learning multiplication facts. Have your child solve several multiplication problems each day using a calculator.

10. Provide practice on multiplication facts using a computer with software programs that give immediate feedback for your child.

11. Use daily drill activities to help your child memorize multiplication facts (e.g., written problems, flash cards, etc.).

12. Have your child perform timed drills in multiplication to reinforce basic math facts. Your child "competes" against his/her own best time.

13. Have your child use a calculator for drill activities of basic multiplication facts.

14. Develop a math facts reference sheet for multiplication for your child to use when solving multiplication problems.

15. Have your child solve half of his/her multiplication problems and use the calculator as reinforcement to complete the other half of the assignment.

16. Make certain your child understands number concepts and the relationship of number symbols to numbers of objects before requiring your child to solve math problems requiring multiplication.

17. Provide your child with opportunities for tutoring from siblings or friends. Allow your child to tutor others when he/she has mastered a concept.

18. Reinforce your child for attempting and completing work. Emphasize the number correct, then encourage your child to see how many he/she can correct without help. Have your child maintain a personal chart of math performance.

19. Provide your child with enjoyable math activities (e.g., computer games, math games, manipulatives, etc.).

20. Have your child recheck all math work. Reinforce your child for each error corrected.

21. Provide your child with shorter math homework assignments throughout the evening (e.g., four problems given several times throughout the evening, etc.).

22. Work the first problem or two of the math homework assignment with your child in order to make certain that your child understands the directions and the operation necessary to solve the problems.

23. Teach your child to use resources in the environment to help in solving math problems (e.g., counting figures, counting numbers of objects, using a calculator, etc.).

24. Have your child talk through the math problems while solving them in order that you can identify errors he/she is making.

25. Make certain your child understands that multiplication is a quick way of adding, by giving him/her examples of how much longer it takes to add than to multiply.

26. Practice skip counting with 2's, 3's, and 5's.

27. Have your child count by equal distances on a number line. Demonstrate that the equal distances represent skip counting or equal addition which is the concept of multiplication.

28. Teach your child the identity element of one. Any number times one is always that number.

29. Have your child practice the multiplication tables each day with a brother/sister or a friend using flash cards.

30. Identify specific multiplication problems your child fails to correctly solve, and target these problems for additional instruction and time to be spent in tutoring and drill activities.

31. Make certain your child knows why he/she is learning a math concept. Provide your child with concrete examples and opportunities to apply these concepts in real-life situations.

32. Make certain your child is not required to learn more information than he/she is capable of at any one time.

33. Make certain that all directions, questions, explanations, and instructions are delivered in a clear and concise manner and at an appropriate pace for your child.

57 Fails to correctly solve math problems requiring division

1. Reward your child for correctly solving math problems requiring division. Possible rewards include verbal praise (e.g., "You did a great job of solving your division problems."), a kiss on the cheek, a hug, having a friend over to play, staying up late, watching a favorite TV show, and playing a game with a parent. (See Appendix for Reward Menu.)

2. Provide your child with a quiet place to work (e.g., "office," desk, etc.). This is used as a means of reducing distracting stimuli and not as a form of punishment.

3. Reduce the emphasis on competition. Competitive activities may cause your child to hurry and solve division problems incorrectly.

4. Have your child solve division problems by manipulating objects and stating the process(es) used.

5. Discuss words and phrases which usually indicate a division operation (e.g., into, share, each, average, quotient, half as many, etc.).

6. Have a sibling or a friend act as a model for your child to demonstrate how to solve division problems.

7. Evaluate the appropriateness of the task to determine: (a) if the task is too difficult, and (b) if the length of time scheduled for the task is appropriate.

8. Provide your child with many concrete experiences to help in remembering math facts. Use popsicle sticks, tongue depressors, paper clips, buttons, fingers, etc., to form groupings to teach division facts.

9. Have your child use a calculator to reinforce learning division. Have your child solve several problems each day using a calculator.

10. Provide practice of division facts using a computer with software programs that give immediate feedback to your child.

11. Use daily drill activities to help your child reinforce basic math facts. Your child "competes" against his/her own best time.

12. Have your child use a calculator for drill activities of basic division facts.

13. Use daily drill activities to help your child memorize division facts (e.g., written problems, flash cards, etc.).

14. Find opportunities for your child to apply division facts to real-life situations (e.g., money, average length of time it takes to do a job, etc.).

15. Develop math fact reference sheets for division for your child to use in solving division problems.

16. Have your child independently solve half of his/her homework problems each evening and use a calculator as reinforcement to complete the other half of the problems.

17. Make certain your child understands number concepts and the relationship of number symbols to numbers of objects before requiring your child to solve math problems requiring division.

18. Make certain that your child knows the concepts of more than, less than, equal, and zero. The use of tangible objects will facilitate the learning process.

19. Give your child several objects (e.g., one inch cubes, connecting links, etc.) and have him/her divide them into groups.

20. Provide your child with opportunities for tutoring from a sibling or friend. Allow your child to tutor others when he/she has mastered a concept.

21. Reinforce your child for attempting and completing work. Emphasize the number correct, then encourage your child to see how many more he/she can correct without help. Have your child maintain a personal chart of math performance.

22. Provide your child with enjoyable math activities (e.g., computer games, math games, manipulatives, etc.).

23. Make certain that the language used to communicate with your child about division is consistent (e.g., "Divide the numbers." "What is the divisor?" "What is the dividend?" etc.).

24. Have your child recheck all math work. Reinforce your child for each error corrected.

25. Make certain your child has mastery of math concepts at each level before introducing a new skill level.

26. Provide your child with shorter math tasks throughout the evening (e.g., four homework problems given several times throughout the evening, etc.).

27. Work the first problem or two of the homework assignment with your child in order to make certain that he/she understands the directions and the operations necessary to solve the problems.

28. Teach your child to use resources in the environment to help him/her solve math problems (e.g., counting figures, counting numbers of objects, using a calculator, etc.).

29. Have your child talk through math problems as he/she solves them in order to identify errors your child is making.

30. Have your child learn to divide numbers of objects. Then have your child pair number symbols with the number of objects while solving simple division problems. Gradually remove the objects as your child demonstrates success in solving simple division problems.

31. Teach your child the identity element of one. Any number divided by one is always that number.

32. Have your child practice the division tables each day with a brother/sister or a friend using flash cards.

33. Identify specific division problems your child fails to correctly solve and target problems for additional instruction and time to be spent in tutoring and drill activities.

34. Make certain your child knows why he/she is learning a math concept. Provide your child with concrete examples and opportunities to apply the concept in real-life situations.

35. Make certain your child is not required to learn more information than he/she is capable of at any one time.

36. Make certain that all directions, questions, explanations, and instructions are delivered in a clear and concise manner and at an appropriate pace for your child.

58 Fails to correctly solve math problems requiring regrouping (e.g., borrowing and carrying)

1. Reward your child for correctly solving math problems requiring regrouping. Possible rewards include verbal praise (e.g., "You did a good job of solving your math problems that required regrouping."), a kiss on the cheek, a hug, having a friend over to play, staying up late, watching a favorite TV show, and playing a game with a parent. (See Appendix for Reward Menu.)

2. Reduce the emphasis on competition. Competitive activities may cause your child to hurry and make mistakes in regrouping.

3. Have your child solve math problems by manipulating objects to experience regrouping.

4. Have a sibling or a friend act as a model for your child and demonstrate how to correctly solve math problems that require regrouping.

5. Evaluate the appropriateness of the task to determine if your child has mastered the skills needed for regrouping.

6. Provide your child with many concrete experiences to help your child learn and remember regrouping skills. Use popsicle sticks, tongue depressors, paper clips, buttons, base ten blocks, etc., to form groups to teach regrouping.

7. Provide practice in regrouping using a computer software program that gives immediate feedback to your child.

8. Use daily drill activities to help your child with regrouping (e.g., written problems, flash cards, etc.).

9. Have your child perform timed drills to reinforce regrouping. Your child "competes" against his/her own best time and score.

10. Find opportunities for your child to apply regrouping to real-life situations (e.g., getting change in a restaurant, figuring how much items cost when added together while shopping, etc.).

11. Develop a regrouping reference sheet for your child to use when solving math problems which require regrouping.

12. Have your child solve half of his/her math problems each day and use the calculator as reinforcement to complete the other half of the math assignment.

13. Make certain your child understands number concepts and the relationship of number symbols to numbers of objects before requiring him/her to solve math problems requiring regrouping.

14. Make certain your child knows the concepts of more than, less than, equal, and zero. The use of tangible objects will facilitate the learning process.

15. Have your child practice the concept of regrouping by "borrowing" and "carrying" from objects in columns set up like math problems.

16. Provide your child with opportunities for tutoring from a sibling or friend. Allow your child to tutor others when he/she has mastered a concept.

17. Reinforce your child for attempting and completing work. Emphasize the number correct, then encourage him/her to see how many more your child can correct without help. Have your child maintain a personal chart of math performance.

18. Provide your child with a few problems several times throughout the evening (e.g., four homework problems given three times a night, etc.).

19. Work the first problem or two of the math homework assignment with your child in order to make certain that your child understands the directions and the operation necessary to solve the problems.

20. Have your child talk through math problems as he/she solves them in order to identify errors that are being made.

21. Require your child to check subtraction problems by adding (i.e., the difference plus the subtrahend equals the minuend). Reinforce your child for each error corrected.

22. Make certain your child has a number line (e.g., a line of numbers, 1, 2, 3, 4, 5, 6, 7, 8, 9, 10, 11, 12, 13, 14, 15, 16, 17, 18, 19, 20) to use as a reference.

23. Have your child talk through math problems while solving them in order that you can identify errors he/she is making.

24. Have your child check his/her math assignments using a calculator. The calculator can also be used to reinforce the learning of math facts.

25. Use manipulative objects (e.g., base ten blocks) to teach your child regrouping.

26. Develop a math reference sheet for your child to keep with him/her (e.g., steps used in doing subtraction problems, addition problems, etc.).

27. Make certain your child understands the concept of place value and that problems move right to left beginning with the ones column.

28. Make certain your child is not required to learn more information than he/she is capable of at any one time.

29. Make certain your child has mastery of math concepts at each level before introducing a new skill level.

59 Works math problems from left to right instead of right to left

1. Reward your child for working math problems from right to left. Possible rewards include verbal praise (e.g.,"You did a great job of solving your math problems."), a kiss on the cheek, a hug, staying up late, watching a favorite TV show, and playing a game with a parent. (See Appendix for Reward Menu.)

2. Reduce the emphasis on competition. Competitive activities may cause your child to hurry and make mistakes in math problems.

3. Have a brother/sister or a friend work with your child each day on working math problems from right to left.

4. Develop a math reference sheet for your child (e.g., steps used in doing addition problems, subtraction problems, multiplication problems, division problems).

5. Have your child check math assignments using a calculator.

6. Use large colored arrows to indicate where your child should begin to work math problems (e.g., right to left).

7. Work the first problems for your child as he/she watches, in order to provide demonstration and set an example.

8. Put your child's math problems on graph paper or vertically lined paper to emphasize columns, with directions to begin each problem at the right.

9. Make certain your child has mastered place value concepts and understands that columns to the left are higher values than those to the right.

10. Require your child to solve math problems by place value (e.g., begin with the ones column, the tens column, hundreds column, etc.).

11. Have your child use a calculator to solve math problems.

12. Speak to your child to explain: (a) what he/she is doing wrong (e.g., working math problems from left to right) and (b) what he/she should be doing (e.g., working math problems from right to left).

13. Write the place value above each math problem in order to remind your child to begin with the ones column to solve the problems.

14. Display a large poster with a message that indicates reading begins to the left and math problems begin on the right (e.g., READING BEGINS ON THE LEFT. MATH BEGINS ON THE RIGHT.).

15. Make certain your child has a number line (e.g., a list of numbers, 1, 2, 3, 4, 5, 6, 7, 8, 9, 10, 11, 12, 13, 14, 15, 16, 17, 18, 19, 20) to use as a reference.

16. Make certain your child knows why he/she is learning a math concept. Provide your child with concrete examples and opportunities to apply these concepts in real-life situations.

17. Have your child talk through math problems while solving them in order to identify errors your child is making.

18. Recognize quality work (e.g., display your child's work, congratulate your child, etc.).

19. Provide practice in math using a computer software program that gives your child immediate feedback.

20. Make certain your child has mastery of math concepts at each level before introducing a new skill level.

21. Reduce the amount of information on a page if it is causing visual distractions for your child (e.g., fewer math problems, less print, etc.).

1. Reward your child for following the necessary steps when solving math problems. Possible rewards include verbal praise (e.g., "You did a nice job on your math homework problems tonight."), a kiss on the cheek, a hug, having a friend over to play, staying up late, watching a favorite TV show, and playing a game with a parent. (See Appendix for Reward Menu.)

2. Evaluate the appropriateness of the task to determine: (a) if the task is too difficult and (b) if the length of time scheduled for the task is appropriate.

3. Reduce the emphasis on competition. Competitive activities may cause your child to hurry and fail to follow necessary steps in math problems.

4. Make certain that your child recognizes all math operation symbols (e.g., ×, -, +, ÷).

5. Use written reminders beside math problems to indicate which step is to be done. Gradually reduce the use of reminders as your child demonstrates success.

6. Put all math problems involving the same steps on a single line, on a separate piece of paper, etc.

7. Make the math operation symbols next to math problems extra large in order that your child will be more likely to observe the symbol.

8. Color code math operation symbols next to the problems in order that your child will be more likely to observe the symbol.

9. Work the first problem or two of a math homework assignment for your child in order that he/she will know what steps to use.

10. Use a separate piece of paper for each type of math problem, gradually introducing different types of problems on the same page.

11. Provide your child with a list of steps necessary for the problems your child is attempting to solve. Have your child keep a list as a reference while solving math problems.

12. List the steps in solving math problems on your child's bulletin board, on a poster, etc.

13. Have a brother/sister or a friend work with your child while he/she learns to follow the steps in math problems.

14. Have your child check his/her answers to math problems on a calculator.

15. Have your child act as a tutor for a younger brother/sister or friend who is learning new math concepts. Explaining steps in basic math problems will help your child cement his/her own skills.

16. Have your child equate math problems to real-life situations in order that he/she will better understand the steps involved in solving the problems (e.g., 4×25 is the same as 4 baskets of apples with 25 apples in each basket. How many apples do you have?).

17. Make certain your child has a number line (e.g., a list of numbers, 1, 2, 3, 4, 5, 6, 7, 8, 9, 10, 11, 12, 13, 14, 15, 16, 17, 18, 19, 20) to use as a reference.

18. Have your child talk through math problems as he/she is solving them in order to identify errors your child is making.

19. Develop a math reference sheet for your child to use (e.g., steps used in doing subtraction, multiplication, addition, and division problems).

20. Have your child check his/her math homework assignments using a calculator. The calculator can also be used to reinforce the learning of math facts.

21. Use vertical lines or graph paper in math to help your child keep math problems in correct order.

22. Make certain your child is not required to learn more information than he/she is capable of at any one time.

23. Provide practice in math using a computer software program that gives your child immediate feedback.

24. Make certain your child has mastery of math concepts at each level before introducing a new skill level.

25. Reduce the amount of information on a page if it is causing visual distractions for your child (e.g., fewer problems on a page, less print, etc.).

61 Has difficulty solving math word problems

1. Make certain that your child's inability to read is not the cause of his/her difficulty solving math word problems.

2. Reward your child for correctly solving math word problems. Possible rewards include verbal praise (e.g., "I like the way you solved all of your math word problems."), a kiss on the cheek, a hug, having a friend over to play, staying up late, watching a favorite TV show, and playing a game with a parent. (See Appendix for Reward Menu.)

3. Have your child question any directions, explanations, or instructions not understood.

4. Provide your child with a quiet place to work (e.g., "office," desk, etc.). This is used as a means of reducing distracting stimuli and not as a form of punishment.

5. Reduce the emphasis on competition. Competitive activities may cause your child to hurry and solve math word problems incorrectly.

6. Have your child read the math word problems first silently and then aloud and identify the mathematical operation required.

7. Work math word problems that require a one-step process with your child, making certain that the sentences are short and concise.

8. Teach your child to look for "clue" or "key" words in word problems that indicate mathematical operations.

9. Have your child orally analyze the steps that are required to solve word problems (e.g., "What is given?" "What is asked?" "What operation(s) are used?" etc.).

10. Represent the numerical amounts, in concrete forms, that are presented in the word problems (e.g., problems involving money can be represented by providing your child with the appropriate amount of real or play money).

11. Have your child write a number sentence (e.g., 4 + 3 = 7) after reading a math word problem. This process will help your child see the numerical operation prior to finding the answer.

12. Have your child create word problems for number sentences. Place the number sentence on a piece of paper and have your child tell or write word problems that could be solved by the number sentences (e.g., 4 + 3 = 7: four apples and three apples equals seven apples).

13. Have your child restate math word problems in his/her own words.

14. Ask your child to identify the primary question that must be answered to solve the given word problem. Continue this activity using more difficult word problems containing two or more questions. Make sure your child understands that questions are often implied rather than directly asked.

15. Have your child make up his/her own word problems. Direct your child to write problems involving specific operations. Brother/sister, friends, parents, etc., could solve the word problems. Your child can also provide answers to his/her own problems.

16. Supplement your child's textbook problems with self-made problems. These problems can deal with everyday experiences. Include your child's name in the word problems to make them more realistic and meaningful to your child.

17. Use word problems that are of interest to your child and related to his/her experiences.

18. Make certain your child reads through the entire word problem before attempting to solve it.

19. Teach your child to break down each math word problem into specific steps.

20. Have your child make notes to "set the problem up" in written form as he/she reads the math word problem.

21. Have your child simulate situations which relate to math word problems (e.g., trading, selling, buying, etc.).

22. Have your child solve math word problems by manipulating objects and stating the process(es) used.

23. Help your child recognize common patterns in math word problems (e.g., how many, add or subtract, etc.).

24. Discuss words/phrases which usually indicate a subtraction operation (e.g., difference between, from, left, how many more or less, how much taller, farther, heavier, withdrawal, spend, lost, remain, more, etc.).

25. Discuss words/phrases which usually indicate a division operation (e.g., into, share, each, average, monthly, daily, weekly, yearly, quotient, half as many, etc.).

26. Discuss and provide your child with a list of words/phrases which usually indicate an addition operation (e.g., together, altogether, sum, in all, both, gained, received, total, won, saved, etc.).

27. Discuss words/phrases which usually indicate a multiplication operation (e.g., area, each, times, product, double, triple, twice, etc.).

28. Teach your child to convert words into their numerical equivalents to solve word problems (e.g., two weeks = 14 days, one-third = 1/3, one year = 12 months, one quarter = 25 cents, one yard = 36 inches, etc.).

29. Allow your child to use a calculator when solving math word problems.

30. Require your child to read math word problems at least twice before beginning to solve them.

31. Have your child begin solving basic word problems which combine a math problem and word problems such as:

$$7 \text{ apples}$$
$$\text{and} \quad 3 \text{ apples}$$
$$\overline{}$$
$$\text{equals 10 apples}$$

Gradually change the problems to math word problems as your child demonstrate success.

32. Before introducing completed word problems, present your child with phrases to be translated to numbers (e.g., six less than ten equals 10 - 6).

33. Have a brother/sister or a friend act as a model for your child to demonstrate how to solve math word problems.

34. Talk to your child's teacher to reduce the number of assigned problems given to your child at one time (e.g., five problems instead of ten, etc.).

35. Demonstrate for your child how to solve word problems by reading the problem and solving the problem on paper step-by-step.

36. Speak with your child to explain: (a) what he/she is doing wrong (e.g., using the wrong operation, failing to read the problem carefully, etc.) and (b) what he/she should be doing (e.g., using the appropriate operation, reading the problem carefully, etc.).

37. Evaluate the appropriateness of the task to determine: (a) if the task is too difficult and (b) if the length of time scheduled to complete the task is appropriate.

38. Correlate word problems with computation procedures just learned at school (e.g., multiplication, operations with multiplication word problems, etc.).

39. Teach your child the meaning of mathematical terms (e.g., sum, dividend, etc.). Frequently review the terms and their meanings.

40. Highlight or underline key words in math word problems (e.g., references to the operation involved, etc.).

41. Provide your child with a checklist to follow in solving math word problems (e.g., what information is given, what question is asked, what operation(s) is used).

42. Make certain your child has a number line (e.g., a line of numbers, 1, 2, 3, 4, 5, 6, 7, 8, 9, 10, 11, 12, 13, 14, 15, 16, 17, 18, 19, 20) to use as a reference.

43. Make certain your child knows why he/she is learning to solve math word problems. Provide your child with concrete examples and opportunities to apply these concepts in real-life situations.

44. Have your child talk through math word problems as he/she is solving them in order to identify errors your child is making.

45. Develop a math reference sheet for your child (e.g., steps used in doing subtraction, multiplication, addition, and division problems).

46. Have your child check his/her word problems using a calculator. The calculator can also be used to reinforce the learning of math facts.

47. Make certain your child knows the concepts of more than, less than, equal, and zero. The use of tangible objects will facilitate the learning process.

48. Recognize quality work (e.g., display your child's work, congratulate your child, etc.).

49. Make certain your child is not required to learn more information than he/she is capable of at any one time.

50. Have your child act as a tutor to teach a brother/sister, friend, etc., a math concept he/she has mastered. This can serve as reinforcement for your child.

51. Provide practice in solving math word problems using a computer software program that gives your child immediate feedback.

52. Make certain your child has mastery of math concepts at each level before introducing a new skill level.

53. Have your child manipulate objects (e.g., apples, oranges, toy cars, toy airplanes, etc.) as you describe the operation.

62 Fails to form letters correctly when printing or writing

1. Reward your child for making correct letters. Possible rewards include verbal praise (e.g., "Your handwriting is beautiful."), a kiss on the cheek, a hug, having a friend over to play, staying up late, watching a favorite TV show, and playing a game with a parent. (See Appendix for Reward Menu.)

2. Evaluate the appropriateness of the task to determine: (a) if the task is too difficult and (b) if the length of time scheduled to complete the task is appropriate.

3. Check your child's posture. Have your child sit erect in an appropriately sized chair with feet touching the floor, his/her back pressed against the back of the chair, shoulders slightly inclined, arms resting comfortably on the desk, and elbows just off the lower edge of the desk.

4. Check your child's writing position. A right-handed person writing in cursive should tilt the paper to the left so the lower left-hand corner points toward the midsection. As writing progresses the paper should shift, not the writing arm.

5. Check your child's grasp. The pencil should be between the thumb and first two fingers, holding the instrument one inch from its tip.

6. Provide your child with an alphabet strip with letters of the same size as he/she is to use.

7. Write the letters on your child's paper and have him/her trace them.

8. Make certain your child is instructed in each letter formation, giving your child oral as well as physical descriptions and demonstrations.

9. Provide your child with physical prompts by moving your child's hand, giving him/her a feeling of directionality.

10. Use arrows to show your child directionality when tracing or using dot-to-dot to form letters.

11. Use color cues for lines (e.g., red for the top line, yellow for the middle line, green for the bottom line) to indicate where letters are to be made.

12. Draw simple shapes and lines for your child to practice forming on lined paper.

13. Highlight the base line or top line on the paper in order to help your child stay within the given spaces.

14. Write the complete letters and have your child trace them. Gradually provide less of the letters for your child to trace (e.g., dashes, then dots) as he/she is successful.

15. Identify those letters your child does not form correctly. Have your child practice the correct form of one or more of the letters each day.

16. To facilitate appropriate holding of a pencil, put colored tape on parts of the pencil to correspond to finger positions. Then put colored tape on your child's fingernails and have your child match colors.

17. Reduce the emphasis on competition. Competitive activities may cause your child to hurry and fail to form letters correctly.

18. Have a brother/sister or a friend act as a model for your child by working daily on drill activities involving letter formation, ending and connecting strokes, spacing, and slant.

19. Have your child practice forming letters correctly using writing activities which are most likely to cause your child to want to be successful (e.g., writing a letter to a friend, rock star or famous athlete; filling out a job application or contest form; etc.).

20. Recognize quality work (e.g., display your child's work, congratulate your child, etc.).

21. Provide your child with quality materials to perform the assignment (e.g., pencil with eraser, paper, handwriting sample, etc.). Be certain that your child has only the necessary materials.

22. Make certain your child has mastery of handwriting concepts at each level before introducing a new skill level.

23. Check your child's handwriting work at various points throughout a handwriting activity to make certain that your child is forming letters correctly.

24. Make certain your child is not required to learn more information than he/she is capable of at any one time.

25. Have your child practice forming letters correctly by tracing over a series of dots.

26. Make certain your child has an alphabet strip to use as a reference.

27. Require your child to proofread all written work. Reinforce your child for each correction made.

63 Uses inappropriate letter size when writing

1. Make certain your child's vision has been checked recently.

2. Reward your child for using appropriate letter size when writing. Possible rewards include verbal praise (e.g., "Your handwriting is beautiful."), a kiss on the cheek, a hug, having a friend over to play, staying up late, watching a favorite TV show, and playing a game with a parent. (See Appendix for Reward Menu.)

3. Evaluate the appropriateness of the task to determine: (a) if the task is too difficult and (b) if the length of the time scheduled to complete the task is appropriate.

4. Check your child's posture. Have your child sit erect in an appropriate sized chair with feet touching the floor, his/her back pressed against the back of the chair, shoulders slightly inclined, arms resting comfortably on the desk, and elbows just off the lower edge of the desk.

5. Check your child's paper position. A right-handed person writing in cursive should tilt the paper to the left so the lower left-hand corner points toward the midsection. As writing progresses the paper should shift, not the writing arm.

6. Check your child's grasp. The pencil should be between the thumb and first two fingers, holding the instrument one inch from its tip.

7. Use paper that has a midline and a descender space.

8. Have your child identify maximum letters (b, d, f, h, k, l,), intermediate letters (t), and minimum letters (a, c, e, g, i, j, m, n, o, p, q, r, s, u, v, w, x, y, z) in order to help your child locate the correct placement of each group.

9. Make certain your child is shifting his/her paper as writing progresses.

10. Provide your child with quality materials to perform the assignment (e.g., pencil with eraser, paper, dictionary, handwriting sample, etc.). Be certain that your child has only the necessary materials.

11. Evaluate writing for alignment by drawing a horizontal line across the tops of the letters that are to be of the same size.

12. Highlight lines on the paper as a reminder for your child in making correct letter size.

13. Have a brother/sister or a friend act as a model for your child to imitate making letters the appropriate size when writing.

14. Be certain your child has samples of letters of the appropriate size for his/her activities requiring letters.

15. Provide your child with an alphabet strip with letters the same size as he/she is to use.

16. Write letters on your child's paper and have him/her trace them.

17. Write letters on your child's paper in a broken line and have your child connect the lines.

18. Darken the lines on your child's paper which are used for correct letter size.

19. Have your child correct mistakes involving inappropriate letter size.

20. Draw boxes to indicate the size on specific letters in relationship to the line.

21. Using examples written on grid paper, have your child copy the examples beneath them.

22. Using tracing paper, have your child trace over specific letters or words.

23. Using a series of dots, have your child trace words or sentences.

24. Provide your child with clearly stated criteria for acceptable work (e.g., neatness, appropriately sized letters, etc.).

25. Recognize quality work (e.g., display your child's work, congratulate your child, etc.).

26. Make certain your child has mastery of handwriting concepts at each level before introducing a new skill level.

27. Check your child's work at various points throughout the assignment to make certain that your child is making letters the appropriate size.

28. Make certain your child an alphabet strip as a reference.

29. Use vertical lines or graph paper to help your child space letters correctly.

30. Provide your child with a different sized pencil or pencil grip.

1. Reward your child for making letters and numbers correctly when writing. Possible rewards include verbal praise (e.g., "Your handwriting homework looks wonderful."), a kiss on the cheek, a hug, having a friend over to play, staying up late, watching a favorite TV show, and playing a game with a parent. (See Appendix for Reward Menu.)

2. Make certain that your child's formation of letters is appropriate and consistently correct. In manuscript writing, all strokes use a forward circle (e.g., circling to the right) for letters that begin with a line (e.g., b), and a backward circle (e.g., circling to the left) for letters in which the circle is written before the line (e.g., d).

3. Use poster board activities (e.g., drawing lines, circles, etc.) to teach your child proper directionality for each letter or numeral.

4. Physically guide your child's hand, providing a feeling of directionality.

5. Have your child trace letters and numbers in magazines, newspapers, etc., which he/she typically reverses when writing.

6. Use direction arrows to remind your child of correct directionality.

7. Identify the letters and numbers your child reverses and have your child practice making one or more of the letters correctly each day.

8. Make certain your child recognizes the correct form of the letters and numbers when he/she writes them (e.g., b, d, 2, 5, etc.).

9. Make certain your child checks all his/her work for those letters and numbers typically reversed. Reinforce your child for correcting any reversed letters and numbers.

10. Provide your child with letters and numbers to trace which he/she typically reverses.

11. Given letters and numbers on separate cards, have your child match the letters and numbers that are the same.

12. Have your child keep a card with the word bed to serve as a reminder of the correct form of b and d in a word he/she knows.

13. Have your child keep a list of the most commonly used words which contain letters he/she reverses. This list can be used as a reference when your child is writing.

14. After identifying those letters and numbers your child reverses, have your child highlight or underline those letters and numbers in a magazine, newspaper, etc.

15. Point out the subtle differences between letters and numbers that your child reverses. Have your child scan five typewritten lines containing only the letters or numbers that are confusing (e.g., nnhnhhnn). Have your child circle the "n's" and the "h's" with different colors.

16. Cursive handwriting may prevent reversals and may be used as an alternative to manuscript.

17. Make certain your child has a number line and alphabet strip to use as a reference to make the correct forms of letters and numbers.

18. Reduce the emphasis on competition. Competitive activities may cause your child to hurry and reverse numbers and letters when writing.

19. Recognize quality work (e.g., display your child's work, congratulate your child, etc.).

20. Have your child practice writing letters, words, and sentences by tracing over a series of dots.

21. Require your child to proofread all written work. Reinforce your child for each correction made.

22. Have your child engage in writing activities designed to cause your child to want to be successful in writing (e.g., writing a letter to a friend, rock star, famous athlete, etc.).

65 Fails to write within a given space

1. Make certain your child's vision has been recently checked.

2. Reward your child for each word and/or sentence that is appropriately spaced. Possible rewards include verbal praise (e.g., "You did a nice job of spacing your words and letters in your writing assignment."), a kiss on the cheek, a hug, having a friend over to play, staying up late, watching a favorite TV show, or playing a game with a parent. (See Appendix for Reward Menu.)

3. Have your child perform a "practice page" before beginning the actual homework assignment.

4. Have your child look at correctly written material to serve as a model for him/her to imitate.

5. Have your child sit erect in an appropriate sized chair with feet touching the floor, back pressed against the back of the chair, shoulders slightly inclined, arms resting on the desk, and with elbows just off the lower edge of the desk.

6. Check your child's paper position. A right-handed person writing in cursive should tilt the paper to the left so the lower left-hand corner points toward the midsection. As writing progresses the paper should shift, not the writing arm.

7. Place dots between letters and have your child use fingers as a spacer between words.

8. Make certain your child is shifting his/her paper when writing.

9. Using appropriate spacing, print or write words or sentences. Have your child trace what is written.

10. Provide your child with samples of handwritten words and sentences he/she can use as a reference for correct spacing.

11. Reduce the emphasis on competition. Competitive activities may cause your child to hurry and fail to use correct spacing when writing words and sentences.

12. Draw vertical lines for your child to use to space letters and words (e.g., | | | |).

13. Teach your child to always look at the next word to determine if there is enough space to the margin.

14. Provide your child with graph paper, instructing him/her to write letters in each block, while skipping a block between words and sentences.

15. Recognize quality work (e.g., display your child's work, congratulate your child, etc.).

16. Provide your child with quality materials to perform the assignment (e.g., pencil with eraser, paper, dictionary, handwriting sample, etc.). Be certain that your child has only the necessary materials.

17. Check your child's work at various points throughout a writing assignment in order to make certain that your child is writing within a given space.

18. Give your child one handwriting task to perform at a time. Introduce the next task only when your child has successfully completed the previous task.

19. Assign your child shorter writing assignments and gradually increase the length of the assignments as your child demonstrates success.

20. Have your child engage in writing activities designed to cause your child to want to be successful in writing (e.g., writing a letter to a friend, rock star, famous athlete, etc.).

66 Cannot copy letters, words, sentences, and numbers from a book, work sheet, etc.

1. Make certain your child's vision has been recently checked.

2. Reward your child for copying letters, words, sentences, and numbers from work sheets, textbooks, etc. Possible rewards include verbal praise (e.g., "I like the way you copied your math problems so neatly."), a kiss on the cheek, a hug, having a friend over to play, watching a favorite TV show, and playing a game with a parent. (See Appendix for Reward Menu.)

3. Evaluate the appropriateness of the task to determine: (a) if the task is too difficult and (b) if the length of time scheduled to complete the task is appropriate.

4. Have your child question any directions, explanations, or instructions not understood.

5. Reduce distracting stimuli (e.g., noise and motion around your child, pictures in the textbook, etc.) in order to enhance your child's ability to copy letters, words, sentences, and numbers.

6. Enlarge the print from which your child is copying.

7. Talk to your child's teacher about changing the format of the material from which your child copies (e.g., have less material to a page, remove or cover pictures on pages, enlarge the print, etc.).

8. Highlight or underline the material your child is to copy.

9. Use a frame or window to cover all material except that which your child is to copy.

10. Have your child copy small amounts of material (e.g., one sentence or line) at a time.

11. Make certain your child's work area is free of all materials except that from which he/she is copying.

12. Provide your child with a private place to work (e.g., a private "office," a quiet desk, etc.). This is used as a means of reducing distracting stimuli and not as a form of punishment.

13. Provide a variety of ways for your child to obtain information without copying it (e.g., commercially produced material, photocopy of the material, self-made material, etc.).

14. Have a brother/sister or a friend assist your child in copying material (e.g., to read the material aloud as your child copies it, copy the material for the student, etc.).

15. Maintain consistency of the format from which your child copies.

16. Identify any particular letters or numbers your child has difficulty copying and have your child practice copying those letters or numbers.

17. Have your child practice writing letters, words, and sentences by tracing over a series of dots.

18. Make certain your child has a number line and alphabet strip to use as a reference for the correct form of letters and numbers in order to reduce errors.

19. Require your child to proofread all written work. Reinforce your child for each correction made.

20. Recognize quality work (e.g., display your child's work, congratulate your child, etc.).

21. Provide your child with quality materials to perform assignments (e.g., pencil with eraser, paper, dictionary, handwriting sample, etc.). Be certain that your child has only the necessary materials on the desk.

22. Reduce the emphasis on competition. Competitive activities may cause your child to hurry and commit any number of errors.

67 Is impulsive

1. Establish a rule (e.g., stop and think before acting). This rule should be consistent and followed by everyone in the home. Talk about the rule often.

2. Reward your child for thinking before acting. Possible rewards include verbal praise (e.g., "I'm proud of you for thinking about your behavior before you acted!"), a kiss on the cheek, a hug, having a friend over to play, staying up late, watching a favorite TV show, and playing a game with a parent. (See Appendix for Reward Menu.)

3. If there are other children or adolescents in the home, reward them for thinking first before acting.

4. Carefully consider your child's age before expecting him/her to always think before acting.

5. Show your child how to stop and think before acting.

6. Make sure that you stop and think before acting in order to teach your child to do the same.

7. When your child acts without thinking, explain exactly what he/she is doing wrong, what should be done and why.

For example: You ask your child to clean his/her room and he/she immediately starts arguing with you. Get your child's attention and say, "William, you are arguing with me. You need to stop and think about your behavior and the consequences that will occur."

8. Write a contract with your child.

For example: I, William, will stop and think before I get angry with others. Each time that I do this, I will earn a nickel.

The contract should be written within the ability level of your child and should focus on only one behavior at a time. (See Appendix for an example of a Behavior Contract.)

9. Allow natural consequences to occur as a result of your child's failure to think before acting.

10. Make certain that your child sees the relationship between his/her behavior and the consequences which follow (e.g., hurting others' feelings, not being allowed to participate in special activities, being avoided by others, etc.).

11. Immediately remove your child from the situation until he/she can demonstrate acceptable behavior and self-control.

12. Supervise in order to make sure your child thinks before acting.

13. Remind your child to "stop and think" when beginning to do something without thinking first.

14. Immediately stop your child from behaving inappropriately and discuss the consequences of the behavior.

15. Provide constant, positive reinforcement for appropriate behavior. Ignore as many inappropriate behaviors as possible.

16. Prevent your child from becoming overstimulated by an activity (e.g., monitor or supervise your child's behavior to limit overexcitement in physical activities, games, parties, etc.).

17. Provide your child with a clearly identified list of consequences for inappropriate behavior.

18. Supervise closely in situations in which your child is likely to act impulsively (e.g., maintain close physical proximity, maintain eye contact, etc.).

19. Talk with your family doctor, a school official, a social worker, a mental health worker, etc., about your child's failure to consider the consequences of the behavior.

20. Teach your child ways to settle down (e.g., counting to 10, saying the alphabet, walking away, etc.) when there is a need to slow down and think about what he/she is doing.

21. Remove your child from a group or activity until he/she can demonstrate self-control.

22. Make it possible for your child to earn those things he/she wants or needs so that your child will not have to engage in inappropriate behavior to get what is desired (e.g., lying or stealing to get something important).

23. Do not make it too difficult for your child to earn those things he/she wants. If it is too difficult to earn something, the negative consequences of getting it in an inappropriate way (e.g., stealing) may seem like a worthwhile risk.

24. Each time a consequence is delivered, whether it is positive or negative, have your child explain to you why it is happening (e.g., "Because I was a helpful shopper, I can have a treat at the checkout line.").

25. Make certain your child understands that consequences naturally follow behavior, whether it is your child's, yours, or someone else's. It is your child's own behavior that makes consequences occur.

26. Discuss consequences before your child begins an activity (e.g., cheating in a game will result in the game ending and people not playing again).

27. Reduce the opportunity to act impulsively by limiting decision-making. Gradually increase opportunities for decision-making as the student demonstrates success.

28. Make necessary adjustments in the environment to prevent your child from experiencing stress, impatience, frustration, etc.

29. Teach your child to verbalize feelings before losing control (e.g., "I'm getting tired of doing this." "I'm getting bored standing here." etc.).

30. Provide your child with a place to go when becoming overly excited (e.g., a quiet corner, a room, etc.).

31. Remind your child when he/she begins to lose control (e.g., by saying, "You need to count to ten." "Calm down." etc.).

32. Teach your child ways to deal with conflict situations (e.g., talking, reasoning, asking an adult to intervene, walking away, etc.).

33. Monitor the behavior of others (e.g., brothers, sisters, friends, etc.) to make certain they are not teasing or otherwise stimulating your child to lose control.

34. Look for the warning signs (e.g., arguing, loud voices, etc.) that your child is getting upset or angry and intervene to change the activity.

35. Prevent your child from becoming so stimulated that he/she reacts with impulsive behavior (i.e., intervene when your child is becoming overexcited in order to prevent loss of self-control).

36. Teach your child to "think" before acting (e.g., ask himself/herself, "What is happening?" "What am I doing?" "What should I do?" "What will be best for me?").

37. Reduce the emphasis on competition. Highly competitive activities may stimulate impulsive behavior.

38. Teach your child decision-making steps: (a) think about how other persons may be influenced, (b) think about consequences, (c) carefully consider the unique situation, (d) think of different courses of action which are possible, and (e) think about what is ultimately best for him/her.

39. Point out natural consequences of impulsive behavior in order that your child can learn that persons who act in a more deliberate fashion are more successful than those who act impulsively (e.g., If you begin before understanding directions or what is needed, you may finish first; but you may do things wrong, things may be broken or destroyed, etc.).

40. "Prepare" your child in advance for those things which you know will occur (e.g., changes in routine, guests, visitors, special events, highly stimulating outings, etc.).

41. Reduce those activities which stimulate your child's impulsive behavior (e.g., "roughhousing," loud music, having friends over, etc.).

42. Maintain as much of a routine as possible for your child to follow in order to increase stable behavior.

43. Go over the rules before your child engages in activities in order to reduce the likelihood of impulsive behavior (e.g., "When we get out of the car, we will hold hands walking across the parking lot.").

A Reminder: Do not confuse impulsive behavior with enthusiasm; impulsive behavior should be controlled while enthusiasm should be encouraged.

1. Sit down and explain changes in routine to your child a few days before they happen, if possible.

2. Encourage your child to tell you why he/she is upset about guests or a baby-sitter in the home. Make sure that your child is not being mistreated in any way.

3. Do not make your child go through changes that are upsetting.

4. Try to give your child as much structure and "sameness" in his/her life as possible.

5. Allow your child to participate in deciding when changes in routine will occur.

6. Have a calendar of family activities and indicate on the calendar when guests will visit, doctors' appointments will occur, baby-sitters will come, etc.

7. Plan things for your child to do when changes in routine occur (e.g., caring for a younger brother or sister, going to see a movie, having a friend spend the night, etc.).

8. Reward your child for accepting changes in routine. Possible rewards include verbal praise (e.g., "I'm proud of you for not getting mad when dinner was late."), a kiss on the cheek, a hug, having a friend over to play, staying up late, watching a favorite TV show, and playing a game with a parent. (See Appendix for Reward Menu.)

9. If there are other children or adolescents in the home, reward them for accepting changes in their routine.

10. Write a contract with your child.

For example: I, William, will not cry when I have to stay with a baby-sitter. When I accomplish this, I can have a friend spend the night.

The contract should be written within the ability level of your child and should focus on only one behavior at a time. (See Appendix for an example of a Behavior Contract.)

11. Try to remain calm and accept changes in your own routine. If you become upset by changes, your child will learn to do the same.

12. When your child has difficulty adjusting to a change in routine, explain exactly what he/she is doing wrong, what should have been done and why.

For example: You tell your child that dinner will be 15 minutes late and he begins to cry and stomp around. Go to your child and say, "William, you are crying. You need to stop crying and wash up so you'll be ready for dinner."

13. Remind your child, as often as possible, of changes that will occur in routine.

14. Try to limit the number of changes in your child's routine whenever possible.

15. Do not leave your child alone with others until your child has a feeling of comfort and safety.

16. Introduce your child to a new baby-sitter and let them spend some time getting acquainted before you leave your child alone with the baby-sitter.

17. Have your child try something new with peers with whom he/she feels uncomfortable (e.g., swim lessons, dancing, baseball, etc.).

18. If your child begins to use "afraid of doing it" as an excuse, take your child to the activity, see him/her into the location, leave, and come back when the activity is over. Make certain the person with whom you are leaving your child understands the situation.

19. Present changes in routine in the most attractive manner possible (e.g., "Rather than going to school this morning, we are going out to eat breakfast and see the dentist.", etc.).

20. Allow your child to take part in changing the routine (e.g., let your child decide which day to visit Grandma, which baby-sitter he/she would like to have, etc.).

21. Be personally available when your child is dealing with changes in routine (e.g., take your child to the first day of swim lessons, have the new baby-sitter come over to play games with your child while you are home, etc.).

22. Do not reinforce your child's fears about changes in daily routine by allowing him/her to get out of participating in a situation because he/she is afraid of change.

23. Carefully consider your child's age and maturity level before expecting him/her to accept changes in routine.

24. Let your child know in advance of any change in the daily routine (e.g., identify the time dinner will be served, what time Dad will be home, what you will be doing for the day, etc.).

25. Help your child plan changes in routine (e.g., a slumber part, visiting relatives, etc.).

26. Have your child attend special events that may be a change in routine with peers with whom he/she feels comfortable (e.g., birthday parties, school, swim lessons, etc.).

27. Give your child a responsibility to perform at special events in order to participate, interact, etc., without experiencing the awkwardness of not knowing what to do or say to others (e.g., taking coats, serving refreshments, etc.).

28. Have your child help plan special events (e.g., family gatherings, parties, etc.) in your home by choosing refreshments, planning a schedule of daily events, etc.

29. Allow your child to attend special events without insisting that he/she socialize when feeling uncomfortable.

30. In order to help your child feel comfortable with a new situation, take your child to meet the new teacher, swim instructor, or dance instructor; visit the dentist before the actual appointment; etc.

31. Provide your child with a revised schedule of daily events which identifies the activities for the day and the time they will occur. (See Appendix for Weekday or Saturday Schedule.)

32. Attempt to limit the number of changes that need to occur in your child's routine.

33. Evaluate the significance of the change in routine in order to determine how much assistance your child will need in the change.

34. Make certain your child understands any directions, explanations, or instructions involved in changing to a new routine.

35. Provide your child with notes on the refrigerator, in his/her room, etc., to remember changes in routine.

36. Provide your child with a verbal reminder of changes in routine.

37. Provide your child with frequent opportunities to become accustomed to changes in the routine (e.g., having guests in your home, having a baby-sitter, etc.).

38. Limit the number of changes in your child's established routine. Gradually increase the number of changes in routine as your child demonstrates success.

39. Make certain that anyone who assumes responsibility in your home (e.g., grandparents, baby-sitter, etc.) is provided with rules, schedules, mealtimes, bedtimes, appropriate activities, consequences, etc., in order that their supervision will be as consistent with yours as possible.

40. Make certain your child understands that you will receive a report of behavior from baby-sitters, grandparents, etc., upon your return.

41. Make certain your child is rewarded for appropriate behavior during any change in routine (e.g., having guests in your home, having a baby-sitter, staying with grandparents, etc.).

A Reminder: Difficulty adjusting to changes in a routine often result from the excitement of doing something out of the ordinary. Make certain your child is well informed in advance of such changes and knows what the rules and expectations will be.

69 Is not able to eat, sleep, or concentrate because of personal or school problems

1. Talk to your family doctor, a school official, a social worker, or a mental health professional about your child's inability to eat, sleep, or concentrate.

2. Encourage your child to tell you when he/she is upset over personal or school problems.

3. Reward your child for talking to you about personal or school problems. Possible rewards include verbal praise (e.g., 'I'm so proud of you for coming to me to talk about your problem with your friend, Jamie.''), a kiss on the cheek, a hug, having a friend over to play, staying up late, watching a favorite TV show, and playing a game with a parent. (See Appendix for Reward Menu.)

4. If there are other children or adolescents in the home, reward them for talking about personal or school problems.

5. By maintaining an open and honest relationship with your child, he/she will feel comfortable coming to you for help in solving personal or school problems.

6. Make a point to ask your child how things are going each day.

7. Write a contract with your child.

For example: I, William, will tell Mother and/or Daddy when I am upset about something that happened in school. When I talk about my feelings I will earn a dime.

The contract should be written within the ability level of your child and should focus on only one behavior at a time. (See Appendix for an example of a Behavior Contract.)

8. Make certain that your child sees the relationship between his/her behavior and the consequences which follow (e.g., not eating and sleeping will cause illness).

9. Maintain trust and confidentiality with your child at all times.

10. Encourage your child to get involved in extracurricular activities (e.g., scouting, sports, clubs, etc.).

11. Encourage your child to talk with other individuals (e.g., guidance counselor, school nurse, social worker, teacher, relative, etc.) if your child is uncomfortable talking with you.

12. Before going to bed, read your child a pleasant bedtime story in order to help your child think about positive thoughts before going to sleep.

13. Have the family eat meals together in order to have conversation and to keep your child's mind off of school or personal problems.

14. Take time to listen so your child realizes that your concern is genuine.

15. Reduce the emphasis on competition. Repeated failures may heighten anxiety about performance.

16. Provide your child with as many enjoyable and interesting activities as possible.

17. Structure the home environment in such a way that time does not permit opportunities for your child to dwell on concerns or worries.

18. Discuss ways in which to practice self-improvement with your child.

19. Encourage your child to discuss problems with you instead of trying to handle problems alone.

20. Encourage your child to talk to a counselor at school about courses.

21. Explain that some concerns or worries, while legitimate, are not unusual for children (e.g., worrying about grades, popularity, dating, sex, etc.). Talking about concerns will only make it easier to deal with them.

22. Teach your child to be a problem-solver when encountering a personal or school problem:

> Step 1: Identify the problem
> Step 2: Identify goals and objectives
> Step 3: Develop strategies
> Step 4: Develop a plan for action
> Step 5: Carry out the plan

23. Teach your child that the best way to deal with a problem is to confront it and solve it (e.g., if he/she is worried about an assignment, the best thing to do is to work on it; if he/she is worried about a test, study with a friend; etc.).

24. Be sensitive to your child's behavior in order to detect concern over personal or school problems and intervene early to help deal with them.

25. Spend time alone with your child in order to give him/her the opportunity to talk with you, share feelings, and feel comfortable sharing concerns over personal or school problems. Involve your child in your activities and get involved in your child's activities, getting to know your child's friends and their interests, concerns, etc.

26. Demonstrate to your child that you can be deliberate as a problem-solver and that you and your child together can solve personal or school problems (e.g., when your child has a problem with homework, help your child with it or communicate with the teacher in order to be able to complete the homework, turn it in on time, and have it accurate).

27. The way you react to your child's personal or school problems will determine whether or not he/she comes to you with a problem again (e.g., by being supportive and helping your child solve problems, your child will want to call upon you for help in the future).

28. Do not appear shocked or surprised by your child's problems. Be supportive and non-judgmental if your child comes to you with problems concerning drugs, sex, dating, boyfriends, girlfriends, etc.

A Reminder: Be sensitive to your child's worries and concerns. They are as real to him/her as yours are to you.

1. Teach your child to stop and think about the consequences of his/her behavior before behaving in a certain manner.

2. Make sure that you consider the consequences of your behavior before behaving in a certain manner.

3. Immediately stop your child from behaving inappropriately and discuss the consequences of the behavior with him/her.

4. Reward your child for considering the consequences of his/her behavior. Possible rewards include verbal praise (e.g., "I'm proud of you for not hitting your sister when she called you a name!"), a kiss on the cheek, a hug, having a friend over to play, staying up late, watching a favorite TV show, and playing a game with a parent. (See Appendix for Reward Menu.)

5. If there are other children or adolescents in the home, reward them for considering the consequences of their behavior.

6. Allow natural consequences to occur due to your child's failure to consider the consequences of his/her behavior (e.g., hitting others will result in being hit in return, stealing will result in being fined, etc.).

7. Make certain that your child sees the relationship between his/her behavior and the consequences which follow (e.g., failing to bring in a bike at night might result in it being stolen).

8. When your child fails to consider the consequences of his/her behavior, explain exactly what he/she did wrong, what should have been done and why.

For example: You get a call from your child's teacher reporting that your child stole a stopwatch from her desk during recess. Go to your child and say, "Billy, I just talked with your teacher. She said you stole a stopwatch from her desk today. You took something that belonged to someone and stealing is wrong. You should not steal from others. If you do, they will not trust you."

9. Write a contract with your child.

For example: I, William, for one day, will stop and consider the consequences of my behavior before behaving in a certain way. When I accomplish this, I can play a game with Mother.

The contract should be written within the ability level of your child and should focus on only one behavior at a time. (See Appendix for an example of a Behavior Contract.)

10. Talk with your family doctor, a school official, a social worker, a mental health worker, etc., about your child's failure to consider the consequences of his/her behavior.

11. Teach your child ways to settle down (e.g., count to 10, say the alphabet, walk away, etc.) when it is necessary to slow down and think about what he/she is doing.

12. Remove your child from a group or activity until he/she can demonstrate self-control.

13. Make certain that consequences are consistently delivered for the behavior that is demonstrated (e.g., appropriate behavior results in positive consequences and inappropriate behavior results in negative consequences.

14. Provide constant, positive reinforcement for appropriate behavior. Ignore as many inappropriate behaviors as possible.

15. Prevent your child from becoming overstimulated by an activity (e.g., monitor or supervise your child's behavior to limit overexcitement in physical activities, games, parties, etc.).

16. Provide your child with a clearly identified list of consequences for inappropriate behavior.

17. Teach your child to be a problem-solver when encountering a personal or school problem:

    Step 1: Identify the problem
    Step 2: Identify goals and objectives
    Step 3: Develop strategies
    Step 4: Develop a plan for action
    Step 5: Carry out the plan

18. Carefully consider your child's age before expecting him/her to always think before acting.

19. Show your child how to stop and think before acting.

20. Remind your child to "stop and think" when beginning to do something without thinking first.

21. Supervise situations in which your child is likely to act impulsively (e.g., maintain close physical proximity, maintain eye contact, etc.).

22. Deliver natural consequences to help your child learn that his/her behavior determines the consequences which follows (e.g., work not done during work time has to be made up during recreational time, what is wasted or destroyed has to be replaced by him/her, etc.).

23. Be certain to take every opportunity to explain to your child that it is his/her behavior that determines the consequences, whether they are positive or negative (e.g., your child may choose a movie to go see or rent because all chores were done for the week, your child has to make the bed and clean his/her room on a Saturday afternoon because it was not done on Saturday morning, etc.).

24. Each time a consequence is delivered, whether it is positive or negative, have your child explain to you why it is happening (e.g., "Because I was a helpful shopper, I can have a treat at the checkout line.").

25. Make it possible for your child to earn those things he/she wants or needs in order that your child will not have to engage in inappropriate behavior to get what is desired (e.g., lying or stealing to get something important).

26. Do not make it too difficult for your child to earn those things he/she wants. If it is too difficult to earn something, the negative consequences of getting it in an inappropriate way (e.g., stealing) may seem like a worthwhile risk.

27. Make certain your child understands that consequences naturally follow behavior. You do not make the consequence happen; it is the behavior that makes the consequence occur.

28. Discuss consequences with your child before beginning an activity (e.g., cheating in a game will result in the game ending and people not playing again).

29. Reduce the opportunity for your child to act impulsively by limiting decision-making. Gradually increase opportunities for decision-making as your child demonstrates success.

A Reminder: Perhaps the most important lesson we will learn in our lifetime is that it is our behavior that determines the consequences which follow.

1. Establish rules for leaving the yard, being home on time for meals, etc. (e.g., leave a note with information such as where you will be, a phone number where you can be reached, and when you will be home; call when you will be late; ask permission to leave the yard; etc.). These rules should be consistent and followed by everyone in the home. Talk about the rules often and reward your child for following the rules.

2. Reward your child for asking permission to leave the yard, being home on time, etc. Possible rewards include verbal praise (e.g., "Thank you for asking permission to leave the yard!" "I appreciate it when you get home in time for dinner." etc.), a kiss on the cheek, a hug, having a friend over to play, staying up late, watching a favorite TV show, and playing a game with a parent. (See Appendix for Reward Menu.)

3. If there are other children or adolescents in the home, reward them for asking permission to leave the yard, being on time for meals, etc.

4. Carefully consider your child's age before expecting him/her to ask permission to leave the yard, know when it is time to come home, etc. Supervise your child and know where he/she is at all times.

5. Let your child know what you are doing by leaving a note telling where you are, the number where you can be reached, and when you will be home. By doing this, your child will learn the importance of letting others know where he/she is at all times.

6. When your child leaves the yard without permission, explain exactly what he/she did wrong, what should have been done and why.

7. Make certain that your child sees the relationship between his/her behavior and the consequences which follow (e.g., getting home late for dinner results in having to eat food that is no longer warm).

8. Remind your child to keep track of time by asking an adult, looking at a watch, etc.

9. Write a contract with your child.

For example: I, William, will be home in time for dinner for 4 days in a row. When I accomplish this, I can have a friend over to spend the night.

The contract should be written within the ability level of your child and should focus on only one behavior at a time. (See Appendix for an example of a Behavior Contract.)

10. Allow natural consequences to occur due to your child's leaving the yard without permission, not coming home for dinner on time, etc. (e.g., not being able to leave the yard, missing dinner, having to eat leftovers, etc.).

11. After giving your child permission to leave the yard, make sure you know where your child will be and tell him/her what time to be home. Have your child repeat to you the time to be home.

12. Have your child keep track of the number of times he/she asks permission to leave the yard, is home on time for dinner, etc., by putting a star or check mark on a list by the behavior performed. Let your child trade in stars or check marks for rewards.

13. Make certain your child understands that the privilege of being away from home is dependent upon letting you know where he/she is at all times, coming home on time, etc.

14. Maintain a list of your child's friends and their telephone numbers in case you need to reach your child.

15. Establish a regular routine for meals and other family activities so that your child will know when to be home.

16. Be consistent in dealing with your child's behavior. Consequences must be delivered each time your child is late, goes somewhere he/she is not to go, etc.

17. Require your child to keep you informed by telephone where he/she is at all times.

18. Keep a notepad in a conspicuous place for your child to leave messages telling you where he/she will be and what time he/she will be home.

19. Make certain your child knows that coming home late without permission will result in loss of privileges (e.g., using the car, dating, etc.).

20. Increase supervision of your child (e.g., direct supervision by you, another adult, older adolescent, etc.).

21. Make certain your child understands that being late frightens and causes concern for the family.

22. Require your child to call home to tell you when and why he/she will be late.

23. If your child is late for a meal, have your child prepare his/her own meal, do without a meal, etc.

24. Make an agreement with your child to call you if the driver of a car in which he/she is riding has been drinking, if he/she has been drinking, if he/she is uncomfortable in a particular situation, etc. Make certain your child understands that there will be no negative consequences for calling, but if he/she does not call there could be negative consequences.

25. Offer your child the opportunity to have friends at your home to watch late movies, order pizza, spend the night, etc.

26. Make certain that baby-sitters, grandparents, visitors in your home, etc., are aware of your child's tendency to leave the yard without permission. Make certain they understand the importance of maintaining consistency in the discipline of your child when he/she leaves the yard without permission.

27. Make certain your child understands that people worry, become upset, etc., when he/she leaves the yard without permission.

28. Make certain that when consequences are delivered for inappropriate behavior, they are not extreme and are directly related to the inappropriate behavior (e.g., If your child leaves the yard without permission, he/she will be grounded to the yard for two hours, one day, etc.).

29. Make certain your child knows what the consequences will be in your home for leaving the yard without permission (e.g., loss of privileges, loss of freedom to be left alone, etc.).

A Reminder: Your child's behavior should determine how much freedom is given to come and go from day to day.

72 Cannot accept constructive criticism

1. Make sure that you criticize your child in a constructive and supportive manner. Do not "pick on your child" or make him/her feel "picked on."

2. Allow your child to make comments and be a part of the problem-solving process when there are behaviors that need to be changed.

3. Do not "make fun" of your child when he/she becomes angry, cries, etc., when others give constructive criticism.

4. Reward your child for accepting constructive criticism in an appropriate manner. Possible rewards include verbal praise (e.g., "I'm so proud of you for sitting and listening to me when I was trying to help you improve your English paper."), a kiss on the cheek, a hug, having a friend over to play, staying up late, watching a favorite TV show, and playing a game with a parent. (See Appendix for Reward Menu.)

5. If there are other children or adolescents in the home, reward them for accepting constructive criticism in an appropriate manner.

6. Show your child how to accept constructive criticism by listening, making appropriate comments, etc.

7. Be a model for accepting constructive criticism.

8. Write a contract with your child.

For example: I, William, for one week, will not cry when Mother tells me to clean my room. When I accomplish this, I can earn a model airplane.

The contract should be written within the ability level of your child and should focus on only one behavior at a time. (See Appendix for an example of a Behavior Contract.)

9. Do not become upset or angry when your child does something wrong. Help your child understand what he/she did wrong by talking calmly about the problem. If you get angry, your child will try to make excuses for the behavior.

10. Do not give your child constructive criticism in front of others. Discuss the need for behavioral changes in private.

11. When your child responds inappropriately to constructive criticism, explain exactly what he/she is doing wrong, what should be done and why.

For example: Your child begins crying when you are helping with an English assignment. Explain by saying, "I'm trying to help you with your English and you are crying. You need to stop crying so we can talk about your errors and discuss changes that need to be made."

12. Offer to help or provide assistance when you give your child constructive criticism.

13. Make sure that other individuals (e.g., teachers, parents of your child's friends, baby-sitters, etc.) are aware of your child's reaction to constructive criticism.

14. Help your child feel comfortable coming to you for assistance with a problem by listening to him/her and helping find a solution to the problem.

15. Make certain that your child sees the relationship between his/her behavior and the consequences which follow (e.g., others avoiding your child, not being allowed to participate in activities, etc.).

16. Help your child understand the intent of others when they say or do something that upsets him/her.

17. Teach your child to deal with feelings of sensitivity.

18. When your child reacts in an overly sensitive manner, explain what happened to cause your child to "overreact" and what could have been done in order to prevent the reaction.

19. Provide your child with a quiet place to go when he/she becomes upset or angry with a friend or friends.

20. Remove your child from a friend or group of friends who may be overly critical of your child.

21. Avoid allowing your child to engage in activities which may not prove successful and which may cause him/her to feel bad about himself/herself.

22. Encourage your child to pursue those activities with which he/she experiences the most success.

23. Make certain that your comments take the form of constructive criticism rather than criticism that can be perceived as personal, threatening, etc. (e.g., instead of saying, "You always make the same mistake." say "A better way to do that might be...").

24. Compliment your child whenever possible.

25. Encourage others to compliment your child.

26. Set up your child for success by finding activities that will result in success; then your child will feel more confident, self-assured, etc., and will likely find more success on his/her own.

27. Do not allow your child to remain in those activities, situations, etc., where there is not a chance of success. Continued failures can be a destructive influence.

28. Do not reinforce your child's sensitivity by feeling sorry for him/her, putting others down, involving yourself in the situation, etc., when your child comes to you saying someone laughed at or made fun of him/her.

29. Identify those things about which your child appears to be overly sensitive. Talk to your child and help overcome the sensitivity by getting a tutor, cutting your child's hair, playing catch, helping to lose weight, etc.

30. Do not tease your child about weight, color of hair, abilities, etc.

31. Talk to peers, brothers/sisters, etc., about being sensitive to your child's feelings.

32. When giving your child constructive criticism, deliver a positive comment before offering criticism (e.g., "Your room looks great, but you need to spend a few extra minutes cleaning your closet." "You did a great job in the baseball game today. Next time you may want to play closer to first base." etc.).

33. Make certain the criticism you are giving your child is constructive in nature.

34. Make certain that others offering your child criticism are doing it in a constructive way.

35. Explain to your child how to take constructive criticism (e.g., say, "OK, thanks for the advice." "Thanks for helping me out." "Great idea." etc.).

36. Explain to your child that constructive criticism is not a put-down, but rather a way to help him/her improve.

37. Use language that reflects support rather than language that proves threatening (e.g., "Another way to do that might be . . ." rather than "That's not the right way to do that. Do it over." etc.).

38. Anytime that constructive criticism is given, begin by saying to your child, "Let me help you."

39. Review those things you are going to say to your child to make certain they are constructive and positive.

40. Make certain your child is receiving adequate, positive reinforcement anytime it is appropriate.

41. Provide constructive criticism when your child is most likely to demonstrate an appropriate response (e.g., instead of giving constructive criticism at the end of a ball game, wait until the next day; etc.).

42. Ask your child if he/she would like to have some constructive criticism. Respect his/her decision.

43. Avoid using such phrases as "don't take this the wrong way, but. . . ", "Don't take this personally, but. . .", "I don't mean to hurt your feelings, but. . . ", when approaching your child with constructive criticism.

A Reminder: We are all sensitive to criticism; be certain to be as positive as possible.

73 Is impatient

1. Establish a rule (e.g., be patient with others). This rule should be consistent and followed by everyone in the home. Talk about the rule often and reward your child for following the rule.

2. Attempt to be patient. If you are impatient, your child will learn to be impatient also.

3. Reward your child for being patient. Possible rewards include verbal praise (e.g., ''Thanks for waiting patiently until I was finished talking on the phone!''), a kiss on the cheek, a hug, having a friend over to play, staying up late, watching a favorite TV show, and playing a game with a parent. (See Appendix for Reward Menu.)

4. If there are other children or adolescents in the home, reward them for being patient.

5. Give your child suggestions of things to do (e.g., counting to 10, saying the alphabet, walking away from the situation and then returning, etc.) in order to help teach more patience.

6. When your child is impatient, explain exactly what he/she is doing wrong, what he/she should be doing and why.

For example: You overhear your child yelling at a friend to hurry. Go to your child and say, ''William, you are yelling at Matt. You need to wait patiently until he is ready to play, or he may not want to play with you.''

7. Write a contract with your child.

For example: I, William, for two days in a row, will wait patiently for my turn to use the telephone. When I accomplish this, I can go to the movies on Saturday.

The contract should be written within the ability level of your child and should focus on only one behavior at a time. (See Appendix for an example of a Behavior Contract.)

8. Provide supervision when your child interacts with others.

9. Immediately remove your child from interacting with others when he/she begins to be impatient.

10. Make certain that your child sees the relationship between his/her behavior and the consequences which follow (e.g., hurting others' feelings, others avoiding your child, etc.).

11. Teach your child how to deal with feelings of frustration in an appropriate manner.

12. Carefully consider your child's age and experience before expecting him/her to always be patient.

13. Encourage your child to ask for help when necessary.

14. Do not make your child wait for long periods of time to get your attention.

15. Make sure that there is something to do if your child has to wait on others (e.g., reading, playing a game, listening to music, etc.).

16. Encourage your child to find something to do when waiting for others.

17. Remind your child how it felt when he/she was learning something new, attempting something new, etc., and help your child see how others might feel in the same situation and that he/she should use patience when around such situations.

18. Do not allow your child to play with children with whom he/she has little patience.

19. Have your child spend short periods of time with younger brothers and/or sisters and friends in order to learn to be more patient with them. Gradually increase the amount of time your child spends with younger brothers and/or sisters and friends as he/she demonstrates increased patience.

20. Identify the thing with which your child is impatient (e.g., younger brothers/sisters or friends, games, homework, etc.). Remind your child to try to use patience before doing something with which he/she is impatient.

21. Make certain that your child is able to get those things that are needed without having to ask others for help. Your child should be able to reach food, dishes, shampoo, clothes, etc., without needing someone's help.

22. Talk to your child in the manner in which you want them to talk to you. Treat them with respect and do not "talk down" to them.

23. Provide your child with a place to go when he/she becomes impatient (e.g., a quiet corner, a room, etc.).

24. When your child begins to get impatient, provide reminders for self-control (e.g., by saying, "You need to count to ten." "Calm down, you're becoming impatient." etc.).

25. After telling your child that he/she cannot do or have something, explain the reason.

26. Teach your child alternative ways to communicate unhappiness (e.g., talking about a problem, asking for help, etc.).

27. Give your child additional responsibilities (e.g., chores, errands, privileges, etc.) in order to provide alternative activities if your child does not get to do what he/she wants.

28. Discourage your child from engaging in those activities which cause unhappiness.

29. Help your child to be able to identify when he/she is beginning to get upset in order to do something to calm down (e.g., walk away, talk about feelings in a socially acceptable way, seek help from an adult, etc.).

30. Involve your child in activities that are likely to result in success and which will help your child feel good about himself/herself. Repeated failures result in frustration and impatience.

31. Do not place emphasis on perfection. If your child feels he/she must meet up to your expectations and cannot, it may cause your child to become impatient with himself/herself.

32. Talk to your child's teacher to make certain that the child is not having trouble in school and becoming impatient with schoolwork.

33. Make necessary adjustments in the environment to prevent your child from experiencing stress, impatience, frustration, etc.

34. Reinforce your child for demonstrating self-control based on the length of time he/she can be successful. Gradually increase the length of time required for reinforcement as your child demonstrates success.

35. Prevent frustrating or anxiety-producing situations from occurring (e.g., only give your child chores, responsibilities, etc., on the appropriate ability level).

36. Teach your child to verbalize feelings before losing control (e.g., "I'm getting tired of doing this." "I'm getting bored standing here." etc.).

37. Monitor the behavior of others (e.g., brothers, sisters, friends, etc.) to make certain they are not teasing or otherwise stimulating your child to become upset or angry.

38. Look for the warning signs (e.g., arguing, loud voices, etc.) that your child is getting upset or angry and intervene to change the activity.

39. Before competitive activities, discuss how your child should react if he/she becomes impatient.

40. Do not allow your child to participate in a situation unless he/she can demonstrate self-control.

41. Make certain that the activities, situations, etc., in which your child is involved are appropriate for your child's age, maturity, developmental level, etc. It may be that your child is not ready for such activities at this particular time.

42. Reduce the emphasis on competition. Highly competitive activities may cause your child to be impatient to win, "beat" someone, etc.

43. Help your child perform those activities which cause him/her to be impatient (e.g., putting a model together, making the bed, etc.). Provide less assistance as your child experiences success.

44. Prevent your child from becoming overly frustrated by activities or situations. Intervene to keep your child from becoming too upset. Repeated frustration/impatience only contributes to more frequent impatience occurring at shorter intervals.

A Reminder: Impatience to participate, get things done, etc., while annoying, is a characteristic of youth. Patience is learned with personal success and by satisfaction with our accomplishments.

1. Teach your child how to respond to friendly teasing (e.g., laugh, tease in return, etc.).

2. Act as a model for friendly teasing by joking with others and dealing with friendly teasing in an appropriate manner.

3. Teach your child how to deal with friendly teasing which upsets him/her (e.g., avoid those individuals who do the teasing, walk away from the situation, move to another location, etc.).

4. Explain to your child that friendly teasing is a positive means by which people show others that they like them and enjoy their company.

5. Reward your chid for dealing with friendly teasing in an acceptable manner. Possible rewards include verbal praise (e.g., "I'm glad that you didn't get angry when Lisa was teasing you today!"), a kiss on the cheek, a hug, having a friend over to play, staying up late, watching a favorite TV show, and playing a game with a parent. (See Appendix for Reward Menu.)

6. If there are other children or adolescents in the home, reward them for dealing with friendly teasing in an acceptable manner.

7. When your child has difficulty dealing with friendly teasing, explain exactly what he/she is doing wrong, what should be done and why.

For example: You overhear your child yelling at his sister because she is teasing him. Go to you child and say, "William, Kim is teasing you and you are yelling at her. She is trying to make you laugh and wants you to tease her in return. If you don't like the teasing , then you need to ask her to stop in a friendly manner or walk away from her. If you start yelling, others will not want to be around you."

8. Supervise your child's interactions with others in order to be sure that the teasing is friendly and to help your child respond in an acceptable manner.

9. Write a contract with your child.

For example: I, William, for three days in a row, will not cry when Kim teases me. When I accomplish this, I can earn a Matchbox car.

The contract should be written within the ability level of your child and should focus on only one behavior at a time. (See Appendix for an example of a Behavior Contract.)

10. Talk with your child about choosing friends who are friendly and sincere.

11. Talk with school personnel and other individuals who spend time with your child in order to make them aware of your child's response to friendly teasing.

12. Point out to your child, when you are teasing others, that no harm is meant and that the same holds true when others tease your child.

13. Make certain that your child sees the relationship between his/her behavior and the consequences which follow (e.g., others avoiding your child, being removed from interacting with others, not being able to participate in special activities, etc.).

14. Immediately remove your child when he/she has difficulty dealing with friendly teasing.

15. Allow natural consequences to occur as a result of your child's inability to deal with friendly teasing (e.g., being removed from interacting with others when reacting inappropriately).

16. Help your child understand the intent of others when they say or do something that is upsetting.

17. Treat your child in a sensitive manner. Do not tease, make fun of, or "talk down" to your child.

18. Help your child feel good about himself/herself by making positive comments and spending one-to-one time with him/her.

19. Do not punish or make fun of your child when he/she reacts in an overly sensitive manner.

20. Encourage your child to play with others who are friendly, cooperative, and kind.

21. Make certain that you accept teasing, joking, etc., in an acceptable way.

22. Do not put your child in a situation where he/she may feel bad about himself/herself (e.g., playing football if unwilling and noncompetitive, dancing if not good at it, etc.).

23. Do not reinforce your child's sensitivity by feeling sorry for him/her, putting others down, involving yourself in the situation, etc., when your child comes to you saying someone laughed at or made fun of him/her.

24. Do not tease your child about weight, color of hair, abilities, etc.

25. Talk to peers, brothers/sisters, etc., about being sensitive to your child's feelings.

26. Make certain your child has many successes in order to feel satisfied with himself/herself.

27. Explain to your child that people often tease in a friendly manner because they like the person they are teasing.

28. Teach your child the difference between "friendly teasing" and "unfriendly teasing."

29. Remove your child from a friend or group of friends who may be overly critical of your child.

30. Encourage others to compliment your child.

31. Pair your child with a younger brother/sister, younger children, etc., in order to enhance your child's feelings of success or accomplishment.

32. Discuss with others your child's sensitivity and difficulty in dealing with friendly teasing in order that they may adjust their behavior accordingly.

33. Discuss with your child topics which are not appropriate for friendly teasing (e.g., death, disease, handicaps, poverty, etc.).

34. Help your child understand that if he/she cannot accept friendly teasing, then it would be best if your child avoided certain situations (e.g., do not join in friendly teasing if you cannot handle the situation when the teasing turns to you).

35. Act as a model for friendly teasing by joking with others and your child and laughing when they tease you.

36. Make certain your child understands that friendly teasing is an accepted means of communication and interaction in our society. If your child can accept friendly teasing and also practice it, he/she will have learned a valuable communication skill.

37. Make certain your child understands that when friends tease, it is "friendly teasing" (i.e., even sarcasm, one-upmanship, etc., constitute "friendly teasing" when it is among "friends").

A Reminder: Impress upon your child that "friendly teasing" is a part of having "friends."

75 Is overly sensitive

1. Reward your child for reacting in an acceptable manner to things others say or do. Possible rewards include verbal praise (e.g., "I am so proud of you for not crying when your friend did not want to play with you today."), a kiss on the cheek, a hug, having a friend over to play, staying up late, watching a favorite TV show, and playing a game with a parent. (See Appendix for Reward Menu.)

2. If there are other children or adolescents in the home, reward them for reacting in an acceptable manner to things others say or do.

3. Help your child understand the intent of others when they say or do something that may be upsetting.

4. Teach your child to deal with his/her feelings of sensitivity.

5. When your child reacts in an overly sensitive manner, explain what happened to cause your child to "overreact" and what could have been done to prevent the reaction.

6. Make certain that your child sees the relationship between his/her behavior and the consequences which follow (e.g., others making fun, others avoiding your child, not being invited to do things with others, etc.).

7. Treat your child in a sensitive manner. Do not tease, make fun of, or "talk down" to your child.

8. Help your child feel good about himself/herself by making positive comments and spending one-to-one time with him/her.

9. Encourage your child to play with others who are friendly, cooperative, and kind.

10. Help your child choose activities that make him/her feel good about himself/herself.

11. Do not put your child in a situation where he/she may feel bad about himself/herself (e.g., playing football if unwilling and noncompetitive, dancing if not good at it, etc.).

12. Do not punish or make fun of your child when he/she is reacting in an overly sensitive manner.

13. Make certain that you accept teasing, joking, change, etc., in an acceptable way.

14. Treat your child with respect. Talk in an objective manner at all times and use a calm, quiet voice without losing your temper.

15. Provide your child with a quiet place to go when he/she becomes upset or angry with a friend or friends.

16. Encourage your child to play with children who do not laugh at and/or make fun of others.

17. Increase supervision of your child when playing with others.

18. Talk to your child about ways to handle feelings when someone laughs at or makes fun of him/her (e.g., laughing along, walking away, counting to 10, etc.).

19. Help your child to see his/her good points and talk about them often in an attempt to help your child feel better about himself/herself.

20. Do not put an emphasis on competition. Repeated failures may cause your child to criticize himself/herself.

21. Talk with your child about individual differences, and discuss strengths and weaknesses of individuals your child knows.

22. Make certain you do not contribute to your child being critical of himself/herself by discussing weight, grades, looks, etc., in public or in front of your child.

23. Make certain that your comments take the form of constructive criticism rather than criticism that can be perceived as personal, threatening, etc. (e.g., instead of saying, "You always make the same mistake." say, "A better way to do that might be...").

24. Remove your child from a friend or group of friends who may be overly critical of your child.

25. Avoid engaging your child in activities in which he/she may not succeed and which may cause your child to have bad feelings about himself/herself.

26. Encourage your child to pursue those activities with which he/she experiences the most success.

27. Encourage your child to learn to accept improvement rather than insisting on excellence (e.g., getting one hit during a game is an improvement over striking out four times, etc.).

28. Encourage others to compliment your child.

29. Set up your child for success by finding activities that will result in success; then your child will feel more confident, self-assured, etc., and will likely find more success on his/her own.

30. Do not reinforce your child's sensitivity by feeling sorry for him/her, putting others down, involving yourself in the situation, etc., when your child comes to you saying someone laughed at or made fun of him/her.

31. Do not allow your child to remain in those activities, situations, etc., where there is no chance of success. Continued failures can be a destructive influence.

32. Talk to teachers at school to make certain that your child is successful in school and to see if there are any problems with schoolwork.

33. Identify those things about which your child appears to be overly sensitive. Talk to your child and help to overcome the sensitivity by getting him/her a tutor, cutting your child's hair, playing catch, helping to lose weight, etc.

34. Do not tease your child about weight, color of hair, abilities, etc.

35. Talk to peers, brothers/sisters, etc., about being sensitive to your child's feelings.

36. Remove your child from others who may make fun of him/her.

37. Make certain your child has many successes in order to feel satisfied with himself/herself.

A Reminder: We are all sensitive to others making fun of or laughing at us. We need to be careful that we afford our children the same respect for their feelings as we do for the feelings of adults.

76 Cannot settle down after becoming excited

1. Establish rules (e.g., do not run or yell in the house, quiet down before you enter a building, etc.). These rules should be consistent and followed by everyone in the home. Talk about the rules often and reward your child for following the rules.

2. Reward your child for settling down after he/she gets excited. Possible rewards include verbal praise (e.g., "Thank you for remembering to walk in the house!"), a kiss on the cheek, a hug, having a friend over to play, watching a favorite TV show, and playing a game with a parent. (See Appendix for Reward Menu.)

3. If there are other children or adolescents in the home, reward them for settling down after getting excited.

4. Supervise your child in order to prevent him/her from getting too excited to settle down.

5. Carefully consider your child's age before expecting him/her to quiet down after getting excited.

6. Provide your child with quiet, calming activities (e.g., listening to music, sitting, lying on a bed, listening to a story, etc.) in order to help your child quiet down after getting excited.

7. Immediately remove your child from an activity when becoming too excited and unable to calm down.

8. When your child cannot calm down, explain exactly what he/she is doing wrong, what should be done and why.

For example: Your child is playing with friends at the pool and begins splashing, pushing, and encouraging friends to behavior inappropriately. Go to your child and say, "William, you are not following the pool rules. You need to stop splashing, pushing, and encouraging your friends to break the pool rules. If you cannot follow the pool rules, we will have to go home."

9. Do not allow your child to go to public places unless the rules can be followed.

10. Write a contract with your child.

For example: I, William, will follow the pool rules today. When I accomplish this, I can invite a friend to go to the pool with me tomorrow.

The contract should be written within the ability level of your child and should focus on only one behavior at a time. (See Appendix for an example of a Behavior Contract.)

11. Make certain that your child sees the relationship between his/her behavior and the consequences which follow (e.g., not being allowed to go somewhere such as the pool or the movies, being avoided by friends, missing out on special activities, etc.).

12. Deliver a special signal when your child is not settling down (e.g., a secret word, a hand signal, etc.).

13. Have your child engage in another activity until settling down and gaining control of behavior is possible.

14. Give your child plenty of time to settle down after a stimulating activity (e.g., have your child stop the activity 20 minutes before coming into the house, turn off the TV one hour before bedtime, stop swimming 15 minutes before it is time to go home, etc.).

15. Let your child know when activities will begin and end, and allow enough time to settle down.

16. Be consistent when expecting your child to settle down after getting excited. Do not allow running in the house one day and expect appropriate behavior the next day.

17. Give your child a schedule of daily activities in order to help your child be aware of when he/she needs to settle down after becoming excited.

18. Be consistent when expecting your child to leave the situation when becoming overly excited (e.g., send your child to his/her room for 10 minutes, make him/her sit in a chair for 15 minutes, etc.).

19. Do not allow your child to participate in activities that cause so much excitement that settling down is not possible.

20. Clearly state the manner in which you expect your child to act before going out in public to a place where your child has never been before.

21. Do not take your child places where he/she will have difficulty settling down and demonstrating acceptable behavior.

22. Read your child a relaxing story, let him/her listen to a tape, tell a story, etc., when it is time to settle down before a quiet activity (e.g., mealtime, bedtime, quiet family time, etc.).

23. Increase supervision of your child when involved in activities that tend to cause overexcitement.

24. Remove your child from the situation when he/she becomes overly excited.

25. Encourage your child to play games, sports, etc., with friends who do not encourage too much excitement.

26. Do not allow your child to participate in games, sports, etc., that may cause too much excitement.

27. Teach your child some ways to settle down when overly excited (e.g., count to 10, say the alphabet, sit in a chair, leave the situation, etc.).

28. Make certain that baby-sitters, grandparents, visitors in your home, teachers, etc., are aware of your child's tendency to get excited and not be able to settle down.

29. Prevent your child from becoming overstimulated by an activity. Supervise your child's behavior in order to limit overexcitement in physical activities, games, parties, etc.

30. Allow a transition period between activities (e.g., playtime and mealtime, watching TV and bedtime, etc.) in order that your child can make adjustments in behaviors. You cannot expect your child to go to bed if the TV is still on and everyone is watching it.

31. Use reminders to prepare your child well in advance (e.g., one hour, thirty minutes, etc.) for such activities as dinner, bathing, etc.

32. Establish definite time limits and provide your child with this information before an activity (e.g., one hour to watch TV, thirty minutes to play before dinner, thirty minutes until bath time, etc.).

33. Make certain all stimulating activities end well before quiet times (e.g., the TV is turned off one hour before bedtime, music is turned off thirty minutes before bedtime, your child must come in thirty minutes before dinner, etc.).

34. Maintain consistency in your child's daily routine.

35. Do not let your child start an activity if there will not be enough time to finish (e.g., do not let your child leave for a bike ride fifteen minutes before dinner time).

36. Prevent your child from becoming so stimulated by an event or activity that behavior cannot be controlled.

37. If your child is easily overexcited, make certain that others (e.g., brothers/sisters, friends, relatives etc.) assist you in preventing overstimulation rather than teasing or otherwise stimulating your child.

38. Provide your child with a list of daily events in order that he/she knows which activity comes next and can prepare for it. (See Appendix for Weekday or Saturday Schedule.)

39. Reduce the emphasis on competition. Competitive activities may cause your child to become overly excited.

40. Remain calm when your child becomes overexcited. Your behavior will have a calming effect on your child.

41. Do not let your child engage in overexciting activities for long periods of time.

A Reminder: Intervene early to keep your child from becoming overly excited.

77 Is easily frustrated

1. Immediately remove your child from a situation when he/she begins to get frustrated.

2. Do not allow your child to participate in a situation unless he/she can demonstrate self-control.

3. Closely supervise your child in order to monitor his/her behavior at all times.

4. Inform individuals who will be spending time with your child about his/her tendency to become easily frustrated.

5. Talk with your family doctor, a school official, a social worker, etc., about your child's behavior if it is causing him/her to have problems getting along with others.

6. Provide your child with a quiet place to go when he/she becomes frustrated.

7. Encourage your child to talk with you when he/she is frustrated.

8. Reward your child for controlling his/her behavior. Possible rewards include verbal praise (e.g., "I'm so proud of you for remaining calm when James called you a name!"), a kiss on the cheek, a hug, having a friend over to play, staying up late, watching a favorite TV show, and playing a game with a parent. (See Appendix for Reward Menu.)

9. If there are other children or adolescents in the home, reward them for controlling their behavior.

10. Treat your child with respect. Talk to him/her in a nonthreatening manner.

11. When your child becomes frustrated, explain exactly what he/she is doing wrong, what he/she is supposed to be doing and why.

For example: You tell your child that it is time to feed the dog and your child starts complaining and arguing with you. Get his/her attention and say, "You are getting frustrated because I told you to feed the dog. You need to get control of yourself and feed the dog because it is your job for this month."

12. Write a contract with your child.

For example: I, William, for one week, will not get frustrated with my little brother/sister. When I accomplish this, I can see a movie on Saturday.

The contract should be written within the ability level of your child and should focus on only one behavior at a time. (See Appendix for an example of a Behavior Contract.)

13. Teach your child to recognize when he/she is becoming frustrated and know ways in which to deal with his/her feelings.

14. Make certain that your child sees the relationship between his/her behavior and the consequences which follow (e.g., being avoided by others, not being able to participate in special activities, etc.).

15. Discuss your child's behavior with him/her in private rather than in front of others.

16. Try to reduce or prevent things from happening which cause your child to become easily frustrated.

17. Provide your child with a place to go when he/she gets frustrated (e.g., a quiet chair, his/her room, a corner, etc.).

18. Teach your child what to do when he/she becomes frustrated (e.g., count to 10, say the alphabet, leave the room, etc.).

19. Do not let your child have his/her way when he/she becomes frustrated. Help him/her work through the situation.

20. Be consistent. Try to deal with your child and his/her behavior in a manner that is as fair as possible.

21. Immediately remove your child from the attention of others when he/she becomes frustrated.

22. Remind your child of the consequences of getting frustrated before going into a store, going to a friend's house, having friends over, etc.

23. After telling your child that he/she cannot do or have something, explain to him/her the reason.

24. Make certain that baby-sitters, grandparents, teachers, etc., understand the importance of maintaining consistency in the discipline of your child.

25. Encourage your child to use problem-solving skills: (a) identify the problem, (b) identify goals and objectives, (c) develop strategies, (d) develop a plan for action, and (e) carry out the plan.

26. Teach your child alternative ways to communicate his/her unhappiness (e.g., talking about a problem, asking for help, etc.).

27. Reduce the emphasis on competition. Repeated failures may cause your child to become frustrated.

28. Provide your child with alternative activities, games, etc., in case some activities prove frustrating.

29. Discourage your child from engaging in those activities which cause him/her unhappiness.

30. Encourage your child to associate with peers with whom he/she gets along well in order to prevent him/her from getting frustrated with a situation.

31. Involve your child in activities in which he/she can be successful and will help him/her feel good about himself/herself. Repeated failures result in frustration and impatience.

32. Do not place an emphasis on perfection. If your child feels he/she must meet up to your expectations and cannot do so, he/she may become frustrated.

33. Talk to your child's teacher to make certain that he/she is not having trouble in school and becoming frustrated.

34. Make certain you set a good example for your child by dealing in a socially acceptable way with situations that may be upsetting to you.

35. Reinforce your child for demonstrating self-control based on the length of time he/she can be successful. Gradually increase the length of time required for reinforcement as he/she demonstrates success.

36. Prevent frustrating or anxiety-producing situations from occurring (e.g., only give your child chores, responsibilities, etc., which are on his/her ability level.).

37. Provide your child with positive feedback which indicates he/she is successful, important, respected, etc.

38. Make necessary adjustments in the environment to prevent your child from experiencing stress, frustration, and anger.

39. Teach your child to verbalize his/her feelings before losing control (e.g., "The work is too hard." "Please leave me alone; you're making me angry." etc.).

40. Monitor the behavior of others (e.g., brothers, sisters, friends, etc.) to make certain they are not teasing or otherwise stimulating your child to become frustrated.

41. Teach your child ways to deal with conflict situations (e.g., talking, reasoning, asking an adult to intervene, walking away, etc.).

42. Look for the warning signs (e.g., arguing, loud voices, etc.) that your child is getting frustrated, and intervene to change the activity.

A Reminder: Learning to control our temper is more difficult for some of us than it is for others. Being a model for your child in demonstrating self-control and displaying appropriate reactions to frustration or disappointment will influence your child's behavior.

78 Is easily distracted by other things happening in the home

1. Carefully consider if your child is capable of performing the responsibilities expected of him/her on his/her own. Do not give him/her too many chores to do at once, make sure he/she gets up early enough to get to school on time, provide more than enough time to perform a chore, and do not expect perfection.

2. Establish rules for performing everyday expectations (e.g., get up on time for school, do your chores right after you get home from school, finish your homework before you watch TV, etc.). These rules should be consistent and followed by everyone in the home. Talk about the rules often and reward your child for following the rules.

3. Establish a routine for your child to follow for getting ready for school, performing chores, doing homework, etc. This will help your child remember what is expected of him/her.

4. Reward your child for getting things done without being distracted. Possible rewards include verbal praise (e.g., "You're on time for school. Good for you!" "Thank you for remembering to finish your homework before you turned on the TV." etc.), a kiss on the cheek, a hug, having a friend over to play, staying up late, watching a favorite TV show, and playing a game with a parent. (See Appendix for Reward Menu.)

5. Model for your child the appropriate ways to get things done without becoming distracted. Show him/her how to follow a routine by following one yourself and getting things done on time.

6. When your child does not get something done because he/she was distracted, explain exactly what he/she did wrong, what should have been done and why.

For example: Your child is supposed to catch the school bus at 7:45 a.m. and he/she is still getting dressed when the bus arrives. Go to your child and tell him that he/she has missed the bus because he/she was not ready on time. Explain that it is unacceptable to miss the bus because you don't have the car to take him/her to school.

7. Write a contract with your child.

For example: I, William, will be ready and waiting for the school bus at 7:40 a.m. for three days in a row. When I accomplish this, I can watch 30 extra minutes of TV.

The contract should be written within the ability level of your child and should focus on only one behavior at a time. (See Appendix for an example of a Behavior Contract.)

8. If there are other children or adolescents in the home, reward them for getting things done without becoming distracted.

9. Make certain that your child sees the relationship between his/her behavior and the consequences which follow (e.g., failing to feed the dog will cause the dog to go hungry.).

10. Allow natural consequences to occur due to your child becoming distracted and not getting things done (e.g., his/her bike being stolen because he/she did not put it in the garage overnight).

11. Along with a directive, provide your child with an incentive statement (e.g., "After you get ready for bed, you may watch TV.").

12. Provide your child with written reminders, such as a list posted in the bathroom, indicating what his/her chores are and when they need to be done. (See Appendix for List of Chores.)

13. Tell your child when it is time to set the table, feed the dog, etc.

14. Allow your child to help decide what his/her routine chores will be.

15. Limit the number of chores for which your child is responsible and gradually increase the number of chores as your child demonstrates the ability to get things done on time.

16. Have your child perform the same chores each day, week, etc.

17. Show your child how to perform a new chore, such as setting the table, several times before expecting him/her to do it on his/her own.

18. Make sure your child has all the necessary materials he/she needs in order to get his/her chores done on time.

19. Explain to your child that responsibilities not done on time will have to be done at other times (e.g., playtime, TV time, weekends, etc.).

20. Reduce distracting activities which interfere with your child performing his/her responsibilities (e.g., turn off the TV when it is time to set the table, do not allow friends to come over when it is time to do homework, etc.).

21. Have your child put a star or check mark beside each chore he/she performs on time and allow him/her to trade in the stars or check marks for rewards.

22. Set aside time each day for everyone in the home to do chores (e.g., after dinner have everyone do their assigned chores).

23. Do not accept your child's excuse of "forgetting" to do chores. Have him/her make up the chores he/she forgets to do during his/her free time, TV time, etc.

24. Provide an atmosphere where everyone works together to get things done around the house.

25. Set aside time each week for your child to straighten his/her room, clothes, toys, etc.

26. Have your child do those things that need to be done when it is discussed instead of later (e.g., put swimsuits in the car now so that when you go to the pool later this afternoon, they will not be forgotten, etc.).

27. Help your child begin a chore (e.g., cleaning up his/her room) in order to help him/her get started.

28. Do not punish your child for becoming distracted during chores, responsibilities, homework, etc.

29. Make certain that responsibilities given to your child are appropriate for his/her level of development and ability.

79 Does not listen to what others are saying

1. Establish rules for listening (e.g., listen when others are talking, ask questions if you do not understand, etc.). These rules should be consistent and followed by everyone in the home. Talk about the rules often and reward your child for following the rules.

2. Reward your child for listening. Possible rewards include verbal praise (e.g., "You did a great job of listening!" "I like the way you listen!" etc.), a kiss on the cheek, a hug, having a friend over to play, staying up late, watching a favorite TV show, and playing a game with a parent. (See Appendix for Reward Menu.)

3. If there are other children or adolescents in the home, reward them for listening.

4. Carefully consider your child's age and experience when expecting him/her to be a good listener.

5. Demonstrate the appropriate way to listen by listening to your child when he/she talks.

6. When your child does not listen to what others are saying, explain exactly what he/she did wrong, what should have been done and why.

7. Write a contract with your child.

For example: I, William, for three days in a row, will listen to what others are saying without having to be reminded. When I accomplish this, I can watch 30 extra minutes of TV.

The contract should be written within the ability level of your child and should focus on only one behavior at a time. (See Appendix for an example of a Behavior Contract.)

8. Make certain that your child sees the relationship between his/her behavior and the consequences which follow (e.g., failing to listen to what others are saying may result in missing directions, instructions, etc.).

9. Allow natural consequences to occur due to your child's failure to listen to others (e.g., missing assignments, missing a ride, etc.).

10. Along with a directive, provide an incentive statement (e.g., "After you listen to what I am saying, you may watch TV.").

11. When your child has difficulty listening to others (e.g., at the grocery store, in the mall, playing a game with family members, etc.), remove him/her from the situation until he/she can demonstrate self-control and listen to what others are saying.

12. In order to help your child be able to listen to what others are saying, turn off the TV, give directions in a room away from his/her friends, etc.

13. In order to determine if your child heard what was said, have him/her repeat it.

14. Deliver directions in a supportive rather than a threatening manner (e.g., "Please take out the trash." rather than "You had better take out the trash or else!").

15. Do not criticize your child. When correcting him/her, be honest yet supportive. Never cause him/her to feel bad about himself/herself.

16. Be consistent when expecting your child to listen to what others are saying. Do not allow him/her to fail to listen one time and expect appropriate behavior the next time.

17. Make a written list of directions you want your child to follow (e.g., feed the dog, take out the trash, etc.). (See Appendix for List of Chores.)

18. Talk to your child before going into a public place and remind him/her of the importance of listening to what others are saying.

19. Make sure your child is paying attention to you when you tell him/her to do something. Have him/her look directly at you to know he/she is listening and have him/her repeat the directions to check for understanding.

20. Do not talk to your child from another room. Go to your child, get his/her undivided attention, and tell him/her what to do.

21. Have your child's hearing checked if you have not done so in the past year.

22. Make certain to give directions in a very simple manner and be specific as to what you want your child to do.

23. Do not ignore your child when he/she wants to tell you something. When you ignore others, your child learns that it is acceptable to ignore people.

24. When your child does not listen to what others are saying, let him/her know that he/she is not listening and he/she needs to listen to what others are saying.

25. Talk to your child in a supportive rather than a threatening manner (e.g., "Please take out the trash." rather than "You had better take out the trash or else!").

26. Treat your child with respect. Talk to him/her in an objective manner at all times.

27. Provide your child with a list of written directions, instructions, etc.

1. Establish rules for listening (e.g., listen to conversations and instructions, ask questions if you do not understand, follow the instructions, etc.). These rules should be consistent and followed by everyone in the home. Talk about the rules often.

2. Reward your child for listening. Possible rewards include verbal praise (e.g., "You did a great job of listening today!" "I like the way you listen!" etc.), a kiss on the cheek, a hug, having a friend over to play, staying up late, watching a favorite TV show, and playing a game with a parent. (See Appendix for Reward Menu.)

3. If there are other children or adolescents in the home, reward them for paying and maintaining attention.

4. Carefully consider your child's age and experience when expecting him/her to pay and maintain attention.

5. Demonstrate the appropriate way to pay and maintain attention (e.g., pay attention to conversations, ask questions, etc.).

6. When your child does not listen, explain exactly what he/she did wrong, what should have been done and why.

7. Write a contract with your child.

For example: I, William, for three days in a row, will listen without having to be told more than once. When I accomplish this, I can watch 30 extra minutes of TV.

The contract should be written within the ability level of your child and should focus on only one behavior at a time. (See Appendix for an example of a Behavior Contract.)

8. Make certain that your child sees the relationship between his/her behavior and the consequences which follow (e.g., failing to listen to instructions to bring in his/her bike at night may result in the bike being stolen).

9. Along with a directive, provide an incentive statement (e.g., "When you eat your peas, you may have dessert." "You may watch TV after you get ready for bed." etc.).

10. When your child has difficulty directing his/her attention in the presence of others (e.g., at the grocery store, in the mall, playing a game with family members, etc.), remove him/her from the situation until he/she can demonstrate self-control and follow directions.

11. Do not give your child more than two- or three-step directions to follow. Directions that involve several steps can be confusing and cause your child to have difficulty following them. An example of a two-step direction is: "Please turn off your light and go to bed."

12. In order to determine if your child heard what was said, have him/her repeat it.

13. Deliver directions in a supportive rather than a threatening manner (e.g., "Please take out the trash." rather than "You had better take out the trash or else!").

14. Do not criticize your child. When correcting him/her, be honest yet supportive. Never cause him/her to feel bad about himself/herself.

15. Be consistent when expecting your child to direct his/her attention to what is said. Do not allow him/her to fail to listen one time and expect appropriate behavior the next time.

16. Make a written list of directions you want your child to follow (e.g., feed the dog, take out the trash, etc.). (See Appendix for List of Chores.)

17. Talk to your child before going into a public place and remind him/her of the importance of listening to what is said.

18. Make sure your child is paying attention to you when you tell him/her to do something. Have him/her look directly at you to know he/she is listening and have him/her repeat the direction to check for understanding.

19. Do not talk to your child from another room. Go to your child and get his/her undivided attention before talking to him/her.

20. Do not punish your child for forgetting, for accidents that interfere with following directions, etc.

21. Make certain to give instructions in a very simple manner and be specific as to what you want your child to do.

22. Have your child do those things that need to be done when it is discussed instead of later (e.g., put swimsuits in the car now so that when you go to the pool later this afternoon, they will not be forgotten, etc.).

23. Make certain that responsibilities given to your child are appropriate for your child's level of development and ability.

24. Let your child know that instructions will only be given once and that you will not remind him/her to follow directions.

25. Have your child's hearing checked if you have not done so in the past year.

26. In order to help your child listen to what is going on around him/her, reduce distractions (e.g., turn off the TV, talk to him/her in a room away from his/her friends, etc.).

27. Do not allow your child to go to public places, friends' homes, etc., if he/she cannot listen to what others are saying to him/her.

28. Allow natural consequences to occur due to your child's inability to direct his/her attention to what others are saying (e.g., having to "sit out" at the pool for not listening, losing pool privileges, etc.).

29. Make certain you direct your attention to others when they are talking to you in order to demonstrate for your child how to listen to others.

1. Establish rules for listening (e.g., listen to directions, ask questions about directions if you do not understand, follow directions, etc.). These rules should be consistent and followed by everyone in the home. Talk about the rules often and reward your child for following the rules.

2. Reward your child for listening. Possible rewards include verbal praise (e.g., "You did a great job picking up your clothes!" "I like the way you follow directions!" etc.), a kiss on the cheek, a hug, having a friend over to play, staying up late, watching a favorite TV show, and playing a game with a parent. (See Appendix for Reward Menu.)

3. If there are other children or adolescents in the home, reward them for listening.

4. Carefully consider your child's age and experience before expecting him/her to be successful in activities that require listening.

5. Demonstrate the appropriate way to follow directions (e.g., give your child directions to feed the dog and then you feed the dog with him/her).

6. When your child does not listen, explain exactly what he/she did wrong, what he/she was supposed to do and why.

7. Write a contract with your child.

For example: I, William, for three days in a row, will listen without having to be told more than once. When I accomplish this, I can watch 30 extra minutes of TV.

The contract should be written within the ability level of your child and should focus on only one behavior at a time. (See Appendix for an example of a Behavior Contract.)

8. Make certain your child sees the relationship between his/her behavior and the consequences which follow (e.g., failing to follow the direction to bring in his/her bike at night may result in the bike being stolen).

9. Allow natural consequences to occur due to your child's failure to follow directions (e.g., his/her bike being stolen, loss of school books, schoolwork not done on time, etc.).

10. Along with a directive, provide an incentive statement (e.g., "When you eat your peas, you may have dessert." "You may watch TV after you get ready for bed.").

11. When your child has difficulty listening and following directions in the presence of others (e.g., at the grocery store, in the mall, playing a game with family members, etc.), remove him/her from the situation until he/she can demonstrate self-control and follow directions.

12. In order to help your child be able to listen to directions, reduce distractions (e.g., turn off the TV, give directions in a room away from his/her friends, etc.).

13. Do not give your child more than two- or three-step directions to follow. Directions that involve several steps can be confusing and cause your child to have difficulty following them. An example of a two-step directions is: "Please turn off your light and go to bed."

14. In order to determine if your child heard what was said, have him/her repeat it.

15. Deliver directions in a supportive rather than a threatening manner (e.g., "Please take out the trash." rather than "You had better take out the trash or else!").

16. Give your child a special responsibility (e.g., answering the door, serving food, cleaning, etc.) in order to teach your child to follow directions.

17. Do not criticize your child. When correcting him/her, be honest yet supportive. Never cause him/her to feel bad about himself/herself.

18. Be consistent when expecting your child to follow directions. Do not allow him/her to neglect to follow directions one time and expect appropriate behavior the next time.

19. Use a timer to help your child know the amount of time he/she has to follow directions given to him/her.

20. Play games with your child to help him/her follow directions, rules, etc.

21. Make a written list of directions you want your child to follow (e.g., feed the dog, take out the trash, etc.). (See Appendix for List of Chores.)

22. Talk to your child before going into a public place and remind him/her of the importance of following directions.

23. Establish a regular routine for your child to follow on a daily basis in order to help him/her "remember" to take care of his/her responsibilities. (See Appendix for Weekday or Saturday Schedule.)

24. Make sure your child is paying attention to you when you tell him/her to do something. Have him/her look directly at you to know he/she is listening and have him/her repeat the direction to check for understanding.

25. Do not give directions to your child from another room. Go to your child, get his/her undivided attention, and tell him/her what to do.

26. Do not punish your child for forgetting, for accidents that interfere with following directions, etc.

27. Make certain to give directions in a simple manner and be specific as to what you want your child to do.

28. Have your child do those things that need to be done when it is discussed instead of later (e.g., put swimsuits in the car now so that when you go to the pool later this afternoon, they will not be forgotten; etc.).

29. Make certain that responsibilities given to your child are appropriate for your child's level of development and ability.

30. Let your child know that directions will only be given once and that you will not remind him/her to follow the directions.

31. In order to help your child remember directions, reduce distractions (e.g., turn off the TV, give directions in a room away from his/her friends, etc.).

32. Make certain that games, activities, etc., in which your child participates, are appropriate for his/her level of development.

33. Make certain your child understands that if he/she does not follow directions when playing games, activities, etc., others will not want to play with him/her.

34. Provide your child with written directions, chores, rules, etc. (See Appendix for List of Chores and Posted Rules.)

1. Establish rules for listening (e.g., listen to directions, ask questions about directions if you do not understand, follow the directions, etc.). These rules should be consistent and followed by everyone in the home. Talk about the rules often and reward your child for following the rules.

2. Reward your child for listening. Possible rewards include verbal praise (e.g., "You did a great job picking up your clothes!" "I like the way you follow directions!" etc.), a kiss on the cheek, a hug, having a friend over to play, staying up late, watching a favorite TV show, and playing a game with a parent. (See Appendix for Reward Menu.)

3. If there are other children or adolescents in the home, reward them for listening.

4. Carefully consider your child's age and experience when expecting him/her to respond to oral questions and directions.

5. Demonstrate the appropriate way to listen to oral questions and directions (e.g., look at the person who is talking to you, ask questions, etc.).

6. When your child does not listen, explain exactly what he/she did wrong, what should have been done and why.

For example: You tell your child to clean up his/her room before 5:00. At 5:00, you tell your child that he/she has not cleaned up his/her room and that he/she needs to follow the direction to clean up his/her room now.

7. Write a contract with your child.

For example: I, William, for three days in a row, will listen without having to be told more than once. When I accomplish this, I can watch 30 extra minutes of TV.

The contract should be written within the ability level of your child and should focus on only one behavior at a time. (See Appendix for an example of a Behavior Contract.)

8. In order to determine if your child heard what was said, have him/her repeat it.

9. Make certain that your child sees the relationship between his/her behavior and the consequences which follow (e.g., failing to follow the direction to bring in his/her bike at night may result in the bike being stolen).

10. Allow natural consequences to occur due to your child's failing to follow directions (e.g., his/her bike being stolen, loss of schoolbooks, schoolwork not done on time, etc.).

11. Along with a directive, provide an incentive statement (e.g., "When you eat your peas, you may have dessert." "You may watch TV after you get ready for bed.").

12. When your child has difficulty listening to directions in front of others (e.g., at the grocery store, in the mall, playing a game with family members, etc.), remove him/her from the situation until he/she can demonstrate self-control and follow directions.

13. In order to help your child be able to listen and follow directions, reduce distractions (e.g., turn off the TV, give directions in a room away from his/her friends, etc.).

14. Do not give your child more than two- or three-step directions to follow. Directions that involve several steps can be confusing and cause your child to have difficulty following them. An example of a two-step direction is: "Please turn off your light and go to bed."

15. Deliver directions and requests in a supportive rather than threatening manner (e.g., "Please take out the trash." rather than "You had better take out the trash or else!").

16. Give your child a special responsibility (e.g., answering the door, serving food, cleaning, etc.) in order to teach your child to follow directions.

17. Do not criticize your child. When correcting him/her, be honest yet supportive. Never cause him/her to feel bad about himself/herself.

18. Be consistent when expecting your child to listen and follow directions. Do not allow him/her to fail to follow directions one time and expect appropriate behavior the next time.

19. Use a timer to help your child be aware of the amount of time he/she has to follow through with directions given to him/her.

20. Make a written list of directions you want your child to follow (e.g., feed the dog, take out the trash, etc.). (See Appendix for Sample List.)

21. Talk to your child before going into a public place and remind him/her of the importance of following directions and listening to what is being said.

22. Make sure your child is paying attention to you when you tell him/her to do something. Have him/her look directly at you to know he/she is listening and have him/her repeat the direction to check for understanding.

23. Do not talk to your child from another room. Go to your child, get his/her undivided attention, and tell him/her what to do.

24. Do not punish your child for forgetting, for accidents that interfere with following directions, for asking questions, etc.

25. Make certain to give directions in a very simple manner and be specific as to what you want your child to do.

26. Have your child do those things that need to be done when it is discussed instead of later (e.g., put swimsuits in the car now so that when you go to the pool later this afternoon, they will not be forgotten; etc.).

27. Make certain that the responsibilities given to your child are appropriate for your child's level of development and ability.

28. Assist your child in performing his/her responsibilities. Gradually require him/her to independently assume responsibility as he/she demonstrates success.

29. Write down directions for your child (e.g., take the dog outside at 3:00, clean your room, etc.).

30. Encourage teachers, school officials, etc., to offer your child a written list of questions along with providing oral directions.

31. Make certain to be specific when telling your child what you want him/her to do.

32. Do not accept your child's excuse of "forgetting" to do chores. Have him/her make up the chores he/she forgets to do during his/her free time, TV time, etc.

33. Limit the number of chores for which your child is responsible and gradually increase the number of chores as your child demonstrates the ability to get them done on time.

1. Make certain the chores assigned to your child are appropriate for his/her level of development and ability.

2. Do not assign your child too many things to do at once, provide him/her with more than enough time to get things done, and do not expect perfection.

3. Help your child begin things (e.g., help to open the dog food can, empty trash with your child, etc.).

4. Establish rules for getting things done (e.g., complete chores right after school, before you watch TV, before you go out with friends, etc.). These rules should be consistent and followed by everyone in the home. Talk about the rules often and reward your child for following the rules.

5. Establish a routine for your child to follow for completing his/her chores, homework, etc. This will help your child remember what is expected of him/her.

6. Reward your child for staying on task. Possible rewards include verbal praise (e.g., "Thank you for setting the table!"), a kiss on the cheek, a hug, having a friend over to play, staying up late, watching a favorite TV show, and playing a game with a parent. (See Appendix for a Reward Menu.)

7. If there are other children or adolescents in the home, reward them for staying on task, following a conversation, etc.

8. Model appropriate behavior for your child by staying on task, following a conversation, etc.

9. Write a contract with your child.

For example: I, William, for four days in a row, will set the table before watching TV. When I accomplish this, I can skip one night of setting the table.

The contract should be written within the ability level of your child and should focus on only one behavior at a time. (See Appendix for an example of a Behavior Contract.)

10. When your child does not stay on task, follow a conversation, etc., explain exactly what he/she did wrong, what should have been done and why.

11. Make certain that your child sees the relationship between his/her behavior and the consequences which follow (e.g., failing to listen to directions will result in not knowing what time to be ready for school).

12. Allow natural consequences to occur as a result of your child's failing to stay on task, follow a conversation, etc. (e.g., not getting homework finished, not knowing where to go, etc.).

13. Along with a directive, provide an incentive statement (e.g., "You can watch TV after you set the table.").

14. Provide your child with written reminders, such as a list posted in his/her room, indicating what his/her chores are and when they need to be completed. (See Appendix for List of Chores.)

15. Tell your child when it is time to complete homework, listen to others, etc.

16. Limit the number of chores for which your child is responsible and gradually increase the number of chores as your child demonstrates the ability to complete his/her current chores, responsibilities, etc.

17. Have your child complete the same chores and responsibilities each day, week, etc.

18. Show your child how to perform a new chore or responsibility such as setting the table, several times before expecting him/her to do it on his/her own.

19. Make sure your child has all the necessary materials he/she needs in order to complete each chore and take care of responsibilities.

20. Explain to your child that chores, homework, responsibilities, etc., not completed will have to be completed at other times (e.g., playtime, TV time, weekends, etc.).

21. Have everyone in the family perform chores and responsibilities at the same time in order to help your child remember to complete his/her chores.

22. Reduce distracting activities which interfere with your child's ability to stay on task (e.g., turn off the TV when it is time to set the table, do not allow friends to come over when it is time to do homework, etc.).

23. Have your child put a star or check mark beside each chore he/she completes and allow him/her to trade in the stars or check marks for rewards.

24. Set a timer for your child, giving him/her a limited amount of time to finish a chore, homework, etc.

25. When giving your child a chore to do, tell him/her what time it needs to be done and how long you think it will take for him/her to do the chore.

26. Have your child earn money or privileges for staying on task, following a conversation, etc.

27. Make certain to give directions in a very simple manner and be specific as to what you want your child to do.

28. Have your child do those things that need to be done when it is discussed instead of later (e.g., put swimsuits in the car now so that when you go to the pool later this afternoon, they will not be forgotten; etc.).

29. Vary your child's chores from time to time in order that he/she does not get tired of doing the same chore.

30. Make certain that the responsibilities given to your child are appropriate for his/her level of development and ability.

31. Assist your child in performing his/her responsibilities. Gradually require him/her to independently assume more responsibility as he/she demonstrates success.

1. Establish a rule for putting things back where they belong so things can be easily found the next time they are needed. This rule should be consistent and followed by everyone in the home. Talk about the rule often.

2. Reward your child for putting things back where they belong. Possible rewards include verbal praise (e.g., "Thank you for putting your toys in the toy box!"), a kiss on the cheek, a hug, having a friend over to play, staying up late, watching a favorite TV show, and playing a game with a parent. (See Appendix for Reward Menu.)

3. If there are other children or adolescents in the home, reward them for being organized.

4. Carefully consider your child's age before expecting him/her to be organized. Help him/her put away toys, clothes, etc.

5. Teach your child to put things back where they belong by returning things to their places after you use them.

6. When your child forgets to put things back where they belong, explain exactly what he/she did wrong, what should have been done and why.

For example: Your child forgets to put a toy back where it belongs. Go to your child and tell him/her that he/she forgot to put away the toy and that it needs to be put back where it belongs so it can be found in the future.

7. Write a contract with your child.

For example: I, William, for 5 days in a row, will put my toys back where they belong after I'm finished with them. When I accomplish this, I can watch a favorite TV show.

The contract should be written within the ability level of your child and should focus on only one behavior at a time. (See Appendix for an example of a Behavior Contract.)

8. Make certain there is a designated place for all items in and around the home.

9. Make certain that your child sees the relationship between his/her behavior and the consequences which follow (e.g., not putting away toys will result in not being able to find them and possibly losing them).

10. Allow natural consequences to occur as a result of your child's failure to put things back where they belong (e.g., not being able to find them, the items being damaged and possibly lost, etc.).

11. Along with a directive, provide an incentive statement (e.g., "You may watch TV after you put your clothes where they belong.").

12. Require your child to put his/her coat, gloves, hat, etc., in a designated place upon entering the home.

13. Set aside time each week for your child to straighten his/her room, clothes, toys, etc.

14. Make a list of your child's most frequently used items and/or materials and have your child make sure that each item and/or material is put in its designated place each day.

15. Identify a place for all members of the household to keep frequently used items (e.g., coats, boots, gloves, hats, keys, pens and pencils, purses, etc.).

16. Set aside time each evening when all family members put away things in their proper places and organize their possessions for the next day (e.g., school clothes, books, lunches, etc.).

17. Have your child put away toys, clothes, etc., before getting out more things to play with or wear.

18. Require your child's room to be neat and organized so there will always be a place to put toys, games, clothes, etc.

19. When your child has a friend over, have them pick up toys and games 15 minutes before the friend leaves so he/she can help your child.

20. If your child fails to pick up his/her clothes, games, toys, etc., before going to bed, pick up the toys and take them away from him/her for a period of time.

21. Make certain to be consistent when expecting your child to pick up toys (e.g., do not leave the house with toys in the yard one time and expect the toys to be picked up the next time).

22. Do not expect your child to pick up toys and games that friends failed to put away. Encourage your child's friends to pick up toys and games.

23. Communicate with parents of your child's friends to make certain that your child helps pick up toys when he/she is spending time at a friend's house.

24. Tell baby-sitters or others who are involved with your child that your child is responsible for picking up and putting away his/her own materials.

25. Show your child the proper way to take care of his/her things (e.g., shining shoes, hosing off his/her bike, taking care of dolls, etc.). This will teach your child a sense of responsibility with his/her own belongings.

26. Do not buy additional toys, games, etc., for your child if he/she is not able to take care of what he/she has.

27. Have your child pay for things he/she wants (e.g., a baseball mitt, a new doll, a new pair of jeans, etc.). If your child has spent some of his/her own money on an item, he/she may be more willing to take care of it.

28. Provide your child with shelving, containers, organizers, etc., for his/her possessions. Label the storage areas and require your child to keep his/her possessions organized.

29. Limit your child's use of those things he/she is not responsible for putting away, returning, etc.

30. Make certain that your child understands that things which are lost, broken, or destroyed must be replaced by him/her.

31. Make certain that the responsibilities given to your child are appropriate for your child's level of development and ability.

32. Assist your child in performing his/her responsibilities. Gradually require him/her to independently assume more responsibility as he/she demonstrates success.

33. Discuss your child's responsibilities at the beginning of each day so he/she knows what is expected of him/her.

85 Does not remain on task to do homework

1. Establish homework rules (e.g., start homework when you get home from school, finish homework before you watch TV or play with others, ask for help when necessary, etc.).

2. Reward your child for following the rules. Possible rewards include verbal praise (e.g., "Thank you for finishing your homework before playing outside."), a kiss on the cheek, a hug, having a friend over to play, staying up late, watching a favorite TV show, and playing a game with a parent. (See Appendix for Reward Menu.)

3. If there are other children or adolescents in the home, reward them for following the homework rules.

4. Make sure your child has a quiet and well lighted place in which to do his/her homework.

5. Reduce distractions (e.g., turn off the radio and/or TV, have people talk quietly, etc.) in order to help your child complete his/her homework.

6. Remind your child when it is time to do his/her homework.

7. Encourage your child to ask for help when necessary.

8. Ask your child's teacher to send home explanations of how to help your child with his/her homework if necessary.

9. Sit with your child when he/she is working on homework. You can read, do needlework, etc., while your child works.

10. Write a contract with your child.

For example: I, William, will complete my homework for 4 days in a row. When I accomplish this, I can stay up an hour later on Friday night.

The contract should be written within the ability level of your child and should focus on only one behavior at a time. (See Appendix for an example of a Behavior Contract.)

11. Make certain that your child sees the relationship between his/her behavior and the consequences which follow (e.g., forgetting to complete homework will result in a low grade).

12. Allow your child to do something he/she enjoys (e.g., playing a game, watching TV, talking with a friend on the phone, etc.) after completing homework for the evening.

13. Allow natural consequences to occur due to your child's failure to complete work (e.g., receiving low grades, being excluded from extracurricular activities, etc.).

14. Allow your child to have a friend come over so they can do their homework together.

15. Have your child put a star or check mark beside each assignment he/she completes and allow him/her to turn in the stars or check marks for rewards.

16. Make positive comments about school and the importance of completing homework.

17. Have your child begin homework as soon as he/she gets home from school in order to prevent putting it off all evening.

18. Find a tutor (e.g., a volunteer in the community, one of your child's classmates, etc.) to help your child complete his/her homework.

19. Arrange to pick up your child's homework each day if he/she has difficulty "remembering" to bring it home.

20. Help your child study for tests, quizzes, etc.

21. If your child appears to need a break, allow some playtime between homework assignments.

22. Set up a homework system with your child's teacher (e.g., 2 days a week drill with flash cards, 3 days a week work on book work sent home, etc.). This will add some variety to your child's homework.

23. Let your child set up an "office" where he/she can finish homework.

24. Develop an assignment sheet with your child's teacher so you are aware of the work that should be completed each night. Send back the assignment sheet the next day so your child's teacher is aware that you saw the sheet.

25. Play educational games with your child so it is more interesting for him/her to do homework (e.g., spelling bee, math races, let your child teach the material to you, etc.).

26. Check over your child's homework when he/she is finished so you can be certain that everything is completed.

27. Assist your child in performing his/her homework responsibilities. Gradually require him/her to independently assume more responsibility as he/she demonstrates success.

28. Make certain you are familiar with the school district's homework policy (e.g., 15 minutes a day for 1st-3rd grade, 30 minutes a day for 4th-6th grade, etc.). If your child is receiving more homework than the district requires, talk with your child's teacher.

29. Along with a directive, provide an incentive statement (e.g., "When you finish your homework, you may watch TV" etc.).

30. Make certain your child understands that homework not completed and turned in on time must still be completed and turned in.

31. Review your child's homework responsibilities with him/her after school so your child knows what is expected that evening.

32. Have another child (e.g., brother, sister, friend) help your child with homework each evening.

33. Have your child and a classmate who has the same assignment do their homework together (e.g., right after school at one home or the other).

34. Set aside quiet time each night when the family turns off the TV's and radios to read, do homework, write letters, etc.

35. Hire a tutor to work with your child to help him/her complete homework.

36. Make sure your child has all the necessary materials to perform homework (e.g., pencils, paper, erasers, etc.).

A Reminder: Homework should be a form of "practice" for what your child has already been taught in school. You should not have to teach your child how to work each problem or activity. Talk with your child's teacher if this is a problem.

Note: If your child cannot be successful completing homework at home, speak to his/her teacher(s) about providing time at school for homework completion.

86 Does not listen to or follow verbal directions

1. Establish rules for listening to and following directions (e.g., listen when someone is giving directions, ask questions about directions if you do not understand, etc.). These rules should be consistent and followed by everyone in the home. Talk about the rules often and reward your child for following the rules.

2. Reward your child for listening to and following directions. Possible rewards include verbal praise (e.g., "You did a great job picking up your clothes!" "I like the way you follow directions!" etc.), a kiss on the cheek, a hug, having a friend over to play, staying up late, watching a favorite TV show, and playing a game with a parent. (See Appendix for Reward Menu.)

3. If there are other children or adolescents in the home, reward them for listening to and following directions.

4. Carefully consider your child's age and experience when expecting him/her to listen to and follow directions.

5. Demonstrate the appropriate way to listen to and follow directions (e.g., you give your child directions to feed the dog and then you feed the dog with him/her).

6. When your child does not listen to and follow a direction, explain exactly what he/she did wrong, what should have been done and why.

For example: You tell your child to clean up his/her room before 5:00. At 5:00, you tell your child that the room has not been cleaned and that he/she needs to follow the direction to clean the room now.

7. Write a contract with your child.

For example: I, William, for three days in a row, will follow directions without having to be told more than once. When I accomplish this, I can watch 30 extra minutes of TV.

The contract should be written within the ability level of your child and should focus on only one behavior at a time. (See Appendix for an example of a Behavior Contract.)

8. Make certain that your child sees the relationship between his/her behavior and the consequences which follow (e.g., failing to listen to and follow the direction to bring in his/her bike at night may result in the bike being stolen).

9. Allow natural consequences to occur due to your child's failure to listen to and follow directions (e.g., his/her bike being stolen, loss of school books, schoolwork not done on time, etc.).

10. Along with a directive, provide an incentive statement (e.g., "When you eat your peas, you may have dessert." "You may watch TV after you get ready for bed." etc.).

11. When your child has difficulty listening to and following directions in front of others (e.g., at the grocery store, in the mall, playing a game with family members, etc.), remove him/her from the situation until he/she can demonstrate self-control and follow directions.

12. In order to help your child be able to listen to and follow directions, reduce distractions (e.g., turn off the TV, give directions in a room away from friends, etc.).

13. Do not give your child more than two- or three-step directions to follow. Directions that involve several steps can be confusing and cause your child to have difficulty following them. An example of a two-step directions is: "Please turn off your light and go to bed."

14. In order to determine if your child heard a direction, have him/her repeat it.

15. Deliver directions in a supportive rather than a threatening manner (e.g., "Please take out the trash." rather than "You had better take out the trash or else!").

16. Give your child a special responsibility (e.g., answering the door, serving food, cleaning, etc.) in order to teach your child to follow directions.

17. Do not criticize your child. When correcting him/her, be honest yet supportive. Never cause your child to feel bad about himself/herself.

18. Be consistent when expecting your child to listen to and follow directions. Do not allow your child to fail to follow directions one time and expect appropriate behavior the next time.

19. Use a timer to help your child know the amount of time he/she has to follow through with directions given to him/her.

20. Make a written list of directions you want your child to follow (e.g., feed the dog, take out the trash, etc.).

21. Talk to your child before going into a public place and remind him/her of the importance of listening to and following directions.

22. Establish a regular routine for your child to follow on a daily basis in order to help him/her "remember" to take care of his/her responsibilities. (See Appendix for Weekday or Saturday Schedule.)

23. Make sure your child is paying attention to you when you tell him/her to do something. Have him/her look directly at you to know he/she is listening and have him/her repeat the direction to check for understanding.

24. Do not give directions to your child from another room. Go to your child, get his/her undivided attention, and tell him/her what to do.

25. Do not punish your child for forgetting, for accidents that interfere with following directions, etc.

26. Make certain to give directions in a very simple manner and be specific as to what you want your child to do.

27. Establish a certain time each day for your child to take care of his/her responsibilities (e.g., feeding the dog, completing homework, etc., right after school).

28. Have your child do those things that need to be done when it is discussed instead of later (e.g., put swimsuits in the car now so that when you go to the pool later this afternoon, they will not be forgotten; etc.).

29. Make certain that the responsibilities given to your child are appropriate for your child's level of development and ability.

30. Assist your child in performing his/her responsibilities. Gradually require him/her to independently assume responsibility as he/she demonstrates success.

31. In order to help your child be able to listen to and follow directions, reduce distractions (e.g., turn off the TV, give directions in a room away from his/her friends, etc.).

32. Make sure you have your child's undivided attention when you are talking to him/her. Stand close to your child, maintain eye contact, and have him/her repeat what you say.

33. Be sure your child hears what you say by having him/her acknowledge you (e.g., by saying, "Okay!" "Will do!" etc.).

34. Make certain your child knows that you expect him/her to listen to you by saying, "William, it is important that you listen carefully to what I have to say. You need to feed the dog now!"

35. Have your child's hearing checked if you have not done so in the past year.

36. Allow natural consequences to occur due to your child's inability to follow the rules in public places (e.g., his/her having to "sit out" at the pool, losing pool privileges, etc.).

37. Do not reinforce your child's inappropriate behavior by laughing when he/she is silly, rude, etc.

38. Always expect your child to behave at home and in public.

39. Ask the employees of the public places that your child visits for a copy of their rules. Review the rules daily with your child.

1. Establish rules for taking care of responsibilities (e.g., perform chores, finish homework before bedtime, take care of personal possessions, etc.). These rules should be consistent and followed by everyone in the home, including the parents. Talk about the rules often and reward your children for following the rules.

2. Reward your child for "remembering" to do things. Possible rewards include verbal praise (e.g., "You did a great job cleaning up your room." "Thank you for taking out the trash." etc.), a kiss on the cheek, a hug, having a friend over to play, staying up late, watching a favorite TV show, and playing a game with a parent. (See Appendix for Reward Menu.)

3. If there are other children or adolescents in the home, reward them for "remembering" to do things.

4. Carefully consider your child's age and experience when assigning him/her responsibilities to be performed in and around the home.

5. Demonstrate for your child the appropriate way to perform a chore and assist him/her in performing the chore several times before letting him/her perform the chore independently.

6. Establish a regular routine for your child to follow on a daily basis in order to help him/her "remember" to take care of his/her responsibilities.

For example:
6:30 a.m. - get up, make bed, get dressed
7:00 a.m. - eat breakfast
7:30 a.m. - leave for school
3:30 p.m. - return from school
4:00 p.m. - feed pets
5:00 p.m. - set the table for dinner
5:30 p.m. - eat dinner
7:00 p.m. - do homework
8:00 p.m. - go to bed

This schedule could be posted in central locations around the home (e.g., on the refrigerator, in your child's room, in the basement, etc.). Seeing the schedule often will increase the likelihood of your child remembering what to do and when to do it. (See Appendix for Weekday or Saturday Schedule.)

7. When your child "forgets" to do something, explain exactly what he/she did wrong, what should have been done and why.

For example: It is 5:20 p.m. and your child is watching TV. Walk up to your child and say directly to him, "William, it is 5:20. You are watching TV and you should be setting the table. You need to set the table now because we are going to eat in 10 minutes."

8. Maintain a chart for your child which indicates his/her responsibilities. Along with your child, place a star beside each responsibility he/she performs for the day. A check mark should be placed next to those responsibilities he/she does not perform successfully. Allow your child to trade his/her stars for rewards listed on a "Reward Menu." The rewards should be things that the child has asked to earn and a specific number of stars should be earned in order to obtain each reward. (See Appendix for a Reward Menu.)

9. Write a contract with your child.

For example: I, William, for one week, will remember to take out the trash after dinner. When I accomplish this, I can stay up until 11:00 p.m. on Friday night.

The contract should be written within the ability level of your child and should focus on only one behavior at a time. (See Appendix for an example of a Behavior Contract.)

10. Require your child to perform his/her chore, responsibility, homework, etc., even though he/she "forgot" to do so at the established time.

11. Make certain that your child sees the relationship between his/her behavior and the consequences which follow (e.g., forgetting to pick up possessions results in their damage or loss, failure to do homework results in a failing grade, etc.).

12. Allow natural consequences to occur due to your child's "forgetting" to take care of his/her responsibilities (e.g., personal possessions being lost, failing a homework assignment, etc.).

13. Schedule your child's chores and responsibilities around highly enjoyable activities (e.g., your child can watch TV after feeding the dog and taking out the trash).

14. In order to help your child be able to remember, reduce distractions (e.g., turn off the TV, give directions in a room away from his/her friends, etc.).

15. Provide an incentive statement for your child to help him/her do his/her chores (e.g., "When you clean your room, you can have a friend over.").

16. Make a written list of directions you want your child to follow (e.g., feed the dog, take out the trash, etc.).

17. Be consistent when expecting your child to finish chores. Do not allow him/her to fail to follow directions one time and expect appropriate behavior the next time.

18. Give your child a special responsibility (e.g., answering the door, serving food, cleaning, etc.).

19. Use a timer to help your child know the amount of time he/she has to follow through with directions given to him/her.

20. Do not give directions to your child from another room. Go to your child, get his/her undivided attention, and tell him/her what to do.

21. Make sure your child is paying attention to you when you tell him/her to do something. Have him/her look directly at you to know he/she is listening and have him/her repeat the direction to check for understanding.

22. Do not punish your child for forgetting, for accidents that interfere with doing things, etc.

23. Make certain to be specific when telling your child what you want him/her to do.

24. Establish a certain time each day for your child to take care of his/her responsibilities (e.g., feeding the dog, completing homework, etc., right after school).

25. Sit down with your child and have him/her write a list of chores he/she would like to do.

26. Have your child do those things that need to be done when it is discussed instead of later (e.g., put swimsuits in the car now so that when you go to the pool later this afternoon, they will not be forgotten, etc.).

27. Make certain that the responsibilities given to your child are appropriate for your child's level of development and ability.

28. Assist your child in performing his/her responsibilities. Gradually require him/her to independently assume responsibility as he/she demonstrates success.

88 Changes from one activity to another without finishing the first, without putting things away, before it is time to move on to the next activity, etc.

1. Establish rules for changing activities (e.g., finish one activity before moving on to another, put things away where they belong, return borrowed items in the same or better condition, complete chores on time, etc.). These rules should be consistent and followed by everyone in the home. Talk about the rules often.

2. Reward your child for following the rules. Possible rewards include verbal praise (e.g., "Thank you for putting your dirty clothes in the hamper!" "I'm so proud of you for finishing your homework before watching TV." etc.), a kiss on the cheek, a hug, having a friend over to play, staying up late, watching a favorite TV show, and playing a game with a parent. (See Appendix for a Reward Menu.)

3. If there are other children or adolescents in the home, reward them for finishing one activity before changing to another activity.

4. Carefully consider your child's age and experience before assigning responsibilities to him/her.

5. Show your child how to finish one activity before moving on to another (e.g., return things to their proper places, return borrowed items in the same or better condition, complete chores, etc.) before expecting him/her to perform the responsibilities on his/her own.

6. When your child is not responsible, explain exactly what he/she is doing wrong, what should have been done and why.

7. Write a contract with your child.

For example: I, William, for 5 nights, will finish my homework before watching TV. When I accomplish this, I can stay up until 11:00 p.m. on Friday night.

The contract should be written within the ability level of your child and should focus on only one behavior at a time. (See Appendix for an example of a Behavior Contract.).

8. Make certain that your child sees the relationship between his/her behavior and the consequences which follow (e.g., failing to finish homework before playing results in a failing grade for homework).

9. Allow natural consequences to occur due to your child's failure to finish a task (e.g., forgetting to do homework will result in failing grades).

10. Establish a certain time each day for your child to take care of his/her responsibilities (e.g., feeding the dog, completing homework, etc., right after school).

11. Act as a model for your child for being responsible at all times.

12. Tell your child when it is time to complete his/her homework, chores, etc.

13. Post a list of your child's responsibilities (e.g., 1. Take out the trash, 2. Feed the dog, 3. Set the table, etc.). Have your child put a check next to each chore he/she completes. Reward your child for completing his/her chores.

14. Discuss your child's responsibilities at the beginning of each day so he/she knows what is expected of him/her.

15. Help your child get out the materials necessary for him/her to complete his/her responsibilities (e.g., paper for homework, cleaning supplies for cleaning his/her room, etc.).

16. Help your child get started with his/her chores and explain to your child where things belong when he/she is finished using them.

17. Make a list of your child's commonly used items and/or materials and have your child make sure that each item and/or material is put in its designated place each day.

18. Make certain there is a designated place for all items in and around the home.

19. Require your child to put his/her coat, gloves, hat, etc., in a designated place upon entering the home.

20. Teach your child to put things back where they belong by putting things back where they belong after you use them.

21. Make certain that responsibilities given to your child are appropriate for your child's level of development and ability.

22. Provide your child with shelving, containers, organizers, etc., for his/her possessions. Label the storage areas and require your child to keep his/her possessions together.

23. Assist your child in performing his/her responsibilities. Gradually require him/her to independently assume more responsibility as he/she demonstrates success.

24. Make certain your child understands that things which are lost, broken, or destroyed must be replaced by him/her.

25. Do not buy additional toys, games, etc., for your child if he/she is not able to take care of what he/she has.

26. Limit your child's use of those things he/she is not responsible for putting away, returning, etc.

27. Tell your child what he/she needs to do to complete an activity (e.g., put all materials away before beginning a new activity, have an adult check your homework before putting it away, etc.).

28. Allow your child to do something he/she enjoys after finishing one activity and putting everything away (e.g., watching TV, playing a game with a parent, playing with a friend, etc.).

29. Along with a directive, provide an incentive statement (e.g., ''You may watch TV after you finish your homework and put away all materials.'').

30. Make certain your child puts away all toys, clothes, etc., before he/she is allowed to get out more toys or clothes.

31. Tell baby-sitters or others who are involved with your child that he/she is responsible for putting away his/her own materials.

32. Show your child the proper way to take care of his/her things (e.g., shining shoes, hosing off his/her bike, taking care of dolls, etc.). This will teach your child a sense of responsibility with his/her own belongings.

33. If your child fails to pick up his/her own clothes, games, toys, etc., after an activity, pick up the toys and take them away from him/her for a period of time.

34. Make certain to be consistent when expecting your child to change from one activity to another (e.g., do not leave the house with toys in the yard one time and expect the toys to be picked up the next time).

35. Reduce distracting activities which interfere with your child's ability to change from one activity to another (e.g., turn off the TV when it is time to set the table, do not allow friends to come over when it is time to do homework, etc.).

1. Reward your child for completing his/her responsibilities in a reasonable amount of time. Possible rewards include verbal praise (e.g., ''I'm so proud of you for getting your homework done on time tonight!''), a kiss on the cheek, a hug, having a friend over to play, staying up late, watching a favorite TV show, and playing a game with a parent. (See Appendix for Reward Menu.)

2. If there are other children or adolescents in the home, reward them for completing responsibilities in a reasonable amount of time.

3. Carefully consider your child's age when expecting him/her to be able to attend to an activity for a specific amount of time.

4. Discuss your concerns regarding your child's attention span with your family doctor, a school official, etc., in order to see if his/her attention span may be interfering with progress at school.

5. Remind your child to do his/her chores and complete his/her responsibilities.

6. Help your child complete his/her chores and responsibilities.

7. Write a contract with your child.

For example: I, William, for one week, will work on my homework for 30 minutes each day. When I accomplish this, I can have a friend spend the night.

The contract should be written within the ability level of your child and should focus on only one behavior at a time. (See Appendix for an example of a Behavior Contract.)

8. Reduce distractions (e.g., turn off the TV and radio, do not allow friends to come over, etc.) in order to help your child attend to his/her chores and responsibilities.

9. Give your child simple, one-step directions to follow.

10. Keep your child's chores and responsibilities short and simple. Do not give him/her things to do that take more than 10-15 minutes to complete.

11. Break down your child's chores and responsibilities into smaller tasks.

12. Make sure that your child understands his/her chores and responsibilities by having him/her tell you what he/she is supposed to do in each case.

13. Provide your child with a quiet place to complete his/her chores and responsibilities.

14. Supervise your child through the completion of his/her chores and responsibilities in order to help him/her stay on task and complete the chores and responsibilities.

15. Evaluate your child's responsibilities in order to determine if they are too complicated for him/her to complete successfully.

16. Allow your child to use a timer to remind him/her to complete his/her chores and responsibilities.

17. Make sure that your child has all necessary materials to successfully complete his/her chores and responsibilities.

18. Teach your child how to manage his/her time so that he/she does not wait until the last minute to complete chores and responsibilities.

19. Establish a regular routine for your child to follow on a daily basis in order to help him/her ''remember'' to take care of his/her responsibilities.

For example:
6:30 a.m. - get up, make bed, get dressed
7:00 a.m. - eat breakfast
7:30 a.m. - leave for school
3:30 p.m. - return from school
4:00 p.m. - feed pets
5:00 p.m. - set the table for dinner
5:30 p.m. - eat dinner
7:00 p.m. - do homework
8:00 p.m. - go to bed

This schedule could be posted in central locations around the home (e.g., on the refrigerator, in your child's room, in the basement, etc.). Seeing the schedule often will increase the likelihood of your child remembering what to do and when to do it. (See Appendix for Weekday or Saturday Schedule.)

20. Maintain a chart for your child that indicates his/her responsibilities. Along with your child, put a star beside each responsibility he/she performs for the day. A check mark should be placed next to those responsibilities he/she did not perform successfully. Allow your child to trade his/her stars for rewards listed on a "Reward Menu." The rewards should be things that the child has asked to earn, and a specific number of stars should be earned in order to obtain each reward. (See Appendix for Reward Menu.)

21. Provide an incentive statement for your child to help him/her do his/her chores (e.g., "When you clean your room, you may have a friend over." etc.).

22. Make a written list of directions you want your child to follow (e.g., feed the dog, take out the trash, etc.).

23. Be consistent when expecting your child to finish chores. Do not allow him/her to fail to complete his/her chores one time and expect appropriate behavior the next time.

24. Make sure your child is paying attention to you when you tell him/her to do something. Have him/her look directly at you to know he/she is listening and have him/her repeat the direction to check for understanding.

25. Establish a certain time each day for your child to take care of his/her responsibilities (e.g., feeding the dog, completing homework, etc., right after school).

26. Have your child do those things that need to be done when it is discussed instead of later (e.g., put swimsuits in the car now so that when you go to the pool later this afternoon, they will not be forgotten; etc.).

27. Make certain that the responsibilities given to your child are appropriate for your child's level of development and ability.

28. Assist your child in performing his/her responsibilities. Gradually require him/her to independently assume responsibility as he/she demonstrates success.

29. Talk to your child's teacher to have your child put into small groups for instruction, have a peer tutor, have assignments shortened, etc.

30. Sit down with your child, one-to-one, for a few minutes at a time to practice schoolwork, read stories, etc. Gradually increase the amount of one-to-one time spent together as your child demonstrates the ability to attend for longer periods of time.

31. Make certain to give directions in a very simple manner and be specific as to what you want your child to do.

32. Be consistent when expecting your child to follow directions. Do not allow him/her to fail to follow directions one time and expect him/her to follow directions the next time.

33. Have everyone in the family work together at the same time in order to help your child get his/her responsibilities done on time.

34. Let your child earn money, privileges, etc., for performing his/her chores.

35. Sit with your child when he/she is working on homework. You could read, do needlework, etc., while your child works.

36. Do not give your child too many things to do at one time.

37. If your child appears to need a break, allow him/her some playtime between homework assignments, chores, etc.

38. Play educational games with your child so it is more interesting for him/her to do homework (e.g., a spelling bee, math races, let your child teach the material to you, etc.).

39. Be certain you are not expecting your child to attend to things that appeal to adults but are of no interest to children (e.g., adult conversations, visiting with older relatives, sightseeing, etc.).

40. Require your child to engage in activities for only brief periods of time. Gradually increase the length of time required for your child to attend to activities.

41. When your child is expected to engage in social situations, interact frequently with him/her in order to maintain his/her attention (e.g., ask him/her questions, ask for his/her opinions, stand close to him/her, etc.).

42. Give your child many short responsibilities (e.g., chores, errands) to increase his/her active involvement and give him/her a feeling of success or accomplishment.

43. Modify or eliminate those situations which cause your child to experience stress or frustration (e.g., make games easier, use teams instead of single players competing against one another, etc.).

44. If your child believes he/she cannot be successful in activities, he/she will have little or no interest in such activities (e.g., homework, school projects, games, etc.).

45. Require your child to clean up, put away, etc., those things he/she is playing with/using before moving on to something else.

46. Make certain to provide your child with a quiet, uncluttered place to do homework, school projects, etc.

47. Establish a regular schedule of daily events so that your child knows what he/she should be doing at any one time and what he/she will be doing next (e.g., watching cartoons, eating lunch, going swimming, etc.). (See Appendix for Weekday or Saturday Schedule.)

48. Assist your child in daily homework, school projects, etc. Gradually reduce the amount of assistance you provide your child as he/she demonstrates success in remaining on task, finishing assignments, etc.

49. Be a model for your child for having an appropriate attention span by reading, conversing, working on a project, etc.

50. Encourage your child to ask for assistance instead of moving on to something else, giving up, etc.

A Reminder: Your child's short attention span is not something he/she demonstrates on purpose. Be supportive by not expecting too much from him/her at one time.

90　Starts but does not complete homework

1. Establish homework rules (e.g., start homework when you get home from school, finish homework before you watch TV or play with others, ask for help when necessary, etc.).

2. Reward your child for following the rules. Possible rewards include verbal praise (e.g., "Thank you for finishing your homework before playing outside."), a kiss on the cheek, a hug, having a friend over to play, staying up late, watching a favorite TV show, and playing a game with a parent. (See Appendix for a Reward Menu.)

3. If there are other children or adolescents in the home, reward them for following the homework rules.

4. Make sure your child has a quiet and well lighted place in which to do his/her homework.

5. Reduce distractions (e.g., turn off the radio and/or TV, have people talk quietly, etc.) in order to help your child complete his/her homework.

6. Remind your child when it is time to do his/her homework.

7. Encourage your child to ask for help when necessary.

8. Ask your child's teacher to send home explanations of how to help your child with his/her homework if necessary.

9. Sit with your child when he/she is working on homework. You can read, do needlework, etc., while your child works.

10. Write a contract with your child.

For example: I, William, will complete my homework for 4 days in a row. When I accomplish this, I can stay up an hour later on Friday night.

The contract should be written within the ability level of your child and should focus on only one behavior at a time. (See Appendix for an example of a Behavior Contract.)

11. Make certain that your child sees the relationship between his/her behavior and the consequences which follow (e.g., forgetting to complete his/her homework will result in a low grade).

12. Allow your child to do something he/she enjoys (e.g., playing a game, watching TV, talking with a friend on the phone, etc.) after completing homework for the evening.

13. Allow natural consequences to occur due to your child's failure to complete his/her homework (e.g., receiving low grades, being excluded from extracurricular activities, etc.).

14. If you feel that your child is being assigned too much homework, talk with his/her teacher about your concerns.

15. Allow your child to have a friend come over so they can do their homework together.

16. Have your child put a star or check mark beside each assignment he/she completes and allow him/her to turn in his/her stars or check marks for rewards. (See Appendix for Reward Menu.)

17. Make positive comments about school and the importance of completing homework.

18. Have your child begin his/her homework as soon as he/she gets home from school in order to prevent him/her from putting it off all evening.

19. Find a tutor (e.g., a volunteer in the community, one of your child's classmates, etc.) to help your child complete his/her homework.

20. Arrange to pick up your child's homework each day if he/she has difficulty "remembering" to bring it home.

21. Help your child study for tests, quizzes, etc.

22. If your child appears to need a break, allow him/her some playtime between homework assignments.

23. Set up a homework system with your child's teacher (e.g., 2 days a week drill with flash cards, 3 days a week work on book work sent home, etc.). This will add some variety to your child's homework.

24. Let your child set up an "office" where he/she can finish homework.

25. Develop an assignment sheet with your child's teacher so you are aware of the work that should be completed each night. Send back the assignment sheet the next day so your child's teacher is aware that you saw the sheet.

26. Play educational games with your child so it is more interesting for him/her to do homework (e.g., a spelling bee, math races, let your child teach the material to you, etc.).

27. Check over your child's homework when he/she is finished so you can be certain that everything is complete.

28. Assist your child in performing his/her homework responsibilities. Gradually require him/her to independently assume more responsibility as he/she demonstrates success.

29. Make certain you are familiar with the school district's homework policy (e.g., 15 min- utes a day for 1st-3rd grade, 30 minutes a day for 4th-6th grade, etc.). If your child is receiving more homework than the district requires, talk with your child's teacher.

30. Along with a directive, provide an incentive statement (e.g., "When you finish your homework, you may watch TV" etc.).

31. Make certain your child understands that homework not completed and turned in on time must still be completed and turned in.

32. Review your child's homework responsibilities with him/her after school so your child knows what he/she is expected to do that evening.

33. Have another child (e.g., brother, sister, friend) help your child with homework each evening.

34. Have your child and a classmate who has the same assignment do their homework together (e.g., right after school at one home or the other).

35. Set aside quiet time each night when the family turns off TV's and radios to read, do their homework, write letters, etc.

36. Hire a tutor to work with your child to help him/her complete homework.

37. Make sure your child has all the necessary materials to perform homework (e.g., pencils, paper, erasers, etc.).

A Reminder: Homework should be a form of "practice" for what your child has already been taught in school. You should not have to teach your child how to work each problem or activity. Talk with your child's teacher if this is a problem.

Note: If your child cannot be successful completing homework at home, speak to your his/her teacher(s) about providing time at school for homework completion.

91 Will not independently perform chores or responsibilities

1. Establish rules (e.g., put things away where they belong, return borrowed items in the same or better condition, complete chores on time, etc.). These rules should be consistent and followed by everyone in the home. Talk about the rules often.

2. Reward your child for following the rules. Possible rewards include verbal praise (e.g., "Thank you for putting your dirty clothes in the hamper!" "I'm so proud of you for finishing your homework before watching TV." etc.), a kiss on the cheek, a hug, having a friend over to play, staying up late, watching a favorite TV show, and playing a game with a parent. (See Appendix for Reward Menu.)

3. If there are other children or adolescents in the home, reward them for taking care of their responsibilities.

4. Carefully consider your child's age and experience before assigning responsibilities to him/her.

5. Show your child how to return things to their proper places, return borrowed items in the same or better condition, complete chores, etc., before expecting him/her to perform the responsibilities on his/her own.

6. When your child is not responsible, explain exactly what he/she is doing wrong, what should be done and why.

For example: If is 9:00 p.m. and your child has not started his/her homework. Go to your child and tell him/her that his/her homework has not been done and that he/she needs to be doing homework because bedtime is at 9:30 p.m.

7. Write a contract with your child.

For example: I, William, will finish my homework by 8:00 p.m. every weeknight for 5 nights in a row. When I accomplish this, I can stay up until 11:00 p.m. on Friday night.

The contract should be written within the ability level of your child and should focus on only one behavior at a time. (See Appendix for an example of a Behavior Contract.)

8. Make certain that your child sees the relationship between his/her behavior and the consequences which follow (e.g., failing to put an object in its proper place results in its being broken).

9. Allow natural consequences to occur due to your child's failure be responsible (e.g., forgetting to do homework will result in low grades).

10. Establish a certain time each day for your child to take care of his/her responsibilities (e.g., feeding the dog, completing homework, etc., right after school).

11. Act as a model for your child for being responsible at all times.

12. Tell your child when it is time to complete homework, chores, etc.

13. Post a list of your child's responsibilities (e.g., 1. Take out the trash, 2. Feed the dog, 3. Set the table, etc.). Have your child put a check mark next to each chore he/she completes. Reward your child for completing his/her chores. (See Appendix for List of Chores.)

14. Discuss your child's responsibilities at the beginning of each day so he/she knows what is expected of him/her.

15. Help your child get out the materials necessary for him/her to complete his/her responsibilities (e.g., paper for homework, cleaning supplies for cleaning his/her room, etc.).

16. Help your child get started with his/her chores and explain to your child where things belong when he/she is finished using them.

17. Set aside time each day for the family to put away all materials that have been used throughout the day (e.g., bikes, toys, lawn equipment, dishes, etc.).

18. Let your child know that materials not put away at the end of the day may be taken away for a period of time due to lack of responsibility.

19. Make a list of your child's frequently used items and/or materials and have your child make sure that each item and/or material is put in its designated place each day.

20. Make certain there is a designated place for all items in and around the home.

21. Require your child to put his/her coat, gloves, hat, etc., in a designated place upon entering the home.

22. Teach your child to put things back where they belong by putting things back where they belong after you use them.

23. Make certain that responsibilities given to your child are appropriate for your child's level of development and ability.

24. Provide your child with shelving, containers, organizers, etc., for his/her possessions. Label the storage areas and require your child to keep his/her possessions together.

25. Assist your child in performing his/her responsibilities. Gradually require him/her to independently assume more responsibility as he/she demonstrates success.

26. Make certain your child understands that things which are lost, broken, or destroyed must be replaced.

27. Do not buy additional toys, games, etc., for your child if he/she is not able to take care of the things he/she already has.

28. Limit your child's use of those things he/she is not responsible for putting away, returning, etc.

29. Do not give your child more than two- or three-step directions to follow. Directions that involve several steps can be confusing and cause your child to have difficulty following them. An example of a two-step direction is: "Please turn off your light and go to bed."

30. In order to determine if your child heard the direction, have him/her repeat it.

31. Deliver directions in a supportive rather than threatening manner (e.g., "Please take out the trash." rather than "You had better take out the trash or else!").

32. Be consistent when expecting your child to take care of his/her responsibilities. Do not allow him/her to fail to follow through with responsibilities one time and expect appropriate behavior the next time.

33. Use a timer to help your child know the amount of time he/she has to follow through with responsibilities given to him/her.

34. Make a written list of directions you want your child to follow (e.g., feed the dog, take out the trash, etc.).

35. Make sure your child is paying attention to you when you tell him/her to do something. Have him/her look directly at you to know he/she is listening and have him/her repeat the direction to check for understanding.

36. Do not give directions to your child from another room. Go to your child, get his/her undivided attention, and tell him/her what to do.

37. Do not punish your child for forgetting, for accidents that interfere with following directions, etc.

38. Limit the number of chores for which your child is responsible and gradually increase the number of chores as your child demonstrates the ability to get them done on time.

39. Show your child how to perform a new chore, such as setting the table, several times before expecting him/her to do it on his/her own.

40. Explain to your child that responsibilities not done on time will have to be done at other times (e.g., playtime, TV time, weekends, etc.).

41. Reduce distracting activities which interfere with your child performing his/her responsibilities (e.g., turn off the TV when it is time to set the table, do not allow friends over when it is time to do homework, etc.).

42. Have your child do those things that need to be done when it is discussed instead of later (e.g., put swimsuits in the car now so that when you go to the pool later this afternoon, they will not be forgotten, etc.).

43. Limit your child's use of belongings until he/she can care for them properly.

44. Allow your child to do something he/she enjoys after caring for his/her belongings (e.g., watch TV, play a game with a parent, play with a friend, etc.).

45. Require your child's room to be neat and organized so there will always be a place to put away toys, games, clothes, etc.

46. Communicate with the parents of a friend your child is visiting to make certain that your child helps pick up toys when he/she is spending time at a friend's house.

47. Do not expect your child to pick up toys and games that his/her friends have left out; encourage his/her friends to help pick up the toys.

48. Tell baby-sitters or others who are involved with your child that your child is responsible for picking up and putting away his/her own materials.

49. Show your child the proper way to take care of his/her things (e.g., shining shoes, hosing off his/her bike, taking care of dolls, etc.). This will teach your child a sense of responsibility with his/her own belongings.

50. Have your child pay for things he/she wants (e.g., a baseball mitt, a doll, a new pair of jeans, etc.). If your child has spent some of his/her own money on an item, he/she may be willing to care for it.

1. Establish rules for studying (e.g., start studying when you get home from school, finish studying before you watch TV or play with others, ask for help when necessary, etc.).

2. Reward your child for following the rules. Possible rewards include verbal praise (e.g., "Thank you for studying before playing outside."), a kiss on the cheek, a hug, having a friend over to play, staying up late, watching a favorite TV show, and playing a game with a parent. (See Appendix for Reward Menu.)

3. If there are other children or adolescents in the home, reward them for following the studying rules.

4. Make sure your child has a quiet and well lighted place in which to do his/her studying.

5. Reduce distractions (e.g., turn off radio and/or TV, have people talk quietly, etc.) in order to help your child study.

6. Remind your child when it is time to study.

7. Encourage your child to ask for help when necessary.

8. Ask your child's teacher to send home explanations of how to help your child with his/her studying.

9. Sit with your child when he/she is studying. You can read, do needlework, etc., while your child studies.

10. Write a contract with your child.

For example: I, William, will study for 4 days in a row. When I accomplish this, I can stay up an hour later on Friday night.

The contract should be written within the ability level of your child and should focus on only one behavior at time. (See Appendix for an example of a Behavior Contract.)

11. Make certain that your child sees the relationship between his/her behavior and the consequences which follow (e.g., forgetting to study will result in a low grade).

12. Allow your child to do something he/she enjoys (e.g., playing a game, watching TV, talking with a friend on the phone, etc.) after he/she studies.

13. Allow natural consequences to occur due to your child's failure to study (e.g., receiving low grades, being excluded from extracurricular activities, etc.).

14. If you feel that your child is being assigned too much homework, talk with his/her teacher about your concerns.

15. Allow your child to have a friend come over so they can study together.

16. Have your child put a star or check mark beside each assignment he/she completes and allow him/her to turn in his/her stars or checks for rewards. (See Appendix for Reward Menu.)

17. Make positive comments about school and the importance of studying.

18. Have your child begin studying as soon as he/she gets home from school in order to prevent him/her from putting it off all evening.

19. Find a tutor (e.g., a volunteer in the community, one of your child's classmates, etc.) to help your child study.

20. Arrange to pick up your child's homework each day if he/she has difficulty "remembering" to bring it home.

21. Help your child study for tests, quizzes, etc.

22. If your child appears to need a break, allow him/her some playtime between study assignments.

23. Set up a homework system with your child's teacher (e.g., 2 days a week drill with flash cards, 3 days a week work on book work sent home, etc.). This will add some variety to your child's studying.

24. Let your child set up an "office" where he/she can study.

25. Develop an assignment sheet with your child's teacher so you are aware of the work that should be completed each night. Send back the assignment sheet the next day so your child's teacher is aware that you saw the sheet.

26. Play educational games with your child so it is more interesting for him/her to study (e.g., a spelling bee, math races, let your child teach the material to you, etc.).

27. Check over your child's homework when he/she is finished so you can be certain that everything is complete.

28. Assist your child in studying. Gradually require him/her to independently assume more responsibility as he/she demonstrates success.

29. Along with a directive, provide an incentive statement (e.g., "When you finish studying, you may watch TV." etc.).

30. Make certain your child understands that homework not completed and turned in on time must still be completed and turned in.

31. Review your child's homework responsibilities with him/her after school so your child knows what is expected that evening.

32. Have another child (e.g., brother, sister, friend) help your child study each evening.

33. Have your child and a classmate who has the same assignment study together (e.g., right after school at one home or the other).

34. Set aside quiet time each night when the family turns off the TV's and radios to read, study, write letters, etc.

35. Hire a tutor to work with your child to help him/her study.

36. Make sure your child has all the necessary materials to study (e.g., pencils, paper, erasers, etc.).

37. Carefully consider your child's age when expecting him/her to be able to study for a specific amount of time.

38. Discuss your concerns regarding your child's attention span with your family doctor, a school official, etc., in order to see if his/her attention span may be interfering with progress at school.

39. Sit down with your child, one-on-one, for a few minutes at a time to practice schoolwork, read stories, etc. Gradually increase the amount of one-on-one time as your child demonstrates the ability to attend for longer periods of time.

A Reminder: If your child cannot be successful in studying at home, speak to his/her teacher(s) about providing time at school for studying.

III. Appendix

IDENTIFYING BEHAVIORS TO BE CHANGED:

CONSIDER ...

1. THE BEHAVIOR THAT OCCURS MOST FREQUENTLY.

2. THE BEHAVIOR THAT IS MOST INAPPROPRIATE.

3. THE BEHAVIOR THAT IS THE CAUSE OF OTHER RELATED BEHAVIORS.

One or all of the above approaches may be used to assist you in selecting behaviors to help your child increase appropriate behavior (e.g., doing chores) or decrease inappropriate behavior (e.g., going to bed too late). Your child's perfection need not be the goal, but helping your child become more successful should be the goal.

Posted Rules

- BE ON TIME FOR DINNER

- PUT AWAY ALL PLAYTHINGS

- BE IN BED BY 9:00 P.M.

- BE READY FOR SCHOOL BY 8:00 A.M.

"Posted Rules" are those behaviors that are of primary importance or are a primary problem. If a behavior is not a problem, such as "Running in the House," then it does not have to be a "Posted Rule." Keep the list of rules short, refer to them often, and "reinforce" the child for following the rules. The "posting" of the rules is as much a reminder for the adults as it is for the child. Find a conspicuous place to post the rules where they can be seen easily and often (e.g., the refrigerator is a good place if it is not already overcrowded with other information).

Sample List

1. PUT DIRTY CLOTHES IN CLOTHES HAMPER

2. TAKE A BATH BEFORE BEDTIME

3. BRUSH TEETH

4. GET CLOTHES READY FOR NEXT DAY

5. LISTEN TO A STORY READ BY MOM OR DAD

For those behaviors for which the child needs "reminders," a list such as the one above is developed and placed in the child's room, by the mirror in the bathroom, on the refrigerator or any place where it will easily and frequently be seen by the child. If a behavior like "Putting Dirty Clothes in the Clothes Hamper" is not a problem, then it will not be on the "List."

WEEKDAY SCHEDULE

7:00 AM-	GET UP, WASH FACE, DRESS, MAKE BED
7:25 AM-	EAT BREAKFAST
7:40 AM-	BRUSH TEETH AND HAIR
7:50 AM-	LEAVE FOR BUS STOP
8:30 AM-	BE AT SCHOOL
4:00 PM-	GET HOME AND PLAY OUTSIDE
4:30 PM-	SET TABLE FOR DINNER AND WASH UP
5:00 PM-	EAT DINNER
5:30 PM-	CLEAN UP KITCHEN
6:00 PM-	HOMEWORK
7:00 PM-	WATCH T.V.
7:30 PM-	TAKE BATH AND BRUSH TEETH
8:00 PM-	CHOOSE CLOTHES FOR NEXT DAY AND ORGANIZE BOOKS AND MATERIALS TO TAKE TO SCHOOL
8:30 PM-	BEDTIME

The "Weekday Schedule" is used when "Getting Up on Time," "Catching the Bus," "Doing Homework," "Watching T.V.," etc., at the appropriate times is a problem. The schedule increases the likelihood that behaviors will occur on time and that "other things" will not destroy the routine that is required for individual and family success. The schedule may be less specific than the sample provided and can be somewhat flexible, but it should improve "getting things done."

SATURDAY SCHEDULE

SATURDAY

7:00 AM –	WAKE UP AND GET DRESSED
7:30 AM –	BREAKFAST
8:00 AM –	CARTOONS
9:30 AM –	SHOPPING
11:45 AM –	LUNCH
12:15 PM –	PLAY WITH FRIENDS
2:45 PM –	SWIMMING CLASS
4:00 PM –	CLEAN-UP CHORES
5:00 PM –	HELP WITH DINNER
5:45 PM –	FAMILY DINNER
6:30 PM –	FAMILY TIME
9:00 PM –	BEDTIME

The "Saturday Schedule" or "Weekend Schedule" is used for the child when "being ready" and "getting things done" on a Saturday or weekend is a problem. By establishing a "schedule" the child, as well as everyone else, knows what is expected; and it increases the likelihood that "must" activities (e.g., meals, shopping, etc.) will take place on time. There is still a lot of time to "have fun." The schedule can be less specific or more specific than the sample and can be as flexible as necessary.

LIST OF CHORES

DAILY

- MAKE YOUR BED
- TAKE DISHES AND SILVERWARE TO THE SINK
- FEED SPOT

WEEKLY

- CLEAN YOUR ROOM
- HELP MOM CLEAN THE HOUSE
  or
- HELP DAD CLEAN THE GARAGE
- HELP WITH THE LAUNDRY
  - FOLDING
  - PUTTING IN DRAWERS AND CLOSETS

A "List of Chores" is posted as a reminder of what is expected. This assures that everyone "knows" exactly what is to be done, there are not surprises, and other activities can be scheduled accordingly.

POINT RECORD

MY BEST BEHAVIOR IS...

_____

DATE	HOW WELL I DID	DATE	HOW WELL I DID

The "Point Record" provides a means of recording the appropriate behavior (e.g., going to bed on time, doing chores, completing homework, etc.) the child accomplishes. The "Point Record" is posted on the refrigerator, kept in a file, or placed wherever is most convenient. The child should be able to see the "Point Record" and know how well he/she is doing. Points are "turned in" for rewards which are determined by the child's preferences. (See Reinforcer Survey in this Appendix.)

SAMPLE POINT RECORD

MY BEST BEHAVIOR IS...

GOING TO BED ON TIME

DATE	HOW WELL I DID	DATE	HOW WELL I DID
JAN. 10	OK ✳		
JAN. 11	A LITTLE LATE		
JAN. 12	OK ✳		
JAN. 13	OK ✳		

This sample "Point Record" represents the behavior "Going to Bed on Time." When the child "earns" a reinforcer for which he/she has been working, a new "Point Record" is started for the same behavior. When "Going to Bed on Time" is no longer a problem, a new behavior, such as "Doing Chores," can be substituted.

BEHAVIOR CONTRACT

_____ AGREES TO

_____

_____

EXPECTATION: EVERY TIME _____

_____

_____ WILL EARN 1 POINT.

REINFORCEMENT: WHEN _____

EARNS _____ POINTS HE WILL BE ABLE

TO CHOOSE A REWARD FROM THE REWARD

MENU.

The "Behavior Contract" is one of the most individualized, personalized, and direct strategies designed to increase appropriate behavior and decrease inappropriate behavior.

The "Behavior Contract" should specify:
- Who is involved in the contract
- What behavior is expected (e.g., chores, homework, etc.)
- The amount of behavior that is expected
- How reinforcement is earned
- When reinforcement is earned
- What reinforcement is available

BEHAVIOR CONTRACT

___William___ AGREES TO

___Pick up clothes in his___

___room each day___

EXPECTATION: EVERY TIME ___that___

___clothes are picked up___

___William___ WILL EARN 1 POINT.

REINFORCEMENT: WHEN ___William___

EARNS ___3___ POINTS HE WILL BE ABLE

TO CHOOSE A REWARD FROM THE REWARD

MENU.

The "Completed Behavior Contract" represents:
- Who is being reinforced
- What behavior is to be performed
- When the child earns reinforcement
- What reinforcement is available

REWARD MENU

REWARD	COST
• MODEL AIRPLANE	100
• TOY BOAT	90
• MOVIE	80
• HAVE A FRIEND STAY OVER	70
• PLAY MONOPOLY	60
• GO SHOPPING SATURDAY	50
• CANDY BAR	40
• GUM	30
• MAGIC MARKER	20

This sample "Reward Menu" is compiled from information gathered from the child responding to the "Reinforcer Survey" or otherwise indicating what the child would like to earn for improved appropriate behavior. The value of a reward is determined by its importance, size, cost, etc. Be certain to include lower cost as well as higher cost rewards in order that your child can work for a long-range goal, but also have smaller rewards for those times when a lot of points have not been earned.

REINFORCER SURVEY

1. MY FAVORITE THINGS TO DO AROUND THE HOUSE ARE _____

_____

2. MY FAVORITE TV PROGRAMS ARE _____

_____

3. MY FAVORITE FOODS ARE _____

_____

4. IF I HAD TEN DOLLARS I'D _____

_____

5. MY BEST FRIENDS ARE _____

_____

6. MY FAVORITE THINGS TO DO WITH THE FAMILY ARE _____

_____

7. IF I COULD HAVE A NEW RECORD, IT WOULD BE _____

_____

8. THE THINGS I LIKE TO DO AFTER SCHOOL ARE _____

_____

9. MY FAVORITE SPORTS ARE _____

_____

10. IF I COULD BUY THREE GAMES THEY WOULD BE _____

_____

The "Reinforcer Survey" is a must in order to know what the child would like to earn for hard work and appropriate behavior. There is no better way to stay in touch with the changing preferences children and youth have for favorite activities, games, and material things that are popular for their age group. The "Reinforcer Survey" should be read to the young child for his/her responses and filled in by the older child. The "results" of the survey then provide the basis for the reward to be earned. The "Reinforcer Survey" can be "conducted" once every month, six weeks, etc.

Schedule of Daily Events

SCHEDULE OF DAILY EVENTS

NAME _____

	#1	#2	#3	#4	#5	#6	#7	#8	#9	#10
Monday										
Tuesday										
Wednesday										
Thursday										
Friday										

SCHEDULE OF DAILY EVENTS

NAME _____

	#1	#2	#3	#4	#5	#6	#7	#8	#9	#10
Tuesday										

Each individual student's Schedule of Daily Events is developed for him/her and attached to his/her desk for a week at a time or for one day at a time. This schedule identifies each activity/task the student is assigned for the day, and the schedule is filled in by the teacher one day at a time. Students tend to know what they are to do next when the schedule is provided, and teachers can expect fewer interruptions for directions when students refer to their schedules.

Schedule of Daily Events Sample

SCHEDULE OF DAILY EVENTS

NAME _____

	#1	#2	#3	#4	#5	#6	#7	#8	#9	#10
Monday	Reading	Art (Clay)	Math	Art (Paint)	Science	Creative Writing	Social Studies	Listening	Music	P.E.
Tuesday										
Wednesday										
Thursday										
Friday										

Assignment Sheet

SUBJECT	ASSIGNMENT	DUE DATE	TEACHER SIGNATURE
	ASSIGNMENT SHEET	**DATE** _____	
Math			
Reading			
Science			
Social Studies			
Spelling			
Other			

Comments:

PARENT SIGNATURE _____

SUBJECT	ASSIGNMENT	DUE DATE	TEACHER SIGNATURE
	ASSIGNMENT SHEET	**DATE** _____	
Math			
History			
Science			
English			
Fine Arts/ Practical Arts			
Other			

Comments:

PARENT SIGNATURE _____

Flash Card Study Aid Sample

<u>Questions</u>   **Topic:** _____

<u>Who:</u>

<u>What:</u>

<u>Where:</u>

<u>When:</u>

<u>How:</u>

<u>Why:</u>

Topic: _____

<u>Who</u>

<u>What</u>

<u>Where</u>

<u>When</u>

<u>How</u>

<u>Why</u>

Flash Card Study Aid Sample

Questions   Topic: Pilgrims

Who: were the first settlers of North America?

What: did the first settlers do upon arrival?

Where: did the first settlers establish a colony?

When: did the first settlers come to North America?

How: did the first settlers survive?

Why: did the first settlers come to North America?

Topic: Pilgrims

Who: Pilgrims

What: Built longhouses

Where: Plymouth, Mass

When: 1620's

How: Learned from Indians

Why Religious freedom

Selected Abbreviations and Symbols

ab.	about		$	money
add.	addition		mo.	month
&	and		natl.	national
bk.	book		no.	number
bldg.	building		#	number
cap.	capital		oz.	ounce
c/o	care of		p., pg.	page
cm.	centimeter		pd.	paid
cent.	century		par.	paragraph
ch., chap.	chapter		pop.	population
co.	company		lb.	pound
cont.	continent		pres.	president
cont.	continued		qt.	quart
corp.	corporation		rd.	road
dept.	department		rep.	representative
dict.	dictionary		Rev.	Reverend
educ.	education		sch.	school
enc.	encyclopedia		sc.	science
Eng.	English		sig.	signature
fig.	figure		s.s.	social studies
geog.	geography		sp.	spelling
govt.	government		sq.	square
gr.	gram		subj.	subject
ht.	height		subt.	subtraction
hist.	history		syn.	synonym
ill., illus.	illustration		temp.	temperature
in.	inch		t.	ton
intro.	introduction		treas.	treasurer
lab.	laboratory		U.S.A.	United States of America
lang.	language		univ.	university
lat.	latitude		v.	verb
leg.	legislature		vs.	versus
lib.	library		v.p.	vice-president
liq.	liquid		wk.	week
max.	maximum		wt.	weight
meas.	measure		w/	with
mi.	mile		yd.	yard
min.	minute		yr.	year
misc.	miscellaneous			

The above list only serves as an example. The student should further develop his/her own list.

Outline Form

SUBJECT: _____

Topic: _____

	General	Specific
Who:		
What:		
Where:		
When:		
How:		
Why:		
Vocabulary:		

DO NOT
X
TOUCH

DO NOT
X
TOUCH

DO NOT
X
TOUCH

DO NOT
X
TOUCH

DO NOT
X
TOUCH

DO NOT
X
TOUCH

DO NOT
X
TOUCH

DO NOT
X
TOUCH

DO NOT
X
TOUCH

DO NOT
X
TOUCH

IV. Index